Boomer's Guide to

Sex That
(Still) Sizzles

Boomer's Guide to

Sex That
(Still) Sizzles

René Hollander, Ph.D.

Francine Hornberger

Michael Levin

ALPHA

A member of Penguin Group (USA) Inc.

Publisher: *Marie Butler-Knight*
Product Manager: *Phil Kitchel*
Senior Managing Editor: *Jennifer Chisholm*
Development Editor: *Tom Stevens*
Senior Production Editor: *Billy Fields*
Copy Editor: *Sara Fink*

Cover Designer: *Doug Wilkins*
Book Designer: *Trina Wurst*
Creative Director: *Robin Lasek*
Indexer: *Aamir Burki*
Layout/Proofreading: *Angela Calvert, Donna Martin*

Contents

Foreword

Sex: What Is It?

The Oxford American Dictionary describes "sex" as such: n. (noun) either of the two main groups (male or female) into which living things are placed according to their reproductive functions.

The implication here is that the important thing about sex is to know what group we are in, male or female. Simple, right? Not exactly.

When most people think of "sex" they do not think in terms of nouns, they think in terms of verbs. They do not think in terms of social distinction, but of sexual intercourse. Sex is an action verb.

Just what is sex? It is a reproductive activity. At the most primitive biological level, it is behavior used to procreate the species. Cleverly—or perhaps even sneakily—sex was designed to be extremely pleasant, to ensure the act would be consummated enough times to proliferate pregnancy and continue the human race. What drives this species is pleasure, and pleasure is what this book is all about.

The sexual act or intercourse is something most of us Baby Boomers had difficulty asking about at a time when we really wanted to know. Back then, when we asked adults why boys and girls are different, a common response was: "When you're old enough, you'll find out."

This led to the creation of an almost unspoken contract about sex: the desire to know more about it had to be contained. Any exposure to greater knowledge about this secret mystery was to be repressed. Lying about sex was required, which is at least one reason it has become almost a reflex for those same children, who have now grown into adults, to lie when questioned about their sexual activities. Add to this the emotional (it can only be experienced when you're married and in love), moral (good girls and good boys don't), religious (it is a sin), societal (what will the neighbors think?), and legal (what about the responsibility for a pregnancy or inflicting someone with a sexually transmitted disease?) implications attached to sex and you can see that Baby Boomers got baggage—and a lot of it. So it comes as no surprise that as seasoned, mature adults, Boomers possess much confusion about this most elemental of all human activities.

Our hope is that *Boomer's Guide to Sex That (Still) Sizzles* will enable Boomers to get back to the visceral joys of sex in concert with the lives they lead, beliefs they hold, and fantasies they may have not allowed themselves to explore. Herein, we will provide ways to communicate desires, overcome obstacles that prevent experiencing yourself with another in safe ways, and explore sex as an experience of complete connection to another human being. We will also show how sex, the most human of all acts, can feed and satisfy the powerful need in all human beings to not feel alone, explore the spiritual potential of this act of life, and suggest methods to create sexual celebrations with your partner that are wanted, needed, doable, and enduring.

Boomer's Guide to Sex That (Still) Sizzles answers the questions you may still be afraid to ask—openly, honestly, and bluntly, without putting you on the spot or the couch, or even in the same room. It is a book for all reasons, a book for a generation raised with secrets, shame, and unanswered questions—the largest generation on earth: the Baby Boomers.

—René Hollander, Ph.D.

Introduction

Just how powerful is sex? Imagine walking into a crowded room and yelling "Sex!" You'd have everyone's attention in a heartbeat. It's hard to think of any other topic that so powerfully commands the attention of just about everyone on the planet.

Human sexual activity can be used to communicate every human emotion. The sex act can bring the experience of feeling totally connected to another human being. This need to not feel alone is powerful for all human beings. Sex, this most human of all acts, can feed and satisfy that desire. Sex leads to the exploration of the spiritual potential of life. It's all about connecting and re-connecting.

As with the other Boomer's Guides, this book will concentrate on sex as it pertains to our generation, right now. We'll be looking at those elements about sex at our age that makes it different from what it was in our twenties and thirties, and how to work through and even embrace those differences and enjoy our sex lives to the fullest.

> The best way to strengthen an emotional relationship is to transform the sexual relationship. While great sex cannot save a truly awful relationship, an improvement of the quality, quantity, and above all, variety of sexual experiences can make a good marriage great.

Kristen, 47

"I've always loved sex. I was pretty wild when I was younger so it was probably a good thing for me to get married—you know, to calm down a little. My husband and I had a sexual chemistry that was unlike anything I'd ever experienced before, which is definitely one of the reasons I married him. In the beginning and even years into our marriage—all we ever did was make love. God knows how either of us have the time to hold down jobs—or the energy, for that matter!

We've been married nearly 20 years now, and we still have great sex—we just don't have it as often. It's probably just as well. Four times a day at our age? We'd be dead by now!

It's not that I mind that we've slowed down—it's that I think we've slowed down too much. Either he's too busy or I'm too tired. And when we do have sex, we do things the same way over and over again. I think in the first five years of our marriage we made love or had oral sex in the bathroom of practically all of our friends' homes. Not to mention my parent's house, his parent's house, changing rooms in department stores, parking garages, airplane bathrooms—I must sound like some kind of sex fiend. Well, we both were, and frankly, I miss it! I don't think we've made love anywhere but in our bedroom for the last few years.

I recently sat down with a group of some old girlfriends—the ones with whom I shared most of those wild young years. I asked them if they were still having great sex with their husbands—and if they were having it as often as they wanted it. I was surprised to learn that many of these once-insatiable party girls had become complacent about their sex lives for a wide variety of reasons, like kids, job pressures, changing hormones, and just plain boredom. Some even admitted to not having had sex with their husbands for years.

The last part of that scared me the most. Sure, I can deal with not having the same libido I did in my twenties. Don't get me wrong, I miss the old days; I wouldn't mind having my old sex life back. But I certainly don't want it to be over!"

Add Rapture to Your Routine

What started to happen between Kristen and her husband over the course of the years is something we can all relate to: the sex they couldn't seem to get enough of at one time in their lives slowed down. Life got in the way. And let's face it: As we get older, we simply don't have the stamina we once had, what with raising kids or just having sent them off to college, as well as being at the height of our careers and dealing with all the draining responsibility that goes along with that.

Lack of energy aside, one of the most powerful sex deterrents is that we just don't have the time. These days, we are so completely over-booked, its seems everything we do over the course of the day has to be entered into our PDAs. Well, guess what? That should include sex.

All our romantic notions aside, our lives are so busy today that if we don't schedule sex, there may simply be no time for it.

In addition to lack of time and energy, we run into the third danger: lack of interest. If we're involved in a marriage or other long-term relationship, we've been involved sexually with the same person for years if not decades. Therefore, routine, predictability, and inertia can be at work in our relationship, conspiring to create a situation where boredom is the norm. It is essential for a strong, healthy relationship to find ways to keep making sex interesting and to fight against taking the other person for granted.

> Naturally, there are some psychological and physical issues that cannot be addressed by a book of this type. Situations involving abuse, incest, violence, and other serious psychological factors can only be helped by a competent medical or psychological professional.

What Can You Expect?

This book is meant for Boomers who want to strengthen their relationships, sexually and emotionally. You'll learn things you may not already know about sex, things that will make you a more skillful, attentive, and therefore better lover. You'll work to overcome any fears, doubts, and insecurities that may have crept into your bedroom over the years. And, most importantly, you'll find ways to work sex back into your daily routine.

At the beginning of each chapter in this book, you'll find a "Sexploration Exercise," a set of five multiple questions to ask yourself and your lover. You can answer them, but be advised that there's no answer key; there are no wrong answers here. The point is to ask yourself these questions and answer them as honestly as possible. They are meant to open your mind to the subject matter in the particular chapter in which they appear and to get you started thinking about all the possibilities you may have been overlooking—or ignoring—to improve the quality of your sex life.

In these chapters, you'll read about people going through many of the same things you are, and you'll see how they've been able to work through their issues with sex, as well as the ramifications of not taking action. We'll provide helpful advice on a number of different sex topics, and hopefully arm you with all the information you'll need to take your erotic life from simmer to scorch.

Remember, just because you've hit middle age doesn't mean your sex life has to be over. Studies show that couples can enjoy great sex even into their 60s, 70s, 80s, and beyond. And even if you and your partner have a fantastic sex life right now, I'll bet our book will only make it even better.

Boomer's Guide to Sex That (Still) Sizzles will help both women and men get back to the basic pleasure of sex in concert with the life you lead, the beliefs you hold, and the fantasies you have not allowed yourself to explore. If we succeed, then your sex life will sizzle as never before!

part 1

Sex and the Baby Boomer

Sexploration Exercise #1

1. When was the last time you and your partner had sex?
   a. Last week
   b. About a month ago
   c. Not for several years
   d. Just last night

2. How much time do you usually devote to foreplay?
   a. Ten to fifteen minutes
   b. Hours and hours
   c. A couple minutes—just to get ready enough
   d. Anywhere from half an hour to an hour

3. Who usually initiates sex?
   a. He does
   b. She does
   c. No one—but someone should
   d. An outside-of-the-relationship lover

4. If you're not having as much sex as you used to have, what's the primary reason?
   a. No time
   b. Not attracted to your partner
   c. Don't have a partner
   d. Don't care about sex anymore

5. What's the number one thing you would change about your sex life right now if you could?
   a. Frequency
   b. Intensity
   c. Duration
   d. Lover

chapter 1

Sex Killers

"A relationship, I think, is like a shark. You know? It has to constantly move forward or it dies. And I think what we got on our hands is a dead shark."
—*Alvy Singer (Woody Allen),* Annie Hall

If sex is so wonderful, how come so many Baby Boomers are so bored with it? Have we become—dare we say it?—like our parents? Sex, the driving force in our younger years, has somehow taken a back seat to anything and everything else in our lives. Why?

Boredom is definitely a big part of the equation. We do "it" practically the same time of day, in the same part of the bed, and so forth. That is, if we do "it" at all. These days, it seems the leisure time we once looked forward to as time to be intimate with our partners has somehow become devoted to fiddling on the computer, checking what's on cable, or seeing what's in the fridge—in other words, anything but having sex.

There can be more to it than simple boredom, however. Other reasons why we're not having that much sex anymore include kids and the strain they can put on us physically as well as emotionally; holding on to old and stale resentments; and, in the worst cases, general apathy. In this chapter, we look at these "sex killers" more closely, and find effective ways to prevent them from slaying our sex drives.

Wake Me When It's Over

Virtually all bored married couples make love practically the same way. Partner A (usually the male, but not always) suggests sex with an off-hand, unromantic comment like, "How 'bout it?" Partner B considers the various items on a to-do list that could have been accomplished had sex not been suggested and weighs their importance against perhaps a sense of marital obligation and a basic desire not to rock the boat.

The couple then proceeds to the exact same spot where they have had sex for the past 17 years. They undress themselves (not each other) without really looking at each other. They generally make small talk about the children, about the house, about taxes, even about the dry-cleaning that has to be picked up.

Then they pile into bed, maybe turning off the TV—or maybe not. Within moments, the woman lies on her back, the man climbs on top, finds his balance, does what he needs to do, maybe helps her do what she needs to do, and it's over.

Does this scenario sound painfully familiar to you? Be honest: When's the last time you broke a sweat, mussed the sheets, passionately kissed, made eye contact, or even stopped thinking about changing the oil in the minivan during sex? This kind of sex, which is all too common, is not really good for anyone. If you can't connect with your partner, if you can't let loose and really be free to enjoy the reckless thrill of a mind-blowing roll in the hay, if you can't muster up enough enthusiasm, but you really wish you could, ask yourself this: How would things be different if you were to put even half of the energy into sex that you used to, before "life" got in the way?

Kids

Nothing can put a damper on your sex life like kids. It takes so much energy to raise children that we can become sexually neutered in the process. We stop thinking in sexual terms and instead view the world simply in terms of "what are the kids doing?" We advocate being great parents because the quality of our children's homework or piano lessons or macaroni and cheese is a lot more important than the quality of our orgasms. And while we don't diminish the importance of any of the above, we must acknowledge that these cannot come at the expense of our erotic lives; we must learn to strike a balance between seeing ourselves as parents and seeing ourselves as vital, sexual beings.

It is essential for parents to have a life apart from their children. Spring for a babysitter once in a while so that you can enjoy dinner and a movie, or even go for a walk. Impose on a sympathetic neighbor or relative, with a promise to return the favor soon. Of course it's okay to let children come between you and your partner, but as a thread that ties you together—not as a wedge you use to avoid each other on a sexual level, which will ultimately only drive you further apart.

What's Love Got to Do with It?

Another factor that gets in the way of connecting with each other sexually is the inability to let go of past grievances. Comedians frequently make fun of the spouse who reminds the other spouse of some wrong committed 11 years, six months, five days, four hours, and 42 minutes earlier. But there is truth to this joke.

Many of us carry a collection of unresolved wrongs about our partners. We wish that they were more this and less that. We wish they wouldn't act in certain ways. They earn too little or spend too much. Whatever the specific nature of the grievances, the fact is that they can accumulate and cast a long shadow over a couple's sex life. Arguments that have

> Working through unresolved differences with your spouse, with a therapist, or both, will go a long way toward solving any sex problem that may have cropped up in the marriage. If you're angry at your partner, it's awfully hard to feel sexually aroused.

nothing to do with sex often lead to denial of sex as a means of striking out, punishment, or simply expressing a lack of interest in the other partner.

Look at Me!

Anger is not the only thing that can tear a couple apart. Less apparent, and much more insidious, is apathy. Sometimes couples can be in a relatively even relationship, unaware that intimacy, sexual or otherwise, is draining away. Such was the case with Alison, 42, and Steve, 45, married eleven years.

"A couple of years ago, I was in a minor car accident. I walked away with little more wrong with me than a bruise over my right eye. I didn't realize this bruise was going to mark a much more serious situation, however. During the week or so it took for the bruise to disappear, I realized that my husband, Steve, never even once commented on it. Had he even noticed it?

It got me thinking. I started watching my husband watching me. It was amazing all the things he didn't seem to notice. So I tried a little experiment. About a week after the accident, I took things one step further by wearing the same T-shirt every night for a week. He didn't notice that, either. Amazing.

Ten days later, I applied makeup to my face to make it look as though the bruise had reoccurred. He didn't mention it. I reapplied the makeup every night for a week, taking it off each morning before work. We even had sex this week and even then, Steve never noticed the 'bruise.' I began to wonder how long it had been that my husband hadn't noticed me at all.

I got so angry with Steve one night while he was washing the dishes in the sink and ignoring everything I was saying—just nodding and shaking his shoulders—that I started to poke him in the back with my finger. 'Are you even listening to me? Don't you hear what I'm saying? Why won't you look at me?' By the end of this tirade, I was actually punching my husband in the back like a maniac. This finally got his attention.

That night, Steve and I finally talked it through. We agreed to go to couples' counseling—and made a pledge to each other to try and notice each other more."

Frighteningly enough, Alison's situation is surprisingly common. It sounds so odd, but few of us look carefully at the person we love. Either a newspaper screens us from them at the breakfast table, or we are sitting side by side, but not facing each other, watching TV. Perhaps one is out of bed half an hour before the other, getting ready for work and out the door before words can be exchanged. Or maybe one or both partners in a relationship travel a lot for work. Even in cases where couples spend almost every evening and weekend together, they still don't take the time to truly look at each other.

And yet, even though it's such a powerful experience to gaze into the face of the beloved, many couples stop doing so a few years into their marriage. Want to have great sex tonight? Take the time today to notice, to truly notice, your partner. Comment and compliment; flatter and flirt. You'll see the results!

Sexploration Exercise #2

1. Which of the following is least likely to appear in your day planner?
   a. Pick up Bobby from soccer practice
   b. Drop off Cindy at play date
   c. Get a gift for Fric and Frac's wedding anniversary
   d. Have sex

2. On average, how many times a week do you and your partner have sex?
   a. Five or more
   b. Less than three
   c. Once a week
   d. It's more like "how many times a year?!"

3. What was the last creative way you initiated sex with your partner?
   a. You walked around in the living room naked
   b. You mailed your partner a naughty note
   c. You greeted your partner at the front door wearing nothing but a light froth of whipped cream
   d. Creative? For sex? Sounds like too much work for me!

4. When was the last time you and your partner cuddled and stroked and kissed one another and didn't end up having sex?
   a. We try that at least once a week.
   b. Our anniversary weekend last month.
   c. Probably not since we were first together.
   d. What's the point of that?

5. How often have you and your partner made love in a place that was not your bed?
   a. Last week, on the dining room table
   b. Last night, on the kitchen floor
   c. Last month, in a rent-by-the-hour, cheesy motel room
   d. We never make love except in our own bed. Anywhere else just seems too dirty.

chapter 2

Banning Boring Bonking

"You take someone to the airport, it's clearly the beginning of the relationship. That's why I have never taken anyone to the airport at the beginning of a relationship."
—Harry Burns (Billy Crystal) to Sally Albright (Meg Ryan) in When Harry Met Sally

In the previous chapter, we looked at some of the main reasons Boomer couples often don't find coupling very compelling. We've got a whole book full of positions, angles, unusual sexual practices, and much more, to help you get your lust life back in full action, but first, we present some suggestions to give you a quick jumpstart.

The five methods presented in this chapter are intended to help you to make immediate and powerful transformations in your sex life, without straining your back, your marriage, or your relations with the town police. They're naughty, they're fun, and best of all, they'll start making you look at sex in a whole new light.

Method One: Prolong the Ecstasy

Take a quick scan of your kitchen. Do you have one of those wind-up portable timers? If you do, great! Grab it. You'll need it for this exercise. If you don't, go out and buy one and come right back to this book.

Bring that timer into your bedroom and set it for thirty minutes. And now the fun begins!

This is the time you and your lover are going to devote to appreciating each other before any actual intercourse occurs. Tease each other by slowly removing your clothes—or removing your partner's clothes. Gently stroke the skin as it becomes more and more exposed. Maybe even cover it with soft kisses.

In addition to making your partner feel special and loved, you will also be getting aroused and excited with the anticipation of what you're going to be doing when that timer runs out—and not before the 30 minutes are through. Don't believe us? Wait for the "ding"—you'll see how crazed with passion you'll be!

You can play this game in your own bedroom, but why not try it out in other venues as well? Check into one of those motels that rent "by the hour" or wherever your next sexual escapade will take place.

Method Two: Get a Room

The problem with having kids is that you can really only have sex when they're asleep. You don't want to risk them hearing you—and you especially want to avoid them walking in on you! That's why we advocate getting out of the house from time to time for sex. Not only will this provide a more exciting experience, but it will allow you to fully release your inhibitions and scream as loud as you want. And we all know how exhilarating that can feel!

Tell your kids that you're going out to dinner and a movie. Don't go to dinner and a movie. Go to a cheap motel, the kind of motel you would only go to if you were having an illicit affair you didn't want your spouse, boss, or the local newspaper to know about. The cost of a few hours at a motel is pretty much the same as the cost of dinner and a movie these days—and in some cases, even cheaper.

Method Three: Shop Around

One way to enjoy communicating with your partner to get what you want sexually is to make a game of it. We particularly like a game that involves some mail-order catalogues, a pair of scissors, a checkbook, an envelope, and a stamp.

On a day when you've gotten the kids out of the house and you're not expecting many interruptions, take the pile of catalogues to the sofa and invite your partner to join you. Tell your partner that you're going to be playing a trade-off game together; you pick something you really want out of one of the catalogs and show it to your partner. Then, let your partner know that you plan to give this gift to yourself, but you know you'll have to earn it.

Tell your partner to start removing his or her clothing, one piece at a time. While he or she is stripping down, you—trying to concentrate— fill out the order form, cut it out, write a check for the amount owed, stick it in the envelope, stamp, seal, and then walk it down to the nearest mailbox. When you come back, you will both be giddy with anticipation—you wondering what will be asked of you; your partner knowing all this time and ready to get his or her due.

And here's the bonus prize: In a couple of weeks, long after you've performed whatever it is your partner asked you for, you'll get a reward in the form of a package that arrives in the mail! Be sure to play this game often—but alternate who gets the gift and who gets the, um, prize!

Method Four: Increase Your Frequency

It's the curse of middle age: Sex doesn't happen enough to satisfy either party. Days can go by, even weeks, sometimes a whole month, and a couple suddenly realizes that sex has somehow fallen out of the marriage. If this is happening in your relationship, it's time for a variation on the shopping approach to alleviate boredom in the bedroom.

In this exercise, ask your partner what he or she would like as a gift—but this time, up the stakes. You don't have to break the bank, but the gift you agree on should be something very special—perhaps something of the cost and caliber you would typically save up to buy.

Visit an establishment in your neighborhood that offers those cards that get punched by the visit—with the purchase of every something or other, you work toward a free something else. Ask the person behind the counter if he won't mind sparing one. If this proves to be too much of a hassle, by all means, make one of your own! This isn't an art contest after all. Write the name of the desired object prominently on the card and place it on your partner's pillow.

When your partner asks what you're up to, tell him or her that every time he or she initiates sex, you will cross off one of the numbers on this card. Make sure your partner knows that as soon as the last number on the card gets crossed off, you're going to buy that item for your partner.

It's more than likely that your partner will see the playfulness in what you've done—and will probably also be inspired to make a card for you!

The purpose of this exercise is to get you and your partner back into a regular rhythm of sexual activity, and to allow yourselves to have a really fun time while you're doing it. It's a heck of a lot cheaper in the long run to buy your partner that expensive gift than to slog through a dozen sessions with a properly trained (and not inexpensive) sex therapist.

> *"Sex between two consenting adults is great. Among five, it's fantastic."*
>
> —Woody Allen

Method Five: Write It In

There's no doubt that we live in the busiest period in human history. We're busy, we're tired, and we're stressed. Work, family, and leisure activities pull us in a thousand directions. So where does sex fit in? Sadly, oftentimes the answer is "nowhere." We've become so busy with what we consider "important" time-eaters, like working on our golf handicap or cleaning out our email inbox, that we don't have time to initiate or say yes to sex—unless of course, we write it into our schedules. But how is that conducive to great sex?

Many believe that sex is supposed to be a spontaneous act that is ruined by advance planning. We say the opposite is true. Busy times require committed partners to add sex to the calendar. Yes, we actually want you to make sex dates with your partner. Put them into your planner, the same way you would plan a movie, business appointment, or golf game. Don't be afraid to plan regular sexual encounters with your partner—and coordinate your schedules, for goodness sake, so that you both remember to turn up in the same bedroom at the same time!

> It's hard to be "in the mood" when you can barely keep your eyes open. That's why planning sex for early in the evening (or even earlier in the day), when both parties are still wide awake and at their physical peak, is a great idea.

Surprisingly, planned sex is often much better than spontaneous sex. That's because planned sex allows both partners to look forward to the event and think through exactly what they'd like to do to each other. In spontaneous sex, one partner has to move very rapidly from a non-sexual, nonphysical mode to a boudoir mentality. It's not always easy to make that switch, especially when we have a lot of other things on our minds. When you add sex to your schedule, you have to make time for it—just like you have to make time to visit the doctor or meet with a difficult client, and certainly sex is a lot more fun than these other events! Of course, you may want to come up with another word for it, in case your boss or your kids happen to see your day planner. Try something modest like "private moment."

We hope that you and your partner will try one, some, or all of the above approaches to banishing bedroom boredom. They'll all make sex more fun—and isn't that what great sex is all about?

> "Oh, Moneypenny, the story of our relationship: close, but no cigar."
>
> —James Bond
> (Pierce Brosnan),
> The World Is Not Enough

Sexploration Exercise #3

1. How long ago did you give birth to your last child?
   a. Within the past year
   b. Within the past five years
   c. More than ten years ago
   d. More than twenty years ago

2. When you were pregnant, you:
   a. Enjoyed a healthy, active sex life.
   b. Lost interest in sex somewhat, but had moments of real interest.
   c. Wanted to have sex all the time, but your partner wouldn't touch you.
   d. Decided that you finally got what you wanted and stopped having sex with your partner all together.

3. Since the onset of menopause, your sex drive is:
   a. Unaffected. You still want sex to the same degree you always did.
   b. Different. You have a little trouble getting properly aroused, which make sometimes makes sex more frustrating than fulfilling.
   c. Amplified. You want it more than you ever did!
   d. All but dead.

4. If you are a man, how are you handling the hormonal changes affecting your partner's pregnancy or menopause—and their effect on your sex life?
   a. They're really not affecting your sex life very much at all.
   b. Your partner somehow doesn't have the same sex drive she used to have.
   c. You are trying to be as patient as possible.
   d. You've had enough tiptoeing around on eggshells and you're ready to head out and look for "a little on the side."

5. Since the arrival of the new baby, sex occurs between you and your partner:
   a. Frequently.
   b. Regularly.
   c. Occasionally.
   d. Seldom—if ever.

chapter 3

Changes in Women

"I know all about your woman's troubles there, Edith, but when I had the hernia that time, I didn't make you wear the truss. If you're gonna have the change of life, you gotta do it right now. I'm gonna give you just 30 seconds. Now c'mon and change!"
—*Archie Bunker (Carrol O'Connor) to wife Edith (Jean Stapleton),* All in the Family

When our parents were our age, most of them had already raised their children—sent them to college, perhaps even married them off—and were on the cusp of a new chapter in their lives: grandparenthood. In our generation, however, marriage is something many of us waited to do until we were settled in our careers and lives. While some of us may have put it off until our late twenties, many waited till our thirties to get married—sometimes even later than that. So in addition to the physical changes our mothers were going through at our age, such as the onset of menopause, women the same age today are also faced with pregnancy and childbirth and the changes these events have on their bodies and their sex lives.

In this chapter, we look at physiological issues female Boomers may be facing today, and how these may be affecting the frequency and intensity of their sex lives.

Jean, 44

"Even while I was growing up, I knew I wanted to devote my life to my career. My mother was a stay-at-home mom, which in those days wasn't uncommon. She seemed happy enough to take care of the demands of the household and raising five kids. As I got older and began to understand that she was not just our mother, but that she was a woman in her own right, I started to feel that there was something missing when I looked into her eyes. It was like even though she was happy with her family, there were so many other things she could be doing, and her brain was slowly dying. She always did really well in her classes—straight As even—right up until the semester she dropped out of college to become my father's wife.

I never wanted to have that blank look in my eye, like I hadn't done anything really significant or important with my life, you know? Like I wasted my talents to raise a house full of kids, and when they grew up and went out on their own, would then just be left with nothing. So I worked hard. Really hard. I thrived at school. Graduated Ivy League at the top of my class even. Aced the L-SATs. Even got into a great law school. All I ever wanted to do was be a successful lawyer. By the time I was 32, I had made partner at a prestigious firm, I knew I had made it.

Being a woman—a young woman—in such a prominent position, I had to work overtime—double time, really, in order to make the senior old school male partners believe they hadn't made a mistake in appointing me. So I barely had time to sleep. I went out on dates, had many different sex partners, but never had the time to commit to developing a serious relationship that might lead to marriage and kids one day. A part of me always felt I wanted to have children, but when was I ever going to find the time?

For my fortieth birthday some friends threw me a party, and that's when I met my now-husband, Greg. He was older than me by a few years and also a workaholic, so he understood my hours and dedication to my job. We were married within a year.

Our marriage was great; we could work as much as we wanted and always come home to regular sex—that is, if we weren't too tired. Well, we were addicted to each other. We were never too tired! But then a new variable came into play: Just after I turned forty-two, I learned I was pregnant. Me! Pregnant! I was more excited than I thought I would be at that kind of news, but I was also very worried. Wasn't I a little old to be having kids?

But that wasn't all that bothered me about being pregnant. The more my body began to change and the more the baby began to show, the less Greg wanted to have sex with me. He never initiated sex, and when I did, he found more and more excuses not to. Well, if you've ever been pregnant, you know what a hormone factory you can become—in terms of wanting sex a lot and also in having your moods fluctuate like crazy. I started to feel that my husband didn't desire me anymore because of how my body had changed. And worse, that the sexy career woman he fell in love with was morphing into a sparkless mother-type—kind of like my mother.

One night I just exploded. I tried coming on to my husband before bed. He kissed me on the cheek and rolled over. I was furious and frustrated. I had had enough. I told Greg I wanted a divorce—that I wanted to be with someone who wanted me. He was baffled and asked me where I got that idea. I told him it was because he never wanted to have sex with me anymore, which seemed to horrify him. 'I always want to have sex with you, Jean. You're the most beautiful woman I've ever known! Don't you know how hard it's been for me to not jump on top of you?' I was confused and I asked him why he felt that he had to keep his hands off me. 'Jesus, Jean. Because of the baby. I can't make love to you while you're so pregnant. Not like we do it. It could hurt the baby!'

Like many men Greg's age, Greg never got the memo about the true resilience of the female anatomy. As soon as I told

> "We'll talk about uncomfortable when you're nine months pregnant!"
>
> —Annelle (Darryl Hannah), Steel Magnolias

him that not only was it okay for us to have sex while I was pregnant, but that it was actually quite healthy, we ended up calling in sick to work—yes, us!—and spent the next three days in bed!"

Pregnancy

Yes, it's true. Jean was not just making this up to trick her husband into having sex with her. Sex during pregnancy, no matter how earth-shakingly powerful, will not cause a woman to spontaneously miscarry a baby. Nor will the release of semen into the woman's body poison or otherwise harm the fetus.

Despite all the scientific evidence at hand to disprove these assumptions, there can still be reluctance on the part of a man, especially an older man who grew up with "the old ways," to have sex with his pregnant wife or lover. Psychologically speaking, men sometimes find it difficult to get past thinking that they're sharing their wife's body with a very small stranger, their unborn child. But more common is that a man may not be comfortable physically expressing his passion for his wife or lover. That he, like Greg, may think that even by penetrating his wife during intercourse, he might be putting the safety of the baby in jeopardy.

The flip side of this is what happened to Jean; namely, that a woman who already knows the baby will not be in any danger ends up feeling rejected by what she perceives is her partner's lack of sexual interest in her. And this lack of sexual interest could only stem from the diminished attraction he feels, watching her body bloat and distort to accommodate the baby. This is a dangerous place. If a couple continues to run on assumptions, if they don't communicate, they only create a rift between one another, making their sex life suffer and causing irreversible damage to the relationship. However, if they bring their feelings to the surface, and share their thoughts and feelings and anxieties like they share the toothpaste in the bathroom, then the relationship can only grow—and make the sex only better!

So while studies have shown that sex during pregnancy can be okay, think of all the ways it can be fantastic! Consider how free you are to have it pretty much any time you want. There's no "that time of the month" that's going to hold squeamish lovers back. Nor does any time need to be wasted worrying about getting pregnant. The deed is already done! And while especially in the later months, you'll find that some positions you may be fond of will probably be impossible to pull off, you still have a veritable banquet of sexual delights available to you to sample and savor. And who knows—this might prove to be a great time to get down with your sense of sexual creativity as you and your partner improvise around the "newcomer."

Hello, Stranger!

Once a child is born, a whole new set of sex-prohibitive obstacles might just rise to the surface. Of course, it's not rational to expect that you're going to bounce right back into your sexual selves after just experiencing childbirth and all the physical and emotional strain that goes along with it. The elation is only going to carry you so far—like back to your home and into your bed to get some much-needed rest. Typically, sex might not come up at all in the first couple of months after a baby is born, even if the doctor says that vaginal intercourse will be possible again within 4 to 6 weeks. It may be longer if the child was delivered Cesarean, which is major surgery, folks. Just be patient!

After childbirth, fatigue plays an unimaginably powerful role—and especially when you don't have the bounce-back-ability and physical stamina of a 25-year-old. Just as you can't stay out all night partying anymore without feeling the ramifications for the rest of the week, so can you not expect to be at peak form after getting up several times a night, every night, to look after an infant. And this goes for sex as much as for anything else. So don't worry if your sex life doesn't fall back into full swing even months after a baby is born. You'll get there!

On top of the exhaustion that comes along with being new parents is the loss of privacy. You're not alone in the house anymore. Noisy partners may find that they have to restrict their exclamations because the baby (or the nanny) might overhear. Also, when you do finally get back to your bedroom business, you may find that you're having more "quickies" than you're used to, simply because that may be all you have time for.

During all of this, however, it's important to keep in mind that your partner is still a sexual being, and one you want to enjoy on every imaginable level, even if you feel he or she is not making enough time for you. Be kind to your partner. Fantasize and flirt when you can. And when you finally feel comfortable enough to leave the baby with a family member or close friend overnight, take some time to be together—just you and your partner. Enjoy long, languorous intimate time and get back in touch with your sensual sides.

Menopause

Menopause is the most significant physiological change that female Baby Boomers are facing today. It is a period of time that may last anywhere from a few years to 15 years, during which ovulation gradually comes to an end. The median age for women to begin menopause is about 50 or 51; however, many women begin to experience fluctuations in their menstrual cycles in their early 40s and even their late 30s, during which time they are described as pre-menopausal.

Symptoms of menopause include hot flashes, sweats, insomnia, an inability to concentrate, vaginal dryness, and sporadic menstrual periods, among others. Psychologically, menopause can be traumatic for some women as its onset serves as a physical reminder of things that may have already been affecting women emotionally, such as the loss of youth and the inability to procreate, which, for some women leads to a loss of vibrancy and a sense of not feeling sexual anymore.

But while it is true that many women report a diminishing of sexual desire during menopause, many also report a revival of sexual feelings. Women in their late 40s and early 50s have boasted sex drives stronger and their sex lives more satisfying than ever, a sharp contrast to the typical belief that menopause deadens sexual drive.

Andrew, 55

"My wife used to be a hellcat in the sack. I'm not kidding. Some days I would come home from an exhausting day in the office to find that she had shipped the kids off to her sister's for the night. She'd greet me at the door wrapped in nothing but cellophane. Or a velvet ribbon. One time, she even opened the front door completely naked, her sexy parts covered in peanut butter—one of my favorite foods!

Shelly couldn't get enough. She was always ready, willing, and, if you'll excuse this graphic statement, always absolutely wet! She never required a lot of foreplay to get revved up; it was like she came out of the box that way, so to speak.

Starting from about a few years ago, the changes began. Shelly was only forty-two at the time; that menopause could be starting didn't occur to either of us because she was much too young. What had occurred to us, however, was that it was taking her much longer to get into it—at least it was taking her body much longer. Shelly just wasn't getting wet enough and as a result, sex started to become painful—for her and also for me. And then the sex just kind of stopped.

Shelly and I had a good relationship. It's not like sex was the only thing that had ever bound us together, so it wasn't like we had nothing left when we stopped having sex. But our relationship was definitely strained.

One day, Shelly came home from a doctor's appointment beaming like I hadn't seen her beam in years. 'What got into you?' I asked, nearly expecting she was going to tell me that her doctor knew how to get her excited and that she was having a raging affair with him. That's how much she was glowing. She continued to smile at me, and then she got a devious look in her eye. 'Pull down your pants. Now!' she ordered, as she started to disrobe right in the middle of the living room. Then she whipped out a brown paper bag from her pocket. Inside was a small bottle of lubricant she had just purchased from the drug store. 'I said, pull them down!'

Apparently, what Shelly learned from her doctor that day was that menopause can start as early as in a woman's thirties, and that one of the symptoms of this change in life was vaginal dryness. Suffice to say, we're both thrilled that the hellcat is back and ready for action!"

Don't Stop! Don't Stop!

Menopause itself didn't put a damper on Shelly's sex drive; rather, it was the symptoms that made her feel less sexy. But as Shelly learned from her doctor, the physiological changes that may affect sexual performance need not signal the end of enjoying sexual activity. Rather, they can serve as motivation to find alternative methods, which in itself can lead to greater sexual satisfaction.

Menopause does not alter or eradicate the physiological ability or emotional desire to engage in healthy, satisfying sex. Sexual desire in human beings does not depend on the ability to procreate. The physio-sexual changes of aging alone will not eliminate your capacity to maintain a satisfying sex life. There are ways to maximize sexual functioning in the later years. Continued physical exercise will help to maintain sexual functioning. Sex alone is a productive physical form of exercise and continued sexual expression throughout the adult years is a crucial factor. Just as it is never too late to stop a bad habit such as smoking, it is never too late, or too soon, to reactivate scheduled sexual activity. It's good for the heart and it burns calories!

In short, we want to share the good news with both women and men that a woman's sexual life does not end with menopause. Rather, for women's sexual response, the 40s and even the 50s are only the beginning!

Sexploration Exercise #4

1. Since you turned forty, how has your sex drive changed as compared to when you were a younger man?
   a. No change—I still want it as much as ever.
   b. Slightly different—I want it a lot, but I don't always have the energy to perform like my younger self did.
   c. Very different—too many other things interest me more than the prospect of having sex.
   d. What sex drive?

2. Overall, how would you rate the physical shape you're in?
   a. Never better.
   b. I've maybe put on a couple of pounds, but I still feel healthy and energetic.
   c. I could probably use a little more exercise.
   d. Walking from the couch to the kitchen can sometimes be taxing.

3. How would you rate your erections at this point in your life?
   a. No change from before—rock solid and ready to rock and roll.
   b. Slightly less powerful, but still up to getting the job done.
   c. Hit or miss. Sometimes they're great, sometimes it requires a bit more work to get them to their maximum potential.
   d. I don't have that many erections any more.

4. If you are a woman, are you still satisfied by your male partner?
   a. Always.
   b. Sometimes.
   c. Not anymore.
   d. Never really was to begin with.

5. What would you most like to change about your sex life after forty?
   a. More sex in general.
   b. Greater passion and intensity—not exactly like it used to be, but also not like we're two corpses just laying there either! We may be older, but we're not dead!
   c. More variety and excitement.
   d. Nothing—everything's just right!

chapter 4

Changes in Men

"I've given up on sex completely. I put a mirror
over the breakfast table."
—Rodney Dangerfield

Just like women, when men get older, their bodies also go through changes. There is no such thing as male menopause, per se, but that doesn't mean men are going to escape age and its effect on their sexuality. The changes can affect sexual performance on many levels—or maybe not even very much at all.

The long and short of it is that changes in a man's sexuality during middle age are to be expected. There is nothing "wrong" with men who experience the changes we're about to discuss. As men reach their 40s, 50s, and beyond, they simply think about sex a lot less often. In addition, they may experience less intense erections, and even lose them altogether from time to time.

In addition, men produce a slightly smaller amount of testosterone, our sexual rocket fuel, each passing year. The first noticeable drop-off typically occurs around age 30; the process accelerates after age 50. But even 50-year-olds still produce tons of testosterone—more than enough to get the job done.

In this chapter, we look at some of these changes and offer advice on how to work with and around them to enjoy a fulfilling, satisfying sex life.

Eric, 44

"I've always had this double-edged relationship with the way I think about sex. It's always dominated my thinking from the time I was 12 years old. I always hoped that at some point as I got up in age I'd stop thinking about it all the time. But now that I actually am at that point, I can't help thinking that something's wrong with me!

I can still get an erection very easily, and sex is no problem. The difference is that today, compared to twenty years ago, if my mind wanders during sex, there goes the erection! I can get it back, but that didn't happen when I was 20. And the other difference is that it takes much longer for me to achieve a second erection after I've ejaculated. That bothered me so much, I actually started to see a therapist about it. I didn't tell my wife at first because I was kind of embarrassed. I also didn't want my wife to think that she was in any way the problem. I did, though, at first, think she was the problem.

The therapist was great. She told me there was nothing odd or unusual about what I was experiencing. And my wife was definitely *not* the problem. She reminded me that I'm not 20, and what was going on with my erections is the reality for most men my age. The good news is that as long as I take care of myself physically, I'll be able to have sex into my sixties and seventies. Or beyond. Although to tell you the truth, I have no idea whether I'll still want to have sex at that age. Oh, who am I kidding? I'll probably still want it as much as I do now!"

Keeping It Up

Men can improve their sexual responsiveness by getting back into shape. They can put down the remote control and the Budweiser and renew their gym membership. They can get on a bicycle, take a walk or a run around the neighborhood. Three 20-minute periods of aerobic activity a week are all a man needs to keep himself in top physical—and as a result, sexual—health.

Countless American males engage in risky behaviors that can influence men's sexual response from middle age onwards. These behaviors include smoking, stress, fatigue, the use and abuse of recreational and prescription drugs, and the great American pastime of overeating. If a man doesn't take proper care of his body, his sexual responsiveness, both mental and physical, will be compromised. Some diminishment in erectile firmness is unavoidable, and there's just not much science or lifestyle can do to affect reduced refraction times; however, to a large degree, the quality of a man's sex life is, to a truly remarkable degree, in his own hands!

Back Off, Jack

For men—and women—advancing age likely also means that our backs are not as strong as they once were, and that we're probably throwing them out with more frequency than we did when we were younger—especially during sex.

How can you make sure back problems don't get in the way of your sex life? Of course you could give up sex all together—but how much fun would that be? A better alternative is to examine some of the sexual options for people in your position. If you have a back condition, try to be on the bottom as much as possible so that you can lay flat and don't arch your back during sex. That doesn't mean you're limited to missionary if it's the female's back that's in trouble or woman on top if it's the male's; there are many positions in which to enjoy sex that can be satisfying for both partners as well as comfortable. Experiment with kneeling, sitting, and other positions before you shut the door on sex. We'll talk more about sexual positions in part three of this book.

The third option is to do something about your back, such as strengthening it by finding a competent physical therapist or personal trainer. Many people with bad backs simply suffer or treat themselves with drugs when the right exercise regimen can not only relieve the pain but do something about the underlying symptoms.

> "*You're not the man I knew ten years ago.*"
> "*It's not the years, honey, it's the mileage.*"
>
> —*Marion (Karen Allen) and Indiana Jones (Harrison Ford),* Raiders of the Lost Ark

Embrace the Changes

Sexual changes that men may be noticing in their own physiology are entirely normal and age-appropriate. Does this mean that Boomer couples cannot have incredibly fulfilling sex? Of course not! However, these natural changes may trigger an emotional response, a sense that the man is no longer attractive, that his sexuality is on the wane, or even that his sex life is about to collapse. It just isn't so. By *believing* that these signs point to the death of one's sexuality, men can actually think themselves into a state of mind in which they come to believe that they cannot maintain an erection at all. In other words, the more men think that they have some sort of sexual problem, the more likely they are to *bring on* a serious sexual problem.

Sexploration Exercise #5

1. How important do you feel communication is in a sexual relationship?
   a. It's the most important thing.
   b. It's fairly important, but you can work around it if need be.
   c. It's really not very important. If you're not getting off, you can just fantasize.
   d. What do you mean, communication—talking? About sex? Jeez, it's bad enough that we even have to do it! Why would we drag it out by talking about it?

2. Do you and your partner communicate your sexual needs to one another?
   a. Every time something comes up that we need to discuss, we talk about it—and that means even while we're doing it!
   b. Sometimes we talk, but mostly we just do!
   c. We generally keep quiet and deal with it unless something feels really wrong or uncomfortable.
   d. Are you kidding me? My partner's so sensitive, if I told them something they were doing wasn't getting me off, they'd be so hurt, they'd probably leave me!

3. How do your sexual conversations come up?
   a. Usually afterwards, in a neutral setting, like over dinner.
   b. Right then and there—if something isn't working, there's no time like the present to make it better.

   c. Typically it's out of frustration and anger, and it doesn't matter when—though we each usually strike while the iron is hot, so to speak.
   d. They don't.

4. When your partner communicates something about your sex life to you, how do you respond?
   a. I am as open and understanding as possible and try to foster an environment of mutual sharing and communication as much as I possibly can.
   b. I try to listen, but I'd be lying if I told you that I never got bent out of shape over it.
   c. It really hurts my feelings when I'm not doing something right because I try really hard. Why doesn't anything I do seem to please my partner?
   d. Hey, if they don't like what I got to give 'em, let 'em find someone else!

5. Have you ever considered counseling as a way to communicate sexually with your partner?
   a. Sometimes
   b. Often
   c. Not usually
   d. Never

chapter 5

Talking It Over

"I find you very attractive. Your assertiveness tells me that you feel the same way about me. But ritual remains that we must do a series of platonic actions before we can have intercourse. But all I really want to do is have sex with you as soon as possible."
—*Nash (Russell Crowe) to Alicia (Jennifer Connelly),* A Beautiful Mind

You don't have to be a relationship expert to know that the key to enjoying a strong, satisfying relationship is healthy, open communication. At this point in our lives, whether we've been involved in a decades-long marriage or we've tested the waters on a mostly solo voyage, paying calls on many different ports, we've seen that the greatest romantic successes result when both partners are free to share ideas and aspirations, comments and constructive criticisms—if we've been paying attention. But while most mature men and women agree that communication is essential, conversational inhibitions persist. Why? The reasons are many. It may be a fear of hurting the other's feelings, the anxiety of anticipated rejection, or in the most dire of cases, general apathy. Of course, if you are reading this book, we're guessing this last category does not apply to you.

Experts argue and agree in their assessments of why men and women don't—or can't—communicate properly: We have different ways we express and interpret information, we've been conditioned by parents and peers to behave in certain ways, we're from different planets. All of this information can spin us in circles and cause us to be frustrated to the point of giving up as oftentimes, what looks good on paper doesn't always translate to real-life interaction and thus, open conversation between the sexes.

This is never more true than when it comes to discussing what goes on behind the bedroom door. But despite the old and ingrained clichés about the differences in communication styles between men and women, open communication assures that partners' needs will be met, and, for the purposes of this book, that the lusciously exciting, life-affirming, cosmically carnal sex we may have had in our twenties and thirties might just become a reality in later years.

But how do we get there?

Margaret, 48

"I met my husband, Erik, when we were both in college. I was just a freshman, while he was a senior. My sexual experience at that time was limited to occasional necking on Saturday night dates; with three partners already under his belt, Erik seemed to have all the know-how and confidence of a world-class lover. Naturally, he still had a lot to learn, but we didn't know that. I, on the other hand, had no idea what I wanted or what sex was all about.

The first time we made love, Erik climbed on top of me, and before I knew it, it was over. I didn't know I could tell him that I didn't feel anything but a stinging pain. That I was expecting—and deserved—much more. As a result, he thought I was satisfied with having sex this way, and I perpetuated the myth by pretending I was satisfied.

By the time I hit my thirties, the typical missionary style we made love in just didn't seem to be enough anymore. I'm embarrassed to say that

I had my first orgasm, nearly by accident, with a high-pressure, detachable showerhead we had recently purchased. As wonderful as that felt, I wished I could share that amazing pleasure with my husband.

When I was 40, I walked in on Erik masturbating to a video in the family room in the middle of the night. Of course I was mortified. I was so humiliated, I wanted to pack my bags and leave my marriage that night. Luckily, Erik wouldn't let me go. I asked him why he needed pornography when he had *me*. He hesitated at first, which made me think he wanted to leave me but didn't know how to tell me. But then he explained that he loved having sex with me, but sometimes it was too tame for him, and that he longed to try out new things with me, but didn't know how to approach me about it. I told him that there might be things I wanted to try, too, but that I had always been afraid of hurting his feelings by asking for them.

Much to my initial embarrassment, Erik suggested we watch the video together, and maybe that way, if I was too shy to actually *tell* him what I wanted, I could comment on what I was seeing, and let him know when I saw something that looked interesting. Needless to say, I thought this was absolutely crazy, but I trusted him. If he thought this would be good for us, the least I could do was give it a try.

All I could do at first was laugh, but once I got over the giggles, I started to get really aroused. I turned to him when I found something that looked really intriguing, a man performing oral sex on a woman, and said, 'What about that?' Erik turned the tape off and tried it out on me. And at last I was able to climax with my husband. We broke down a huge obstacle that night and used our video method several times until we got comfortable enough to just ask. We don't need those videos anymore, but sometimes we'll put one on just for fun!"

The Door Swings Both Ways

In the case of Margaret and Erik, a relationship-long lack of sexual communication led each to seek out other ways to find sexual satisfaction—Erik with the VCR and Margaret with bathroom hardware—when all they really needed was an open door for communication. No one's saying that adult videos are the answer, but, as in the case of Margaret and Erik, that's simply what worked. We'll learn more about it in Chapter 31.

Essentially, what's needed is for someone to simply open that door. And why not make that someone you? There are many ways to do this—from mild to wild. The trick is to try. To experiment and explore. To share. Because, sadly, the outside venue your partner seeks out to fulfill what's lacking in your bed could end up being another person.

A Two-Way Street

Even in these progressive times, sex for many remains a topic closed for conversation, for the reasons we have already expressed and others. Aside from general shyness, a person who expresses his or her sexual desires runs many risks, including rejection, or that these expressions may be interpreted as criticism of sexual "style," or of seeming too forward, too perverted, too deviant. We may be the generation that sparked the sexual revolution, but that doesn't mean we always know as we get further from the recklessness of youth what to do with all that sexual freedom now.

As is the case in any marriage or long-term relationship, there's the fear that anything either party says can become part of the permanent record, and the other party can read back that testimony at any time, now or in the future. This increases the anxiety and sense of caution. So what's the solution? How can couples have a fruitful discussion about sex, without lighting all kinds of new, unpleasant fires? As we touched on earlier, there is no shortage of guidance for couples in this area.

One of the many sex books out there that offers some of the best advice about communication in the sexual arena is the granddaddy of them all, *Sex In Human Loving*, by Masters and Johnson. The basic idea that Masters and Johnson offer can be summed up in four words: *know before you go*. In other words, think through in advance exactly what you want to say to your partner and how. The more time you spend thinking it through, the clearer you are likely to be. It is important for us to express our feelings about our sex lives to our partners clearly, thoughtfully, gently, and not over-emotionally. We want to be specific, reassuring, and we never, ever, want to appear accusatory.

For that reason, it's important to avoid absolutes. The words "always" and "never" have the unfortunate effect of putting the other immediately on the defensive, and for good reason: In any situation, there are no absolutes. It's like saying "You never take out the garbage," when what we really mean to say is, "It would help if you took out the garbage more than once a week." By speaking to our partners in accusatory absolutes, we instill in them a sense that we believe not only have they never provided us with a satisfying experience, but we highly doubt that they could ever do so in the future.

Another word you want to omit when talking about sex is the word "you" as a launch point. When we start a sentence with the word "you," we automatically place the other person on the defensive. Think about the other areas of your life. If anyone—a parent, a teacher, or a boss—begins a sentence with the words "you do X," our first thought—and often our first response—will be to blurt out, "No, I don't." We end up with a situation in which there is more heat than light, and the common word for such situations is "argument." Instead, pull the focus onto yourself, simply by starting with the word "I." And always focus first on the positive, such as "I like it when you ...," then be as specific and flattering as is possible.

Ladies, you might try: "I like the way you massage my clitoris gently at first, and then when you know I'm getting closer to coming, you apply more pressure and massage me faster and faster." If your partner has a tendency to get too excited, like maybe he forgets where he is and what he's doing—maybe it seems like he thinks he's scrubbing the paint off a car with a toothbrush—don't say, "Then you rub me much too hard, and I almost can't come because it actually begins to hurt." Think about how you'd feel in his shoes. Certainly, you want to know the truth, but only in the most positive light. Try instead: "What I think might be great to try is if you continue to tease me, and press down lighter than usual as I'm about to come. I've heard you can make an orgasm last longer that way." In that way, you'll have accomplished three things:

1. You'll have made your lover feel really good about being able to drive you mad with ecstasy.

2. You'll not have needlessly hurt your partner's feelings by making him think he doesn't have what it takes to properly bring you to orgasm.

3. You'll now be able to have the satisfaction you crave.

And gentlemen, there are tactful ways for you to approach a similar uncomfortable situation with your partner. If your lover has a tendency to hold your penis incorrectly when manually stimulating you, perhaps creating painful friction by inadvertently pinching the tender skin between her fingers, don't tell her: "Hey—quit it! That really hurts!" Instead, and maybe even at another time, try: "I love when you stimulate me with your hands. That kind of pleasure feels like nothing else. And you know, I've heard the slippery sensation you get from using a lubricant is amazing. Is that something you may be interested in trying?"

> *"He hates it when I cry. It reminds him of our wedding night."*
> —Marie Barone (Doris Roberts),
> Everyone Loves Raymond

To sum up: Think before you speak. Don't blurt things out in annoyance and frustration during the very vulnerable sex act; talk to your partner the way you want to be talked to. Later maybe. And remember to be as specific as you possibly can, because the clearer the instructions your partner receives, the happier you will both be.

The bottom line on asking for what you want: Take your time, think it through, be specific, don't accuse and "kitchen sink" (throwing everything but the kitchen sink into your criticisms) it. When you avoid putting the other person on the defensive, you'll soon be opening new ways to communicate you may never even have dreamed of.

Shaking It Up

It comes as a surprise to no one that men think about sex all the time, while many women, on top of thinking about sex often, also spend a lot of time wrapped up in other priorities that are at least as important—such as taking care of the children, their jobs, or the home. So, men, be advised to not take the rejection of an offer of sex while your wife or girlfriend is wrapped up in these other pursuits as a blow to your sexual self-esteem. Instead of jumping her over a sink of dirty dishes, you might say, "I sure hope we can make time later to be alone. There's something about you today. I just can't take my eyes off you."

What effect does this have? First, it makes her feel wanted and attractive, suds to the elbows and all. It also makes her feel like you appreciate and value the other contributions she makes to the relationship, and free to refuse sex at the moment, without missing out at a more opportune time. (It may just also get her ready, thinking about what's to come!)

And ladies, try to accept that your lover may be plagued with the male condition of constant sex on the brain. It's okay to be annoyed, but don't angrily wave him away and make him feel unattractive and deviant. If there is to be a "later," playfully remind him about the garbage that needs to go out—and then why not make a game of it? You can tell him he'll get what's coming to him if he's a good boy. And then pretend to be a naughty taskmistress as you inspect and judge that the job has been completed to your satisfaction. If not, why not keep him panting with the knowledge that great sex will be the reward for a job well done. We'll talk more about role play in Chapter 27.

By All Means, Talk—But Don't Forget to Listen!

You have to expect, and, in fact, hope, that when you open this channel of conversation, you may just get a few suggestions from your partner about things you can do to please him or her more effectively. Be advised: Unless you and your partner are reading this book together, you may not be on the same page when you broach the topic. You have to accept that your partner may not know to phrase his or her needs as gently or tactfully. Take that under consideration and be as understanding as you can be, no matter how much like bullets tearing through your sexual self-esteem the words of your partner may seem.

When you have been able to express yourself, and your partner has been able to contribute what he or she needs to, explain to your partner that your mission is to please him or her—be that in the bedroom or in everyday life. And by all means, gently tell your partner how *you'd* like to be told these things. While some of this certainly sounds like rudimentary common sense, in the heat of a charged moment, we all know that basic common sense has a tendency to elude even the most grounded soul.

If you can't resolve your issues just by yourselves, remember that couples' counseling is a great way to help yourselves become more objective about your particular situation. Sometimes you may need a third-party to mediate, even if just temporarily. There's no shame in that. Just be prepared: The state of a couple's sex life may mirror the overall relationship. If things are one-sided sexually, chances are that the entire relationship may be imbalanced. So if you think it might be bigger than you can properly and effectively handle together, by all means, seek outside guidance from an expert.

Remember that just because your parents and grandparents never looked to another person for guidance about their sexual relationships doesn't mean you should not. (And keep in mind that just because you were not made aware that counseling happened doesn't mean it didn't.) Never before in our society have we been as knowledgeable and open about the nature of sexual relations as now. Books, television programs, videos, and websites dealing with relations between the sexes abound. The real tragedy of our lives today is that we've never had so many life preservers to throw to couples, and yet so many relationships are drowning in a sea of misinformation, old ideas, or fear. If you feel help is necessary, don't try to handle it by yourself.

Sexploration Exercise #6

1. As a single Baby Boomer, do you find things have drastically changed since you first started dating in the 1960s and 1970s?
   a. Extremely so
   b. Somewhat
   c. Not very much
   d. Not at all

2. If you've already had your first post-marital sexual experience, how did it make you feel?
   a. Energized and alive
   b. Dirty and sinful—but in a very good way
   c. Hungry and anxious for your next attack—like a predator with a jungle to dominate and conquer
   d. Guilty and remorseful—as if you had just cheated on your former partner

3. If you haven't, what's holding you back?
   a. I'd like to take a little more time to heal before I inflict myself on others.
   b. My ex has made me hate every member of the opposite sex, and unless I'm planning on switching teams anytime soon, you can be sure I'll be sleeping alone for a long time to come!
   c. I don't think I'd know how to do it with someone else.
   d. I'd sooner leap into my spouse's grave than jump into bed with someone new.

4. Are you considering trying to date a person ten or more years younger than you are?
   a. No way! I don't want to have to teach someone everything I know!
   b. Oh yes! I'd love to teach someone everything I know!
   c. I don't know—I feel like these kids might know something I don't know and that might be embarrassing for me.
   d. Why not? You'll never know what you have to offer—or what someone else can offer you—if you don't give it a try!

5. What are you looking for in a partner at this point in your life?
   a. A playmate. Someone strictly to fool around with.
   b. A boyfriend or girlfriend. Someone with whom I can do things like go to dinner and the movies, and with whom I can enjoy lots of great sex.
   c. A companion. Someone with whom I'd like to do those activities, but without the sex.
   d. A spouse. Someone with whom you can build a brand new, lifelong relationship.

chapter 6

Sex and the Widowed or Divorced Boomer

"Oh, okay! How it's been so long since you've had sex and wondering if they've changed it?!"
—Phoebe Bouffay (Lisa Kudrow), Friends

So you've read this book up to this point so far, and you may already be thinking: Wait a minute—this book isn't for me. This is for Boomers involved in a relationship or marriage. But I've never been married and I haven't had a relationship since 19-I-have-no-idea-when!

If you've never been married and you're not in a relationship right now—or haven't been for a while—*and* you've been enjoying a healthy and active adult sex life to this point … well, you could probably tell us things we don't even know. However, we hope we still have lots to share with you in this chapter and beyond.

Now, if on the other hand, you were married for a long period of time, maybe to your high school or college sweetheart, and you've just recently divorced, we can definitely help you jog your memory about all the ins and outs of courting. Or if perhaps your other half has passed away, and you've finally gained the courage to go out and get back into the dating scene, we're going to give you the facts about the twenty-first century dating world as gently as we can. Whatever your scenario, we'll try to guide you into what can be an exciting new life in this chapter.

Keep in mind, we have very limited space here to address the more serious issues involved with divorce or death of a spouse. Bookstores and libraries abound with resources to help you get over the initial obstacles of your new life style. If you haven't sought help from these other books, or even professional counseling, to deal with the change, we strongly recommend you do so. Only when you are in a right mind to date again and consider the possibility of actually being intimate with another person should you return to this chapter—to this whole book. Don't worry. We'll be here when you get back.

Now, for those of you who have gone through all the stages of your recovery, and who are now ready to get back into the dating scene, there are a few things you need to know before you head out there again. First of all, if you're coming out into the world after being with the same partner for many years, we have to warn you: Things have changed. Standards of acceptable dating behavior have been updated—which can be good or bad, but we think it is good.

The dating society you're facing now is a far cry from the more proper one you may have been raised in. While the ideal scenario is to make love to a partner you are committed to, there are other very acceptable paths to forge.

In this chapter, we'll give you some advice on what you can expect as you venture out into the brand new suddenly single world.

Kimberly, 46

"I just had my first date the other night. Well, not my first, but the first at least since my divorce became final. I was worried initially—and after my first experience, I can't lie and say I don't feel at least some trepidation, but millions of people do this every day. I'm sure I'll adjust. But that first experience—wow! What a nightmare! Let's just say I now know what my teenage daughter means when she says 'date from hell!'

The guy I was fixed up with, Rick, seemed like a nice enough guy at first. He was the older brother of a college friend of mine, so it's not like he was a stranger or anything. But I wish he were. I don't want to have to see this guy again at any events any time soon.

We spoke on the phone four times before I agreed to have dinner with him. We seemed to have a lot in common. Thankfully, he was also divorced—or so I thought. I stupidly thought that meant we were going to be on the same page about many things—especially sex. Was I ever wrong about that!

Rick made reservations at a nice little restaurant—one that we had talked about and that I had mentioned being interested in trying out. And especially because it was kind of exclusive, and a bit on the pricey side, I put the sensible woman behind me and sent my inner girl out with this guy. I even agreed to let him pick me up instead of taking my own car. That turned out to be a huge mistake.

Everything seemed fine until we got to the restaurant. And then it started heading downhill and fast. Rick ordered a double scotch on the rocks, then another, and then a third—even before the entrée arrived. Well, I like a glass of wine myself with dinner, but it was clear to me that Rick had a problem.

And then he started talking—I mean talking like spilling his guts talking. It was Stella this and Stella that—you guessed it, his ex. He went from angry to manic to depressed, but with each sip he took, and as much as I tried to change the subject, we were never able to get off of Stella. He ended up getting pretty drunk—and after paying the check, he insisted on driving.

Mistake number two: I got in the car with him.

We got maybe a mile or two into the country; by that time it was clear he was way too drunk to be driving. I gently suggested that I get behind the wheel instead. He became verbally abusive, and that was that. Or so I wished. I had no idea what I was really in for.

I told him to stop the car and I tried to get out. 'Where do you think you're going?' he slurred. 'We're just getting started, baby.' And then he pulled over on the side of the road and tried to jump on top of me. I finally got myself out of the car and started to walk away from him. He actually drove off and left me there. Worse, when I tried to use my cell phone to call a taxi, it was dead—I'd forgotten to recharge it. I walked into town and hoped like hell that I would find a payphone—and quick.

I finally came to a gas station and begged to use their phone. I called my daughter who, thankfully, was home after having one of her famous 'dates from hell' and she came and picked me up. I only hope her awful date was nothing like mine!"

> "*What is* tiramisu? … *Some woman is gonna want me to do it to her and I'm not gonna know what it is!*"
>
> —Sam Baldwin (Tom Hanks), Sleepless in Seattle

Taking the First Step

We're not going to lie to you. The first date you go on is probably not going to be very great. Although, it hopefully won't be as horrible as it was for Kimberly. That certainly was an extreme circumstance, but it begs a lesson: You're not going out with someone you've known for years, like your spouse. It can't—and shouldn't—mean that you're going to trust the person you're with. You're going to be making new alliances. The person you're starting to date won't know about your likes and dislikes; about your smallest insecurities. And after spending so much time with one person, that might take a little getting used to.

So it's okay to feel a little nervous—even a lot nervous. In fact, it's good to be nervous and keep your guard up—at least at first. That way, you can be sure you won't end up in the vulnerable situation in which Kimberly found herself.

Attraction 101

So what's the first step in dating? Well, take the time to really care about your appearance. Feeling good about how you look will help you relax, at least a little, and that will allow you to at least be able to speak and move the date along.

Appearances are most important in the beginning. On a first date, we typically pay more attention to the outside of the person sitting across the table from us—and they do the same with us. Don't kid yourself. We're all human, and it's a very human tendency to sniff out a physical attraction before deciding to be bothered with a brain, a personality, or a soul.

That said, you should definitely make an effort to look your best. It'll send a clear signal that this night is important to you, and it will convey the same message to the one you're going out with.

Send that suit or dress to the dry cleaner's if necessary. (And men, always check your tie for grease stains.) Choose clothes that accentuate your strong points—yes, you still have plenty of them. Learn how to make the best of your appearance—you'll have fun because you'll feel confident and relaxed.

Speaking of relaxing, however, the relaxation of dress codes in recent years makes it easy to get the impression that no one really cares how you look. Don't be fooled—how you dress sends some very clear messages to those who'll be seeing you. Do not underestimate the power of dressing well—clothing can suggest intelligence, youth, and creativity.

How Far Do You Go?

Don't hold your breath for the answer to the question: How far do you go? We're not here to act as your moral barometer. If you have been holding your breath, let go. Immediately. How far you go and exactly when you decide to go that far is all up to your own grown-up self.

As you move through this book, you'll be getting new ideas about sexy things to try, and perhaps sparking old, cobweb-covered concepts about things you used to do and stopped doing with your former spouse. Hopefully, if we've done our job right, we've presented these options to you as objectively as possible. We're not here to tell you what to do; we're just here to give you the information with which to arm yourself as you get closer and closer to having sex with someone new.

That said, as you forge deeper and deeper into the dating world, you are going to face certain pressures in—and perhaps obstacles to—enjoying a comfortable, satisfying, and fulfilling sex life.

People move at their own pace—whether they're eighteen, twenty-five, or fifty-five. You may want sex before the person you're dating is ready—and perhaps the opposite will be true. The key is to make your intentions and needs known as soon as it is comfortable, and to have patience to understand that the person you're dating may want to move faster or more slowly than you. Talk it out. Communicate. Being able to talk to one another is what will cement your relationship in the first place. The physical stuff will come if it's meant to in this particular new relationship. Just be patient.

Should You Seek "Greener" Pastures?

You can probably guess that by "greener," what we mean to say is "younger." It's a very good question, but as you can probably guess by now, it's not one we'll answer for you. You're going to have to experiment and sample different things and see what works for you.

One temptation most older folks have is the urge to fool around with a younger partner. Certainly there's nothing wrong with this at all. A younger partner can teach you things about the world of sex you may have been sheltered from when you were first getting acquainted with the subject. But if we have any advice here, it's this: Go for it, but be careful. No matter how mature a younger person is—or immature an older person—generation gaps will always exist, and misunderstandings are the typical ramifications of these gaps.

But now for the good part. Younger men have lots of stamina and drive. It's likely that they will be able to run circles around the kind of lover your former spouse was. However, keep in mind that for as much as they know, and as much enthusiasm they embody, they won't always have the same finesse or patience that comes with experience. So while the sex may be aplenty, it might not always be as good.

The same can be said for younger women. Sure, everything may still be firm and perky on their bodies, and they may be completely insatiable, but a younger woman might still be learning all the small details that are involved in properly pleasing a man. And, if you have heart issues, be especially careful with the amount of rigorous exercise you can endure. It's a lot like being on the treadmill at the gym: You don't want to overdo and end up in the ICU ward!

And remember what we said earlier: Your younger lovers may have some really great sex experience, but you are the one who has the life experience, and therefore, the mantle of responsibility for communication in the relationship ultimately rests on you.

And let's face it, we should all assume responsibility for proper communication whether our lovers are older or younger than us. Make it your job to be sure that everyone gets on the same page and stays there. What do we mean by this? If you are just getting out there again and you don't want to be tied down, it is your responsibility to express this to the person you are rolling around with presently.

Even if you think it's understood, you may still have to explain it from time to time and make sure your new partner understands. And, conversely, if you are feeling ready to settle down and are on the hunt for a person to join you in contented monogamous bliss, than this should also be made known. Naturally, you don't make the mistake of projectile vomiting all of this information on a first date. However, you don't want to wait until it's too late, either, and you end up hurting someone else. Use your discretion. You'll know when the right time arises.

> *"Sex with an ex can be depressing. If it's good, you don't have it anymore and if it's bad, you've just had sex with an ex."*
>
> —Samantha Jones (Kim Catrall), Sex and the City

Frank, 57

"For a while, I was having a little trouble letting go of my ex-wife, Hannah. She was a vixen, even into her fifties. But she was also an evil heartbreaker. A cheater. A demoralizer. But man, was she an angel in the sack!

When our marriage first started falling apart, she was especially promiscuous. And to cover up for her actions, she would constantly bait and criticize me. A heated fight would inevitably ensue, followed by a more heated session of raw sex. Sure, my body was happy—but my heart was broken. And not to mention what it did to my self-esteem! When she finally told me it was time to divorce, that one of her paramours was now going to be her full-time concentration, well, even then I clung to her. I couldn't let that sex go. I was a mess.

And speaking of messes, our divorce was a huge one. Even after she got me to consent to the split, she was still ruthless with me. And I still took it. She took the house and the Mercedes; I took all the abuse she could give me and then some—if only in the hopes of ending up in bed with her.

Even after I moved out, she wouldn't leave me alone. She'd get bored of the new sucker and then start coming around and bothering me. And you can bet I didn't mind. I had so many delusions about that.

I knew I should stop seeing her, but I just couldn't let go. That is, until I met Maria, and everything changed. Well, almost. Maria was about as different from my ex-wife as any woman could be. She was gentle and caring. The relationship was doomed from the start—and especially because Hannah was still kind of tied up in my life. Hannah got to be very jealous of the new woman in my life, and tried to play more and more of her games to keep me under her thumb. For a while, it worked.

One day, Maria innocently walked in on me and Hannah … and then I lost Maria, too. That was a while ago now, and I've made a concerted effort to try and get over the both of them, but just sometimes, well, I can't lie and say I still don't crave Hannah sometimes. I'd like to pretend I miss Maria more than I do. But I at least like to think that I've now finally grown out of Hannah and can at least find someone like Maria and be happy again. If only Hannah would lose my phone number, that is! What a mess!"

Sex with Your Ex?

It is the most normal, natural, and annoying knee-jerk response of a break-up: falling back into bed with your soon-to-be or long-time ex. This time, we have advice for you and we are going to try and enforce it: Fight nature as best you can in this situation.

Okay, we couldn't tell you what to do when it was time to decide whether or not you were going to have sex with someone new in the first place, or whether or not you should have a sexual relationship with a younger person, and we're certainly not going to hold your hand and tell you what to do here.

And of course, you already know what you *should* do, whether your heart wants to let go or not.

Only under the most extraordinary circumstances do exes reconcile—and even then, it's never the same once the rift has been drawn. There's usually a very good reason people get divorced. It's a lot of aggravation to go through to extricate yourself from someone's life; why drag it back into the bedroom? Save yourself the grief. If you keep going back because you're lonely or sex-starved, why not spend some quality time mastering the art of self-pleasuring instead, even investing in one of the adult toys in Chapter 33 if you need some "instant company."

Well, it looks like you're about ready to learn all about what's going on in the world of sex out there. Launch yourself into the rest of this book and enjoy the ride!

part 2

The Basics

Sexploration Exercise #7

1. When's the last time you and your lover enjoyed a long, languorous kiss?
   a. Ten minutes ago.
   b. Ten days ago.
   c. Ten years ago.
   d. We've never shared a kiss like that.

2. Do you think kissing is an important element of sexual expression?
   a. It is *the* most important.
   b. It's definitely up there, but other elements—like penetration—are much more important.
   c. It's fine to get things started, but once you get into the action, you really don't need to worry about it that much.
   d. Kissing is for kids who don't do anything else.

3. To me, kissing should be:
   a. Reaffirming—like a cool, breezy rain lightly falling on a sweltering summer's day.
   b. Sensual—like licking the sweet, sticky juice of a ripe peach from your fingers.
   c. Eager—like eating an entire Thanksgiving dinner in three bites.
   d. Obligatory—like paying a toll so you can cross a bridge.

4. Do you still remember your first kiss?
   a. Like it was yesterday. I remember the name of the person I kissed, the day of the week it was, what I was wearing…
   b. It was in eighth grade with someone from my math class—that's about all I remember.
   c. I remember I was twelve, but nothing else.
   d. I can't remember what I did yesterday and you want me to remember my first kiss?

5. What is your all-time favorite movie kiss?
   a. When Harry kisses Sally after running through New York City on New Year's Eve to find her in *When Harry Met Sally*.
   b. When Rhett kisses Scarlett just before swooping her off her feet and up the stairs in *Gone With the Wind*.
   c. The kissing montage in *Cinema Paradiso*.
   d. When Michael Corleone kisses his next hit square on the mouth in *The Godfather*.

chapter 7

Kissing 101

"Hold it, hold it! What is this? Are you trying to trick me? Where's the sports? Is this a kissing book?"
—*Grandson (Fred Savage),* The Princess Bride

Do you remember your first kiss? It wasn't all that long ago. Maybe thirty, forty years? Come on … think back. Do you remember that wonderful time in your life when your body was just starting to change—or maybe you hadn't even yet embarked on that strange journey to sexual maturity. Think back to the time when you started to see members of the opposite sex as more than just the enemy, more than just foreign beings to taunt and tease on the playground.

Remember that day when you ditched your friends to walk home from school with one of those foreign beings because, though you might not have been able to explain exactly why, you just wanted to be close to them? Maybe you already knew what was going to happen at the time. You may have planned to walk this person home with the intent of stealing a kiss. Or maybe when it happened, you were caught totally off guard. In either case, the electricity you felt at that moment was unlike anything else you had ever experienced before. It was the awakening of your future sexual self.

(Hrana Janto)

Take time with a kiss, and don't forget your hands.

Today, well into our forties or fifties, and maybe with the same partner for all these years, we just don't kiss like we used to. Maybe there's a quick peck on the mouth when you part for work in the morning or just before sleep. But can you remember the last time you shared a long, luxurious, languorous session of just plain kissing?

In this chapter, we look at the lost art of kissing. We'll remind you of how special the simple act of kissing is, and how to bring it back into your boudoir.

Cori, 44

"When we were dating, my husband, Rick, used to kiss me all the time. I'll never forget our first kiss. It happened the night of our first date and even almost 30 years later, I've never forgotten it.

I liked Rick for such a long time. I met him when he was my lab partner in an advanced biology class. He was a senior. I was just a sophomore and I never thought he'd notice me for more than just the notes he borrowed. But one day he did.

The day he asked me out for our first date, I walked around the rest of the afternoon in a love-struck haze. I think I spent the rest of the week in that wonderful place, anticipating our date and what might happen that night. Ask me about any other week of high school and you can bet I won't remember a thing. But this week, I just can't explain it. It was just so special.

Rick picked me up that Saturday night and I was so nervous the entire date, I don't even know how I held up my end of the conversation. I must have talked, though, because I remember how much we laughed and how much we had in common. In fact, we got along so well, we nearly lost track of time and I almost missed curfew. I never wanted that date to end, but at the same time, I wanted it to end so badly. Why? Because I hoped he would kiss me, of course.

When we got back to my house, Rick stopped the car and walked me to my front door. He was all romance, and that entire walk, I can remember thinking how happy I was that he was a gentleman and hadn't tried to get fresh with me. At the same time, I was so nervous that he'd be such a gentleman that he wouldn't kiss me. He nearly didn't.

When we got to the door, Rick leaned in to shake my hand and I misunderstood his leaning in as him trying to kiss me, so I threw my arms around his neck and pulled my face to his so quickly and clumsily, I knocked my cheekbone right into his chin. I was embarrassed; he was amused. 'Oh, so someone wants a kiss, does she?' he asked. I thought he sounded kind of smug about it and I got mad. So I turned around to my front door in a huff and slipped my key in the lock. He whisked me around and kissed me right on the mouth—first gently and then so fiercely, it was like we were both going to die if we didn't keep kissing each other.

He was the world's greatest kisser. I'd never been kissed the way he kissed me. It may sound crazy, but the way he kissed me made me want to marry him. Even that night.

Of course we were still in school at the time. And even though it was the height of the sexual revolution, we both grew up in very Catholic families. We didn't believe in sex until we were married. Kissing was about as physical as we got—almost—because we both felt strongly about waiting. But when he kissed me, I was on fire. After we got married, even though we could now do other things, we would still spend hours just cuddling and kissing—before sex, after sex. Whenever.

But as the years went by and we had kids and started to get busy, well, it seems like somewhere down the line, Rick just forgot how to kiss.

My husband barely kisses me anymore these days. A peck on the cheek, sometimes, as he heads to the airport for another business trip. But it's not like it used to be.

Sometimes I think there's something wrong with me, that I'm less attractive to him. I've talked a lot about this with my girlfriends and they say the same thing is true in their marriages or relationships. Men just aren't as romantic as women, and when it comes to sex, they just want to get to the point.

We got to that point one day, and it's like we never looked back. Well, at least it's like *he* never looked back. We still have plenty of sex for people our age—maybe once a week, sometimes less, sometimes more. But I do miss all that making out that we used to do!"

Just Remember This: A Kiss Is *Not* Just a Kiss

Cori is not alone. Many couples, as they grow into their lives together, simply stop kissing. And it's a mystery, really, because kissing is the simplest route to seduction. Kissing shows how much you still really care about your partner. It's one of the easiest ways to show your partner that you don't take them for granted. That you still crave the magic you felt when your lips first touched.

Are you like many Boomers, so out of practice that by this time you have perhaps forgotten how to kiss? No problem. In this chapter, we give you pointers to get you back into the most intimate of expressions of passion there is.

Getting Ready

If you are a man, start out by shaving. If your chin is covered in stubble, all she's going to feel is a sandpaper-like sensation on her chin and cheeks. A turn-on? No. Few women if any want to show up at work the next day looking as though their faces got caught in a belt sander.

Women, one of the things men love most about you is the inherent softness you possess. Unlike men, who by this age have skin that's rough and weathered by time, women's skin remains petal soft. It's one of the main reasons men can't keep their hands off you. So your job is to keep that skin soft. Apply a non-greasy moisturizer to your face and neck and even shoulders—anywhere you'd like your lip service to be reciprocated during your next make-out session.

Men and women both: A clean mouth is a kissable mouth. That's one thing you see on TV that you can really believe. Before showering your lover in a cascade of kisses, brush, floss, even rinse out your mouth with mouthwash. And for the piece de resistance, remember that lip balm is your friend. Soft, sultry kisses will not come across that way if your lips are cracked and ragged.

Keep in the back of your mind (and by that, we mean all the way in the back of your mind) as you gear up for a night of pure, unadulterated kissing that once you've set the sensual pot to simmer, your partner's lips may not be the only place your kisses will be welcomed!

Kisses to Kill For

Keep in mind that the steps we're taking you through in this section are suggestions. Once you get the basic gist down, by all means vary as the mood strikes! Also, in order to keep the language succinct and easy to follow, we'll use the feminine pronoun to talk about your lover. But don't think for a minute that this brand of affection doling will only be enjoyed by a woman! Men and women both enjoy tenderness as well as some of the rougher, edgier stuff—it's all about the mood.

The first step to perfect kissing involves no physical contact whatsoever. Before you lock lips, lock eyes. Let your desire as well as your affection show in your face. When it comes to ultimate pleasure, sometimes a look is worth a hundred salacious acts.

Start out by planting a soft kiss on the tip of your lover's nose, and perhaps one each on her eyelids. Move to the side of her face and lightly move your lips across her earlobes. Slide the tip of your tongue delicately around the creases of your lover's ear. Gently caress the side of her face with your fingertips as you alternate soft kisses and light licks from her earlobe to the base of her chin. Brush her lips with yours as you cradle her face in your hands and look into her eyes. Plant small kisses on her lips—even if you are just simply brushing your open lips upon hers. The anticipation of what's to come will send shivers of electricity between the two of you as you move into more serious kissing.

Don't crush the moment by ramming your tongue into your lover's mouth right away. As you build your crescendo of

> "No, I don't think I will kiss you, although you need kissing, badly. That's what's wrong with you! You should be kissed and often, and by someone who knows how."
>
> —Rhett Butler (Clark Gable), Gone With the Wind

passion, delicately lap just the tip of your tongue at her lips, parting them more fully with every stroke. The more gingerly your tongue enters, the more welcome the reception it will find. Carefully play with the tip of your lover's tongue with your own.

And while you are enjoying the sensation of slowly building the moment, don't forget about your hands. Touch, caress, and even gently grope your partner. Run your hands through her hair. Hold her. Hug her. Don't be predictable; let the element of surprise be your guide. Most importantly, enjoy this kissing—at least for the time being—for what it is: namely, kissing. Just like when you were teenagers, kissing doesn't always need to lead right to full-on sex. Keep your lover on her toes—and keep her curling those toes—simply by allowing yourselves to savor the moment for what it is. Don't stop abruptly, throw her down onto the bed, and start ravaging her. Not right away. Take your time and savor the sweetness.

Even if the most mind-blowing, earth-shaking, bed-breaking sex is the result of all this, don't forget about the kissing throughout (as positions permit, of course). What sensation in the world compares to reaching climax while kissing your lover?

And don't think that once the action stops that the kissing must also halt as well. Save a little of that kissing for afterwards. Learn your lover's other favorite spots to be kissed, and gently move your mouth across them while you are lying there in each other's arms, basking in your post-coital glow. Look at your lover while you kiss those spots. Let her know—through the way you look at her, through the way you speak to her, and the way you kiss her—that you love those parts of her body as much as she does—and some special others. This is what true intimacy is all about and intimacy is what makes sex great.

As busy as you are in your lives, as well as you know each other, and as long as you've been together, never forget that the fulfillment of pure ecstasy can begin simply with a little kiss.

> "... I believe in the sweet spot, soft-core pornography, opening your presents Christmas morning rather than Christmas Eve and I believe in long, slow, deep, soft, wet kisses that last three days. [pause] Goodnight."
>
> —Crash Davis (Kevin Costner), Bull Durham

Sexploration Exercise #8

1. What is your overall feeling about masturbation?
    a. It's a healthy activity that one—or two—can enjoy.
    b. It's something you resort to when you don't have another person to fool around with.
    c. It's something you can do when you're in a relationship, but you'd better be as secretive about it as possible or you're sure to hurt your lover's feelings.
    d. It's a filthy act that will buy you a one-way ticket to damnation.

2. Have you—or would you—masturbate in front of your partner?
    a. Masturbation is a regular activity in our sex life, whether we masturbate ourselves for our lovers to watch, or we masturbate each other.
    b. I don't mind if my partner masturbates in front of me, but I'm much too shy to do it in front of my partner.
    c. I would feel pretty inadequate if my partner masturbated in front of me—like I wasn't doing a good enough job of pleasuring them and they had to give me a lesson or something.
    d. I don't masturbate. Ever. Under any circumstances.

3. If you do masturbate, how many times a week would you say you do on average?
    a. Week? I don't know about that. It's more like maybe once or twice a month.
    b. Once a week.
    c. Several times per week.
    d. Several times per day.

4. How did you first broach the topic of masturbation with your partner?
    a. It came up on an early date we were on after we'd had a lot of wine to drink.
    b. One of the first times we were ever in bed together, I asked her to show me what felt good for her, how she liked to be touched—and then she asked me to show her.
    c. He, um, walked in on me and my favorite vibrator.
    d. We don't talk about it. I know we both do it, but we never discuss it.

5. What's your favorite time of day to masturbate?
    a. In the morning—right when I wake up and hopefully coming off a really hot dream.
    b. Before I go to sleep at night. It relaxes me.
    c. I like to masturbate right after a heavy meal and burn the calories off!
    d. I get really aroused by the thought of getting caught, so for me, a bathroom stall at work in the middle of the day does the trick!

chapter 8

The Joy of Self-Pleasure

"Hey, don't knock masturbation. It's sex with someone I love."
—*Alvy Singer (Woody Allen),* Annie Hall

Traditionally, masturbation has gotten a bad rap. It's been known as the "dirty little secret." The thing that you did behind a double-locked door with the window shades pulled down tight. The evil act you performed because you simply couldn't help yourself but had to perform so quietly that you could barely breathe because you were sure the receptionist at your father's office 20 miles away could hear you.

Even the term "masturbation" implies improper behavior. Masturbation derives from Latin words meaning "to disturb or destroy with the hand." But what could be further from the truth? Masturbation is not a means to destroy, rather a way to create a sense of well-being within yourself, to explore sexuality, to bring yourself pleasure without hurting anyone.

And guess what: Most people do it—even Boomers! Don't get us wrong, we are not trying to go against anyone's beliefs by insisting that everyone *should* masturbate. If masturbation goes against your convictions, by all means feel free to skip this chapter. We'll show you plenty of other ways to find sexual satisfaction in this book!

Ever since the sexual revolution, society has sought to de-stigmatize masturbation and remove the guilt, shame, and remorse attached to it. In fact, a whole cottage industry has sprung up around masturbation, including videos, books, clinics, websites, and more, all designed to show people the ins and outs of self-pleasure. We don't have to teach anyone how to masturbate; nor would we presume to tell you anything you didn't already know about your own bodies by this point in your life. Our purpose is simply to show you how you can make masturbation a healthy, integral part of your sexual routine.

In this chapter, we try to free you from some of the inhibitions you may be harboring about masturbation and even teach you how to share it with your partner.

Annie, 53

"No one talked about masturbation when I was growing up—and certainly no one ever admitted to actually doing it! So how could I possibly know that touching that special spot at night before I went to sleep was not only normal, but actually very healthy? I didn't even know that spot had a name. All I knew was that the nights I touched it, I slept better than the nights I didn't.

In high school health class, I learned that what I was doing was called 'masturbation,' and that it was generally frowned upon. The rumor was that you could actually go blind if you did it enough! I have to admit that I was willing to take my chances. Surely, with the amount I did it, if I was going to go blind, it would have happened already?

When I got to college, I had a roommate, Alison, who was very wrapped up in the burgeoning sexual revolution and who had no qualms about what she was doing under the sheets—even with me right across the room from her! She bustled away every night—and even made noises. I had always wanted to let loose like that, but how could I when someone might actually hear me and know what I was up to.

It still didn't make me comfortable about touching myself, and for the first few months of school, I didn't. As a result, I had all the anxieties of being in a new life in a strange place, and no outlet into which to release this anxiety.

I had many boyfriends those first months. And while I didn't have sex with any of them, I did allow some pretty intense petting to go on. The problem was that none of these men ever knew how to bring me to that special place I could get myself to all of these years. Sure, I faked it. I wanted them to feel good about themselves. I wanted them to call me again. But I was going nuts. I just couldn't take it anymore!

One night, when I thought Alison was going to be gone for the weekend, I had to help myself out. On top of all the sexual energy I already had, what with being an eighteen-year-old girl and all, compounded by the fact that I had been rolling around with boys and not been satisfied, I was about to explode. So I locked the door to my dorm room, pulled down the shade, and climbed into bed.

All that pent-up energy resulted in a release like I had never experienced before. It was like I was transported to another place—I was nearly unconscious!

When I came off that high, however, I knew exactly where I was. I was in my dorm room at school, and this fact was made evermore apparent when I opened my eyes and saw that Alison had come in. 'So Miz Prude does play with herself after all! Thank God,' she giggled. 'I thought I was living with a nun!'

I was so embarrassed, my face must have been bright red and eight hundred degrees. 'Hey, don't sweat it,' she laughed. 'Everyone does it. It's totally normal.' I told her that I always had done it but I didn't think it had to be anyone else's business. 'Of course it doesn't. And by all means, let me know when you need a little privacy. I'll leave you alone.'

Over the course of that semester, Alison continued her solo adventures, but at least I knew I could also do it when I wanted to and have my privacy. I learned a lot from Alison. She was always comfortable sharing advice, solicited or not, and even gave me some books and pamphlets to read.

These proved to be the biggest eye-openers of all. When I tried some of the stuff out, namely inserting a finger in my vagina, I learned that it was impossible for a woman to truly fake an orgasm—that all the screaming in the world couldn't fake all those amazing contractions.

> *"For me, the nicest thing about masturbation is afterward, the cuddling time."*
>
> —Val Waxman (Woody Allen),
> Hollywood Ending

Suffice to say, I never faked it again. And I was finally able to show others how to bring me to my special place. But that didn't mean I never went there myself again. I've been married for more years than I care to admit—but I always make a little time for myself. It's like a little gift, a treat I give myself sometimes."

Going Solo

It's likely that if you're reading this book, you've tried masturbation before—and more likely, many times. When Annie let go of the guilt and trepidation she felt about masturbation, her sex life and interactions with others only improved. But just as important, she learned that she could treat herself to an orgasm as a special gift to herself—married or not.

There are very few ways we can really treat ourselves without leaving the privacy of our own bedrooms—and so cost-effectively to boot! Think about the other things you might do when you want to do something special for yourself, like going out for a nice dinner, buying a new golf club or a new pair of shoes? You're talking a hundred or more dollars. And here, for hardly any cost at all, you can give yourself the treat of a lifetime.

Does this seem like an odd concept—treating yourself to masturbation? To make it a reward for devoting your Saturday to volunteering for a good cause or working through a difficult situation at work that week? Then it's time to change your thinking. Masturbation is a wonderful way to, and please pardon the pun, get in touch with yourself. To appreciate the person you are and all the things you do.

When we make love to our partners, we appreciate them with kisses and soft caresses. We make them feel special by taking the time to get in touch with them by touching them. We'll look more at the various ways to touch our partners in other chapters. But for our purposes here, why wouldn't we warrant the same attention?

And taking this time for ourselves can actually enhance the time we spend with our lovers. When you become intimate and experienced with those parts of yourself that make you crazy with lust, you open new doors for your together time. The more you know what you like and don't like, the better you will be at expressing and demonstrating these aspects of your sexuality to your partner.

Another benefit of masturbation becomes apparent to the point of obvious when you're not involved in a relationship. As adult human beings, we all have sexual needs. Through masturbation, you can satisfy, at least to a point, these needs for yourself, which is guaranteed protection from the scary world of disease and emotional complications with emotionally complicated strangers.

Carl, 49

"I'm not even going to lie about this: I *love* masturbation. Ever since I was a teenager, I've masturbated several times a week—okay, when I was a teenager, it was more like several times a day. It didn't matter if I was involved in a sexual relationship or not. I've just always had a lot of sexual energy to work off.

Now ask me if I ever lied about it before. Of course I have! I've been involved in relationships with many women—and that includes two wives. Even though I've only been 'caught' once and that was by my first wife, Emily, it was always my suspicion that a woman just doesn't need to know what you're up to behind the bathroom door.

To this day, I'll never forget how Emily acted when she barged in on me—I had forgotten to lock the door—and found me caught up in a heated moment with that month's *Penthouse*. You would have thought I was drowning puppies.

'How could you do this to me?' she cried, and as I tried to explain to her that it had nothing to do with her, I seemed to be getting in deeper and deeper trouble. Apparently my wife was almost as offended by what she perceived as my 'having sex' without her—and with one of the women in that magazine—as she was about me 'sneaking it.' It was like I was cheating on her. With myself!

Now I can't say Emily and I always had the greatest relationship. We got together when we were very young and I don't think we ever really learned how to talk to each other—you know, like adults. That small incident escalated over the course of several years. There was resentment on her part that she wasn't enough for me to feel sexually satisfied; there was resentment on my part that I was living in a police state and had to watch everything I did. The marriage eventually self-destructed.

So, suffice to say, before I met my second wife, Irene, I always adopted a 'don't ask, don't tell' policy. I didn't need the hassle of offending another woman who didn't understand me.

It must be that marriage makes a man careless, because lo and behold, within a few months of being married to Irene, she accidentally walked in on me getting busy with myself. I had forgotten to lock the door again! 'What are you doing?' she asked. And all I could think was, *Way to go, Carl. Another marriage busted because you couldn't keep your filthy hands off yourself.* 'It has nothing to do with you,' I tried to tell her, immediately cursing myself for not choosing my words more carefully. She didn't say anything.

Irene pursed her lips and stared at the magazine. 'So let's see ... who is she?' she asked, first looking at the page I had been on and then proceeding to flip through the magazine. 'This is just too bad,' she said as she shook her head. I could only expect the worst. 'Tsk, tsk. Just too bad.' 'Irene, please, I can explain ...' 'So tell me, Carl. Why shouldn't this have anything to do with me?'

I started to speak but she cut me off. 'I'm not annoyed because you're doing it,' she said. 'Darling, everybody does it. I'm annoyed that you think you have to hide in the bathroom like a kid.' You can imagine at this point I was totally confused. Irene took me by the hand and pulled me into the bedroom. 'Come on and show me what you like to do to yourself,' she smiled, 'and if you're a really good boy, then maybe I'll show you.'

> "I used to masturbate to a busboy who was rude to me once. What do you think that means?"
>
> —Miranda (Cynthia Nixon),
> Sex and the City

That night was a real eye-opener. Irene had always been a fantastic lover, but once

I was able to actually show her how I liked to be touched, she became a phenomenal lover. And not to mention all the new things I learned about her!"

Table for Two

Sharing what we do during masturbation with our partner? Okay, well that was all well and good for Carl and Irene, but for many of us, that's just crossing the line! Or is it?

Why not consider masturbating in front of your partner. You may be surprised, if you ask, how much your partner might actually be interested in watching. Couples who have had wonderful sex lives for a dozen years or more, who may have discussed or negotiated virtually every issue under the sun, may never have even brought up the subject of masturbation with their partners. And if it has been brought up, no doubt it's been to chide one partner for "sneaking" something behind the other's back.

There are many reasons one masturbates. For men, masturbation is in part a way to release the enormous sexual energy testosterone provides so that they're not on top of their partners all the time. Not that the women would necessarily mind. In fact, many women in their 40s and 50s feel far more sexual than ever, and are often quite desirous of sex. And guess what? A large percentage of these women admit to masturbating to work off that sexual steam.

But why not talk about—and demonstrate—masturbation? There are several reasons for trying this permitted voyeurism. First, anything that brings variety and spice to a potentially flagging or repetitive sex life is most likely a good thing. Second, we think it's an opportunity for both partners to learn something new about how the other likes to be pleased.

Something is lost and something is gained from the kind of day-to-day constant intimacy of a long-term relationship. The good news is that you get to know the other person inside and out, upside down and backward. The bad news is that you get to know the other person inside and out, upside down and backward. It's really tough for couples to find something about which they can have an eye-opening, consciousness-raising conversation. An act of solitary splendor might become a breath of fresh air that can actually serve to strengthen and benefit a marriage.

Sexploration Exercise #9

1. What do you think is the most sexually sensitive part of the male anatomy?
   a. the shaft of the penis
   b. the testicles
   c. the neck
   d. the tip of the penis

2. When fondling a penis, should you:
   a. Hold on tight and yank away like your very life depended on it?
   b. Hold the shaft delicately, with a loose hold on the skin of the penis?
   c. Tap repeatedly on the squishy head of the penis?
   d. Take a firm but not tight hold on the shaft of the penis, just below the head, with your index and thumb curled together at the corona, and repeatedly slide the skin up and down the head?

3. What's your favorite lubrication?
   a. Saliva
   b. Honey
   c. Lotion or Vaseline
   d. A water-based lube, such as Astroglide

4. When's the last time you brought your male partner to orgasm with your hand?
   a. A few nights ago.
   b. A few weeks ago.
   c. It's been years now—it seems like an awful lot of work.
   d. I never do. Let him do that for himself—I have lots of other ways to please him that he can't do for himself!

5. Most commonly, your partner likes to be handled:
   a. Strong and rough, like you're taming a wild horse.
   b. Firm and fast, like you're working diligently and efficiently to complete a task.
   c. Slow and delicate, like you're polishing fine glassware.
   d. I never thought of it—I just do what seems right at the time.

chapter 9

How to Touch a Man

"Holding my penis ... what a wonderful way of saying how much you like me."
—*Parry (Robin Williams),* The Fisher King

In the last chapter, we got to know ourselves a little better by allowing ourselves to explore our most private of parts. But we've lived with our own equipment for years, and intimately at that. The real mystery lies in our partner's body. Even if we've lived with a person for years, do we ever really know it as intimately as our own?

On top of that, and especially in dealing with the same person sexually for years, you might not be taking the time or care anymore to explore your partner's body and learn new things, and that's no good. Part of what we want to accomplish in these chapters is to do away with that marital myopia and take you back to the thrilling days of yesteryear, when foreplay meant a conscious effort to take your partner to the heights of pleasure long before insertion. As we learned in Chapter 6, couples who have been together a long time don't kiss very much if at all, and, just as the kissing goes, so does any form of touching for the sake of giving pleasure.

This chapter and the next teach you how to deal with the body on the other side of the bed. Here, we're talking about the square-framed, probably hairy, leathery one with all that external equipment. What are the spots that really excite him?

Chances are if you have permitted—even encouraged—your male partner to masturbate in front of you, you've learned what gets him going. This chapter, ladies, is meant for you to understand why—and maybe even teach him a thing or two about his body he might not already know about.

The male sexual being can be a lot more complicated than you may think. While it's true that the pleasure center is his penis, his body, like yours, is a minefield of erogenous spots, with many luscious options to explore that will make him explode with pleasure when given the chance to be touched.

Rebecca, 48

"This will sound so silly, I can't even believe I'm going to tell you this, but it used to be that when I was in bed with a man, even past the first few awkward encounters, I sometimes felt like I was on a job interview. You know that feeling you get—where you're about ten times clumsier than usual—not only with your conversation, but with your hands as well. In a job interview, I never know where to put my hands. It's the same thing when I'm with a man.

My ex-husband, Artie, was never really very understanding about this—I guess that's part of the reason that he's now my ex-husband! All he ever seemed to want me to touch was his penis. A little variety, anyone? And never mind that. In going right for the, um, prize, the sex would be over before I even knew it had begun.

My last boyfriend, Frank, was a lot more understanding about this. Because I had been conditioned by Artie all those years to go right to the source when I wanted sex, I would grab his penis with both hands and pull at him like I was wringing laundry out of the washing machine. He seemed to like it. He got aroused and eventually flipped me over on my back and had sex with me. That's just how it worked.

Luckily, however, Frank wouldn't allow this tendency of mine to persist. One day when I was, well, 'doing the laundry,' he gently grabbed my hands and let me in on a little known fact—at least for me it was. He carefully asked me if when he wanted sex, he should just go right for my clitoris, and stop any of the other stuff I was doing beforehand. I was terrified. 'Oh, God, no. I love it when you rub my back and shoulders. When you stroke my breasts and kiss my nipples like you do. That's what really gets me revved up.' And then he asked me something that had never even occurred to me before: 'What makes you think that it's all that different for me?'

After all those years with Artie, I had no idea how to answer that. First of all, I wasn't used to talking about sex so candidly, but also, in the Artie years, my training ground for relations between men and women, it never came up that Artie might have wanted more—or even that I might be doing what I was doing the wrong way.

Then Frank had an idea: He talked me through exactly what he wanted me to do to him—every motion, every stroke, every application of pressure. I was so aroused knowing what I could do for him—exactly what he needed me to do to give him the greatest possible pleasure, that it was all the foreplay I even needed that night. When it was time for the actual penetration to begin, I was so primed and ready, I climaxed within minutes—we both did!"

The Midas Touch

What can make your lover feel like gold? As we learned with Frank and Rebecca, it's not far off from what makes you feel good—and we mean aside from the rush of a perfect orgasm taking over his entire body. Getting good with the physical begins with the emotional. Simply put, it's the way you treat him. It's your openness to communication and your willingness to take the time to learn what really pleases him. So even for the most insatiable satyr, the starting point for appealing to a man's sexuality is through his mind.

Even in these progressive times, men have societal pressures, real or imagined, that weigh on them and may affect their libido. While words like "breadwinner" seem antiquated by today's standards, there is still an enormous amount of pressure for a man to perform—both in and out of the bedroom. If things aren't going so well on the other side the bedroom door, they can sometimes affect what goes on inside the bedroom.

Much like yourself, your partner needs to know that there's no one else in the world who can do for you what he does, as well as he does it. Your partner doesn't need to know that he's not measuring up to your standards, no matter how hard he tries. That's his boss's or clients' domain. In these times, and especially as you approach your retirement years, it becomes more and more likely that people are losing jobs to younger people with considerable less experience but smaller price tags. On top of that, the more advanced in age you become, the more advanced in your career, and therefore are probably at or approaching the top of the pyramid, making the situation that much more dire.

We could get into any of the situations that may be affecting your partner's psychological and emotional well-being to the point that they will be affecting his performance in the bedroom, but that's not really the point here.

Think back to your earliest days of sexual activity, when every square millimeter (and some of the round ones) of your partner's body was an object of intense fascination for you. As the years have passed, it's only natural that we've become more perfunctory in our attitudes both towards sex and towards our partner's body. But it doesn't have to be that way—not all the time. No one's saying you'll have the time or energy to conduct your sex life with the same verve you did when you were younger, but that doesn't mean you can't spring for it once in a while.

The Big "P"

There are essentially two parts of his body a man wants you to touch: The first is his penis, and the second is everything else. Unlike women, men do center virtually all of their sexual feeling in their genitals, but like women, it's not the only sexual place on their bodies.

Like it was for Rebecca, women are sometimes afraid to touch their partner's penis. For one, it might still harbor some great mystery for them and they are afraid to manipulate the member incorrectly. And then there's the simplest reason of all: There's the fear that by touching the penis, they are signaling that they want sex right now. Men can rightfully be accused of misreading that signal.

So how can you touch his penis without immediately being thrown over the nearest chair and, um, rewarded? Caress, stroke, touch, play with his penis, but when you do so, remain in control. Don't let him get the idea that you're ready to go all the way if you're not. If it looks like he's getting too excited and will be on top of you in a matter of minutes, gently push him away and focus on some other part of his body, which we'll get into later in this chapter. He may be somewhat surprised at first, but if men like sex right now, the thing they like even more is sex a few minutes from now. In other words, you can keep him on a low flame just by the way you touch him.

Handle With Flair

Let's turn now to the second most exciting place on a man's penis: the underside of his penis, just below the tip. Women know that no two penises were created equally. Not all women realize that different parts of the penis have different levels of sensitivity. For example, the base of the penis has perhaps one-twentieth of the sexual arousal capability as does the tip. Men like it when you run your fingers or tongue over the part of the shaft nearest the body. But keep in mind that the closer to the tip you go, the more exciting and vibrant the experience.

The tip itself is almost unbearably alive, so much so that direct stroking of the tip offers more sensation than a man can comfortably bear. Your fingers on the tip of his penis, no matter how gentle you may be touching him, is almost a sure-fire recipe for pain. The tip of the penis, while it may be the most sensitive part of the shaft, is not where men want to be stimulated the most. "I knew my ex-wife meant well," says Frederick, 51. "But I just couldn't convince her that massaging the tip of my penis was more painful than pleasurable. It's very hard to tell your wife exactly what you want, anyway."

The best place to touch a penis is actually the underside of the penis close to, but not touching, the very tip. When we say the underside of the penis, we are referring to the part that would be facing downward if a man standing had an erection that was roughly parallel to the ground.

Think of this spot as the "fingerprint" spot for two reasons: If his penis was a finger, the place where the fingerprint would be taken is the spot we're talking about. Second, that's the exact spot where the man wants you to leave your fingerprints, as often as possible. This "fingerprint" spot is the closest analogue to the clitoris on the man's body. You can approach it the same way you would approach your own clitoris—initially with sensitivity, and with increasing pressure as the man becomes more and more aroused.

You can also think of that fingerprint spot as an on/off switch for the man's track to orgasm. Touch it, rub it, moisten your finger and make lazy circles on it, and you'll bring him closer and closer to climax. Move away from it, stroke the shaft, play with the rest of the penis, make a circle of your thumb and forefinger and rub the entire circumference of the penis, and he'll thank you for it, but it will either slow him down or slow the progress toward orgasm. Works like a charm, every time.

Jack, 49

"I went from adolescence to middle age without ever having even heard of the *perineum*. If you'd ask me what it was, I would have said it was part of a basketball court. Okay, I was wrong. But I didn't know that!

I've spent most of my life being something of a playboy. I never wanted to settle down. For me, life has always been about new experiences. To each his own. So you can imagine that I've never been with any woman enough times that she could get to know me intimately enough to show me something about myself I didn't already know.

I first learned what my perineum was when I met Maddie. I blush to admit that she was a fellow slut with whom I had worked remotely for several years. We spent a lot of time playing around on email, on the phone, until we were finally able to get it together in person at a conference we were both planning to attend.

Needless to say, it took one quick dinner out and a bottle of wine before we ended up in the sack. Oh man, was that sex ever explosive. We went at it like teenagers, even missing a couple of the next day's seminars!

Now I'm quite used to teaching women new things to do in bed. Most women I've been with have only been with a handful of partners and therefore only have that limited kind of experience. With me and Maddie, well, I knew we'd have maybe one or two tricks to pull out of the bag that may have been new to the other.

Hard as I tried to dazzle her, I have to hand it to Maddie. She trumped me with this perineum thing. At one point of the night, we wrapped up in a pretty heated 69 session. All of a sudden I felt something like an electric shock course through me, and I immediately shuddered in a thunderous orgasm.

Of course I had to ask her what she did. She smiled, victoriously, and explained it to me. I've never been able to find another woman who could do that to me like Maddie. It almost makes me think it might be time to settle down ..."

> "God gave man a penis and a brain. And only enough blood to run one at a time."
>
> —Robin Williams, Live on Broadway

Private Pleasure Parts

The perineum is actually one of the most sensitive spots on a man's body. The Chinese call this the "million-dollar spot" because touching it is a cheap and easy way to make your man feel like a million dollars. Who knew! Probably not your man. In fact, most men have no idea that any sexual feeling resides in this spot, let alone its enormous potential for sexual pleasure.

So what is the perineum? It's the area covered by the scrotum, located between the base of the scrotum and the lowest part of the anus. This thrilling place for men is, ironically, the part of the man's anatomy that he is least likely to have ever even noticed. After all, it's covered by the testicles a good part of the time, so a guy could go his whole life barely seeing it, let alone thinking much about it. In addition, it has no distinguishing features or particular size. But there's a lot a woman can do to bring her man's perineum to life.

Fortunately, the perineum is a fairly simple body part to operate and manipulate. Gently lift the testicles up and out of the way. All you have to do to engage the perineum is to touch it. It's that simple. Apply light—and we emphasize the word "light"—pressure as the man is approaching orgasm. Direct stimulation of the perineum will enhance the experience of building toward orgasm like nothing you can imagine. We do want to reemphasize the delicacy with which you want to handle that part of his anatomy.

There's another important "P" part on the male anatomy, but we'll save that for later. (If you simply can't wait, head directly to Chapter 10, but don't forget to come back here!)

The Big Picture

What other parts of the man's body could be considered erogenous zones? Just like you, nearly *every* part of the man's body is fair game for your advances. Play with his hair. Or, if there isn't all that much hair left, play with his scalp. There is something very sexy about a woman touching a man's hair—it's both a come-on, and it's a turn-on. And while you're at it, why not cover your man's eyes with one hand while you stroke and kiss him about the scalp and face.

Cover his eyes with your hand while you are stroking his face with the other. When you cover a man's eyes, he loses control and doesn't know what to expect next. It's a very easy way for you to get into the driver's seat, if that's where you want to be this time around!

Remove your hand from his eyes and kiss his eyelids. When he's getting this aroused, he will feel it to the very end of his nose and the tips of his toes. We'll get to his toes a little later; for now, stroke his face and his nose with your fingertips, perhaps alternating with small kisses. Move those fingertips down to his mouth and trace his lips before planting sumptuous kisses on them. Bring the action to his ears. He'll be squirming in no time.

Then there's his neck. Kiss it, touch it, caress it—just don't neglect it. Deep down, your rough, tough man is a big softy (most of him, anyway) waiting for your attention and care. Lavish it on him.

If he has showered lately, think about kissing him under or around the armpit. This is a highly sensitive region that can go decades without proper care.

Moving down his body are your lover's nipples. It's easy for long-together couples to forget that his nipples can be just as sensitive as hers. When was the last time you tweaked them, brushed your breasts against them, or otherwise paid attention to them?

Turn him over and rub his back. Maybe you have some massage oil you've been waiting to try? Warm it first in your cupped hands, and rub it on him with firm, weighty, strokes. And while you're at it, don't neglect that tush. Knead that squishy thing like a mound of dough. And if you're feeling a little playful, why not give it a playful little surprise spank!

How sensitive are a man's legs? Sensitive enough that if you pinch them, rub them, or play with them, some part of him will stand up and take notice. Keep in mind that the closer you approach his genitals, the more excited he's going to become.

At the bottom of the legs are his feet. While this last part isn't for everyone, you might try kissing and sucking on his toes. While some are not too keen on receiving this unique form of pleasure, others may never even have experienced it before and are delightfully surprised to see how wonderful it can be—especially if the feet and toes are otherwise ticklish.

Sexploration Exercise #10

1. What do you think is the most sexually sensitive part of the female anatomy?
   a. The clitoris
   b. The breasts
   c. The shoulders
   d. Her entire body

2. When's the last time you brought your female partner to orgasm with your hand?
   a. A few nights ago.
   b. A few weeks ago.
   c. It's been years now—it seems like an awful lot of work.
   d. I never do. Let her do that for herself—I have lots of other ways to please her that she can't do for herself!

3. Most commonly, your partner likes to be handled:
   a. Strong and rough, like you're taming a wild horse.
   b. Firm and fast, like you're working diligently and efficiently to complete a task
   c. Slow and delicate, like you're polishing fine glassware
   d. I never thought of it—I just do what I think I would like.

4. When digitally stimulating your female partner, you should:
   a. Press firmly, directly on the clitoris, and move your hand in a fast and furious motion.
   b. Rub around the entire vaginal area, never making contact with the ultra-sensitive clitoris even once.
   c. Don't do any sort of rubbing at all; instead penetrate her over and over again with as many fingers as possible.
   d. Work your way around the vaginal area, gently massaging around, but not directly on top of the clitoris, until the woman is about to climax.

5. How long does it typically take a woman to climax?
   a. One minute
   b. Five minutes
   c. Twenty minutes
   d. Forty-five minutes

chapter 10

How to Touch a Woman

*"I could never be a woman, 'cause I'd just stay home
and play with my breasts all day."*
—*Harris K. Telemacher (Steve Martin),* L.A. Story

In the previous chapter, we taught women tricks to turning a man on. Gentlemen, it's now your turn.

Have you started to see your partner's body as, well, maybe something you own, like the sofa in your living room or even the TV in the family room? Like something you have gotten used to always being there, something that gives you comfort or entertainment—but something you don't really consider too much outside that realm?

Think back to before you purchased that sofa or TV, when there was a void in the room that needed to be filled. When you shopped for those items, you scrutinized the options, examined the pillows, seams, even the frame of the sofa. For the TV, you played with it endlessly in the store, evaluating picture and sound quality, becoming evermore excited by the various options one model held over all the others.

The day you brought that sofa or TV home, you couldn't wait to tear away at the boxes and wrappings. For weeks, you savored lounging around on your new sofa as you watched your new TV—and you paid attention to these new things. In fact, they were all you could think about. They were what you looked forward to seeing when you got home from work at night. But, after a while, they lost the same appeal for you. You got used to them, and, instead of being new, exciting toys, they just blended in with the rest of the room.

It's the same with a long-time partner. You courted her. All of her facets—and body parts—were a source of pure delight and discovery. But do you see your partner that way anymore? Not as something you've broken in and have gotten used to, but as a collection of soft sensual parts to be won, and once won, caressed, aroused, and ultimately made love to?

Taking the time to really concentrate on how to touch your partner is not only a validation of continuing sexual appeal, it's also a way to express enthusiasm at being with this person. We told your partner and now we tell you: Just because you've been with the same person sexually for years, it doesn't mean you build up sexual credits with the things you *used* to do. You can't bank sexual favors. Each sexual experience is a new one, a fresh opportunity to rediscover your lover and the things that bring her pleasure. Every time you are together is a new chance for you to express your desire and affection for her. And what better way to do this than by touching her?

Adam, 40

"I'm divorced. Anyone who knew my wife and I would not be surprised about that—at least not around the end of my marriage. At the beginning, well that's another story.

Terri and I met when we were in grad school. We were both in our early thirties. We had both waited to get established in our careers before getting back into the school thing again, and neither of us left our jobs to pursue our studies. We were also both shameless overachievers, so we were also each taking a maximum course load. Suffice to say, we were both really busy. But at least we understood each other—at least about time constraints and things like that.

But there was a whole world of things we never understood each other about because we never had—or found—the time to. Especially sex.

Don't get me wrong. In the beginning, the sex was very exciting. We'd sometimes call each other up after a night of studying—sometimes even at three in the morning—just to get together and hook up. We went at it like rabbits, squeezing in just enough time to get a few winks of sleep and start our crazy lives over in the morning.

We decided to move in together in our last year of school, looking forward to graduation and actually having time to plan a wedding and spend our lives together without midterms and the other pressures of school hanging over us.

The first year we were married didn't turn out as well as we thought it would. After the rush of always having to run somewhere and do something else, we were now faced with the luxury, and, unexpectedly, the strain, of spending a lot more time together than we were accustomed to.

Unfortunately, we never learned how to use our time together effectively. And that went double for the bedroom! We were still on that urgent, 'quickie' speed, and as time went on, we began to realize that we didn't quite know each other's bodies as we thought we had. In fact, we hardly knew anything at all.

Sex started to get strained, and Terri started to get very, well, reticent in bed. She never seemed satisfied. I suppose I could have talked to her about it, but I always figured that she was the woman, she would tell me if something were wrong. She never did. I guess she just thought that eventually I'd figure it out. I never did.

Around the end of our relationship, the frustration felt in the bedroom began to seep into our daily lives. Terri treated me tersely and was always aggravated at me for something or other. At first I tried, I really did. I bent over backwards to suck up to her, but after a while, I began to lose my patience with that. It was demoralizing. It was humiliating. And so I became a monster right back to her.

The sex we had began to get more and more strained, and as Terri had been snapping at me in life, one night she started snapping at me in bed. I was just trying to give her pleasure. I thought maybe one good orgasm would bring back the woman I thought she was. The woman I fell in love with. But the harder I tried, the more enthusiastically I stimulated her, the angrier she got. 'Not like that. To the left. No, your *other* left.' And then the worst ever: 'Ugh. Just forget it. You're useless. I'll just get out old faithful again.' Her vibrator.

I never had a problem with her having that thing before. In fact, we used to really enjoy using it together because it got her off so fast, it was unbelievable—and unbelievably handy when we had a full schedule of meetings and finals to deal with the next day. But now that we had the time, I wanted so much to be able to give her that kind of pleasure myself. It seems with everything I tried, though, I was never going to know how.

> "Friction, friction, friction, orgasm. Fishism. Are we going to dance or not?"
>
> —Richard Fish (Greg Germann), Ally McBeal

The resentment that had built between us had become too much to bear. Within three years of saying 'I do,' Terri and I threw in the towel and said 'I divorce.'"

Making It New Again

The case of Adam and Terri seems extreme, but it is certainly not out of the realm of reality. Lack of communication in sex can translate to ineffective communication in the whole of a relationship. When you're involved in a relationship, both aspects of your life are inextricably intertwined.

Even if you don't have the exact same problems as Adam and Terri, if you've been with your partner a long time, chances are you've experienced these kinds of difficulties in one way or another. This happens for many reasons.

For one, unless you've been able to completely evade Mother Nature—or you have an extensive budget for cosmetic surgery—it's a fairly safe assumption that you and your partner both are not wrapped in the same physical packages you were when you first fell in lust with each other. She might not look like a Victoria's Secret model anymore, but your Adonis days are likely also long behind you. What society tells us is sexy is not always the truth. We all know this in the rational parts of ourselves, but that doesn't mean these images don't burn on women's minds. There's just no getting around it. Multiple pregnancies might make washboard abs a physical impossibility; it doesn't matter that much to you, but does she know it? Make sure she does. Taking the time to touch her is one way you can.

So what does a woman want from a man's hands? In a word: *everything*. Women do not want a man to think that foreplay consists of a quick kiss, brief, if however heartfelt, attention to her nipples, a tap on the clit, and suddenly it's time to close the deal. Think about it, guys. Put yourself in her head and think about her body and her needs. If you were her, what would turn you on? Men often think of their sexuality as confined to the penis and the immediate surrounding area. They overlay that same template on women's sexuality and begin to forget that her erogenous zone is much more than the entrance to her vagina.

How should you get started? You might start looking at your partner—at all of her—as if she were a random woman walking down the street who has given some basic indication that she would not be totally adverse to your sexual advances. She is totally new to you now. Yours to explore and sample and tease and learn how to pleasure all over again. Now, read on!

Getting Started

Even if you're both really pressed for time, never start the seduction of your female partner at her clitoris. You wouldn't want her to signal that she wanted sex by squeezing the tip of your penis, would you? And if you think the tip of your penis can be sensitive, you can't imagine how painful, annoying, and frustrating it is to have your clitoris so incredibly over-stimulated that you can't even feel it anymore. But we'll get to the clitoris later. Our purpose in this section is to explore the whole sexual being that is your female partner.

Whether you've been with your partner four days, four years, or forty years, one thing's generally for sure: You are with this woman because you find her desirable and you'd like to be on top of her as often as possible. You can let her know that without simply jumping her every time you see her, however. There are better ways.

Stare at her. We know this sounds silly, and you shouldn't, of course, gawk at her like she's a freak in the circus, but just look at her. Likely, you'll make her uncomfortable by doing so, so if you do, just assure her that you're just admiring her. Thats she's never looked so beautiful to you as she does at this very moment.

Cuddle her. When's the last time you and your partner had a good cuddle? Probably when you watch TV at night in the living room, one of you sits on the couch and the other on a nearby chair. Go join her on the couch. Put an arm around her and tell her you just wanted to be close to her.

Stroke her. While you're sitting there together, gently trace lazy circles on her arms with your fingertips. She'll probably jump at first in surprise, but she'll soon be nuzzling your neck, pleased at this unexpected show of affection. Move the circles up her arm and to her shoulder. Then, lightly scratch the nape of her neck with your fingernails.

Kiss her. Not full on the mouth—not right away. Go back to Chapter 6 if you need some pointers. Her ears will be easiest for you to get at. Stroke them lightly with your fingertips, then give them gentle little kisses. While you're kissing her ear, move those fingertips back to the nape of her neck, and begin tracing those little circles again. Reposition yourself so that you can begin kissing the nape of her neck, and while you do so, do not forget to have those fingers pay attention to her arms again, her throat, and even lightly caress her breasts. Pay attention to her sighs and gasps; learn the spots that provide her with the most pleasure.

Undress her. Not in one fell swoop. While you're kissing and stroking, remove articles of her clothing, piece by piece, paying attention with your fingers and your mouth to the newly exposed areas. Do not, and we repeat, do *not* fully undress her. Leave her bra and panties intact. Leave her wondering where all this is headed.

Turn off the TV. Kneel down in front of her and look into her eyes as you continue to stroke her arms and shoulders. Now you can move to her breasts—but not at the expense of the rest of her body. Women love having their breasts caressed and fondled, but perhaps not as much as men like to caress and fondle them. Pay attention to them, running your fingers over her bra straps and cups. Then gently remove her bra. Lightly stroke and kiss her nipples, stroking one while you kiss the other.

Move your caresses southward. Stroking her legs from the ankles to the thighs, and then down again. Teasingly touch her around the panty line, "accidentally" letting a finger slip under the fabric from time to time.

Remove her panties. Likely, you're going to be about as excited as she is at this point, and don't worry, it's almost time to go in for the kill. Just not yet.

Lie her down. Either by herself on the couch or slide yourself to the back of the couch and let her lean against you. Touch and kiss each part of her body as if you have never seen anything so beautiful before.

Once you've gotten her to this phase of "ready," it's time to complete bringing her the greatest pleasure she's ever known. We'll give you tips on how to do this manually later in this chapter. Chapter 20 will give you great tips on how to pleasure her orally.

> *Home Bed Advantage— The confident feeling one gets while making love in one's own surroundings.*
>
> —*Jerry Seinfeld*

Remember, foreplay should not be thought of as something you *used* to do; it's something you want to work to perfect for as long as you both shall live. As you are beginning to remember by now, like you, your partner has an apex of sexual stimulation, but her entire body can be seen as one gorgeous sexual organ. The experience of climbing a mountain can—and should—be as rewarding as making it to the peak and planting your flag, so to speak.

Now we're certainly not suggesting you take this approach every time you have sex. No one has that kind of time. But you can always do a little of it here, a little there. There's always time for a little foreplay.

Samantha, 48

"I love my husband, Ian, with all my heart—don't get me wrong—but he used to be the clumsiest lover who ever lived. When we were first married, I thought, okay, he just needs some practice and he'll get better. But as the years went on, he never did. I think he may have even gotten a little worse for a while there.

Don't misunderstand me: My husband is not an ogre. He's a kind and gentle man, and he's wonderfully sensitive and understanding. How else could I have stayed married to him for so long? And it isn't like he doesn't try. He may be a clumsy lover but he's always been nothing if not earnest, loving, and determined. Sometimes he was just a bit too determined, though.

About ten years ago, I met another man at my office, Phil, and while I'm not proud to admit it, I strayed. Phil was handsome and charming—and he was a total player, which was great for me. I didn't want to be in a relationship with someone. I didn't need romance and love—I was still very much in love with my husband.

But I was curious. I'd never had sex with anyone but my husband before. I wanted to know if all men were the same when it came to giving a woman pleasure. I found out.

Sex with Phil was outrageous. I guess you could say that having all those partners really paid off for him—and for me. Phil always took what he wanted first, don't get me wrong. But when it came to me, well, let's just say that Phil played my body like an expert pianist giving a concert at Carnegie Hall. Every stroke had a purpose; there was a thrill in every touch. I know that part of this was the element of danger, but I also knew that a lot of it came down to just plain skill.

I only had sex a few times with Phil. And when I came home to my darling Ian afterwards, I could never look him in the eye. I realized that if it came down to having mind-blowing sex for the rest of my life or being with Ian, there was no contest. I'd give up anything for Ian. I had to tell him what I had been up to. I couldn't take it anymore.

Needless to say, he was devastated. He didn't talk to me for two days and slept on the couch instead of in our bed with me. It was a devastating time. I missed the warmth of his body beside me at night, even the gentle purr of his snoring.

But our bond was a strong one and so we opted for counseling instead of opting out of the marriage. In counseling I was finally able to explain to

Ian why I sought the outside stimulation. 'But why didn't you just tell me I was doing it wrong?' he asked me, in tears. 'You tell me when I cook something wrong or paint the bedroom wrong. How was I supposed to know you didn't like the way I was touching you?'

It took a little time to heal his hurt, but Ian eventually started to sleep in our bed again. And then one night, we even had sex again.

That first night, Ian insisted that I talk him through everything I wanted. In time, we made up signals I could tap onto his back for 'too hard,' 'too fast,' 'to the left,' and so on. Our sex life is better than ever before—and Ian's technique just gets better and better every time!"

> "Yes. Good. Nibbling the earlobe, uhh, kneading the buttocks, and so on and so forth. So, we have all these possibilities before we stampede towards the clitoris, Watson."
>
> —Humphrey Williams (John Cleese), Monty Python's The Meaning of Life

The Grand Finale

Chances are if you have permitted—even encouraged—your female partner to masturbate in front of you, you've learned how she touches herself to get herself going. This section will give you pointers on giving her maximum pleasure when it's your turn to act.

Don't be scared: This will not be one of those graphic play-by-plays with explicit illustrations or anything like that. At your age, we trust that you have at least a rudimentary knowledge of female genitalia, so we'll spare you the gruesome cross-sections and diagrams.

The angle you approach her at should depend on the position in which she feels most comfortable. If she likes to be lying down, please do not insist that she be sitting in a chair because you feel like you can get a more effective angle on her that way. She's in charge; let her lead. You can lie down next to her, or even behind her. You can sit on the edge of the bed or couch next to her. If she likes to sit, you can sit on the floor in front of the bed or chair, or wrap your legs behind her on the bed.

Please be sure to remember that while the clitoris is the headquarters of her sexuality, it is not the only part of the vaginal region that feels sensitivity and responds to touch. Whatever you do, don't go right for it. Build a mission that culminates in clitoral massage; don't make it the entire mission.

The key word to remember when stimulating a woman's genitalia is gentle. You may like a rough touch on your own penis, that too light a touch can be irritating and uncomfortable, but most women like to be touched very lightly—at least at first.

For maximum effect, wet your fingers with your mouth before touching her. As you appreciate the sensation of lubricated friction, she adores it. Move your fingers around her labia, consciously remembering to touch her lightly and gingerly. Move your fingers around the clitoris, but not directly on the clitoris. Too much contact with the clitoris results in over-stimulation and can make orgasm more difficult to achieve—if not impossible.

Gently insert a finger into the vagina, but don't forget about her other parts and do this exclusively. It might be doing wonders for you, and it will seem for her as you will be able to more fully experience her natural lubrication process unfolding, but it's not what she needs.

Pay attention to her moans and the way she squirms. Don't touch that clitoris until you're sure she is ready. When she is, move your fingertips to her clitoris and lightly rub it. As she gets closer and closer to orgasm, you can build the speed and pressure with which you are stimulating her. A wonderful orgasm will be the result.

Sexploration Exercise #11

1. Are you and your lover typically willing to try out new things in the bedroom?
   a. Always—you name it, we're up for it.
   b. Sometimes—there are things we'll try, but we definitely draw the line at some things.
   c. Not usually—we like our sex basic, with maybe a little spice thrown in from time to time.
   d. Never—there's the right way to do it, and then there's the Devil's way.

2. Have you or your partner ever had a G-spot orgasm?
   a. Once we found my G-spot, we've been able to work it in just about every time we have sex now.
   b. I'm sure I've found it on her and we've tried, but so far, no dice.
   c. I think I had one—I had that "peeing" feeling they talk about, but then everything just went kind of dead.
   d. I'd be lucky if my husband even tried once to locate it—let alone do anything with it when he found it!

3. Have you ever tried to locate and stimulate the prostate gland?
   a. We tried, and the sensation was great!
   b. We tried, and while the orgasm was really powerful and cool, I'd rather she just stick with my front parts.
   c. Are you kidding? I don't want her to go up there!

   d. His orgasms are powerful enough. He doesn't need to learn to have a new kind.

4. Which position have you heard best stimulates the G-spot?
   a. Missionary
   b. Woman on top
   c. Rear entry
   d. Standing

5. Which sex toys work best to stimulate the prostate gland?
   a. Dildo
   b. Anal beads
   c. Butt plugs
   d. Vibrator

chapter 11

Bonus Pleasure Spots

*"If you laid all the girls from Smith and
Mt. Holyoke end to end, I wouldn't be surprised."*
—Dorothy Parker

In the past two chapters, we covered the standard pleasure zones for women and men. Many of these you already know quite a bit about already, and have been using with great success for years. To recap, the female's seat of pleasure is the clitoris; for the male, it's the penis. But, as we have certainly also learned in the last two chapters, the human body is loaded with special trigger points that, when properly stimulated, can produce enormous, intense waves of pleasure.

In this chapter, we move slightly off the typical path in terms of places from which men and women can derive pleasure. These spots are the G-spot in women and the prostate in men.

Elizabeth, 46

"I never believed in the whole mystery of the G-spot thing. I never found the thing. No one I had ever been with had ever found it in me. And, if you think that maybe it's just that I'm some kind of mutant, none of my girlfriends had ever found theirs either. We used to think it was just another bunch of bull to make women buy books. And then I met Ben.

Ben was not the typical guy I usually dated. He was kind of short, portly—like that sidekick guy on Seinfeld? George, I think, was the character's name? Anyway, it doesn't matter. The whole point is that I had hit a dry spell in the dating pool, and there was Ben, short, stout, and bald as a bowling ball. Desperate times, you know how it goes. Stay home with your vibrator or let some poor slob buy you a meal and maybe you sleep with him—who knows ....

Well, Ben certainly taught me a lesson. No, he wasn't handsome, but he was really smart. Not book smart, you know, like he knew a lot of obscure things that no one cares about. I mean smart like *clever* smart. The kind of guy who could make you wet yourself laughing. And, as I was about to find out, he could make you wet yourself in other ways as well.

We went out for an amazing dinner. The whole night, and I promise you this, totally in spite of myself, I actually found myself being more and more drawn to this troll-like little man. His laugh was actually quite sexy .... I can't explain it.

When Ben suggested we go back to my place, I didn't even flinch. In the manner of a fire drill, we quietly dropped our napkins to the table, paid the bill, exited the restaurant single file, and slipped into a cab.

We didn't talk until we got back to my place. Once through the front door, we remained in strict business mode. I didn't even let a chuckle escape when I had to remove my shoes because he couldn't reach my lips standing in front of me with both feet on the floor. If I wasn't under his spell, no doubt I would have offered a phone book, a step stool— something, you know?

Once in bed, he went right to work on me. All of a sudden, I had this weird feeling down there, you know, like I was going to pee all over the place or something. I squirmed to get away from him but he held me down. 'Don't worry. It will pass. You're not going to urinate, I promise you. Just relax and enjoy this.'

As soon as I let myself not be afraid of peeing all over him, I started to relax a little bit. And then a lot. All of a sudden, this wave washed over me. I can't explain it. It was the most amazing orgasm I ever had.

When I could breathe again, I sat up in bed and looked over at him. I could barely utter a meek, 'How?' He smiled. 'That's your G-spot, Sugar.' "

G-Spot Primer

What is a G-spot? It is a small mass of nerve tissue located about an inch to two from the entrance to and on the top part of the vagina.

The G-spot received its name during the early years of the Reagan Administration, when authors John Perry and Beverly Whipple wrote a book called *The G-Spot and Other Recent Discoveries About Human Sexuality.* The co-authors named this intriguing part of the female anatomy after the German doctor Dr. Ernst Grafenberg, who first described it, to a grateful German nation, in 1950.

How can you find the G-spot? Insert one or two clean, lubricated fingers about one to two inches into the vagina, with fingertips facing the front wall, and gently feel around. You'll know it when you find it.

Making It Work

Once you've found the G-spot, be sure to massage it as gently as you possibly can, and don't be afraid to ask if you're doing it right. The greatest degree of gentleness and sensitivity is required to make the experience as utterly pleasurable as possible.

If you really want to add another dimension to the pleasure you are providing your partner, lie her down on the bed and massage her G-spot with the fingers of one hand and her clitoris with the fingers of the other. And, if you really want to make it interesting, try orally stimulating the region simultaneously. Just be sure not to put too much direct pressure on the clitoris.

Different sex positions offer different levels of stimulation to the G-spot. For example, rear-entry provides great direct stimulation of the G-spot. In this position, the penis comes into contact with the top of the vagina, the location of the G-spot. This is why many women find it easier to achieve a vaginal orgasm through rear-entry sex, whether they are standing or kneeling. (We'll talk more about the various sexual positions in the coming chapters.)

Some women, at the moment of vaginal orgasm, will ejaculate a clear fluid. Stimulation of the G-spot can increase the flow of this liquid, but doctors and scientists do not know exactly what triggers that flow, why some women ejaculate and others don't, or whether it plays a role in the orgasm itself. What is known is that the fluid is not urine.

"How can we possibly use sex to get what we want? Sex is what we want."

—*Frasier Crane (Kelsey Grammar),* Frasier

Don't be discouraged if you have a hard time finding the G-spot. Nature, in its mysterious way, did not design it to be found all that easily. Perhaps the gentleness of touch, the emotional care that probing for the G-spot requires, was actually part of Nature's plan to bring a couple that much closer together.

You Mean Guys Have One, Too?

Although men do not have a true G-spot, the part of the anatomy we are about to discuss has several similarities to the female G-spot: It's hidden away and it requires the same sort of insertion and finger-wiggling to stimulate. What are we talking about here? The prostate gland.

The prostate is actually one of the most sexually sensitive parts of the male anatomy. Typically, men do not associate pleasure with their prostate. The prostate is something that men think about only when it fails.

The prostate gland is described to be approximately the size of a typical walnut. Now comes what may be the bad news for some. The prostate gland is located a few inches up inside the anus, generally at the level of the man's naval. In order to reach it, you may want to put a condom on your finger. Be sure to cover it with a lubricant.

Insert your finger well into his anus until you reach the prostate. The thrill that he will get from the sensation you provide will more than outweigh any initial discomfort you or he may feel performing this act. Don't hesitate to have sex with him while stroking his prostate gently with your finger. It will give him a thunderous orgasm. Also, you don't need to use your finger to stimulate his prostate; a sex toy (see Chapter 33) will also do nicely.

Thomas, 45

"My sex life with my wife of thirteen years, Margaret, was getting stale. When we first met, and even years into our marriage, we had sex all the time. But there came a time when we exhausted everything new there was to do pretty early on—or so we thought—and with no new ground left to forge, we fell into a complacent, standard, step-by-step routine.

I think it started just after our ten-year anniversary. Our relationship began to deteriorate. Our boredom with each other in the bedroom began to seep into the events of our daily lives, and we started to spend less and less time together, and when we did, we hardly even talked at all.

This wasn't sitting well with either of us, but for a long time, neither of us acted because we were simply too afraid to act. That we loved each other very much was never in question. If what was happening between us was going to lead us to divorce court, I think we were both content to live in silence together than to confront it and risk not being together at all.

When a couple we knew who had married around the same time we did told us they were going to be calling it quits, we were shaken into action. It was one thing to speculate that our kinds of problems could lead to divorce; it was quite another thing to watch our friends go through the process.

One night before going to sleep, Margaret leaned over to my side of the bed. 'I don't want to end up like Charles and Eileen,' she whispered, and I could tell she was crying. I threw my arms around her. 'We won't, honey. We won't,' I comforted her, not sure if I was lying to both of us with this. 'We have to get help,' she told me. I agreed.

Marriage counseling was kind of weird at first. I mean, having to have someone else there so you could talk to your wife—the person you'd married, in part, because you knew they were the person you could talk to better than anyone else you had ever known? But we went. And a great thing happened because of it.

We started to bond all over again with the exercises we were given—and we even forged a special bond at our counselor, Alice's, expense. She had a really weird way of scratching at her scalp and sniffing her finger every time she made a new observation about my wife and myself, and we both noticed it. So, during our sessions, when she scratched and sniffed, my wife and I would tap and kick each other lightly under the table, each trying to get the other one to crack up laughing. We actually had a great time with this, and when we used to leave our sessions, we would crack up laughing till our sides hurt.

In one of our sessions, Alice asked us about our sex life. It took a while for us to be honest that it wasn't what it used to be and that we were desperate to try and find something to make it new and exciting for us. She recommended a couple of books for us to look into that might give us some new ideas about how to give pleasure to each other and make our sex lives exciting again.

We looked through one of the books together one night. We came to a section about male sexual stimulation and the prostate gland. Even though the book could not say enough about how exciting it can be for a man to have his prostate stimulated during sex, I was not about to accept anything up what I firmly considered a one-way street. Margaret was more willing to try it out, so I figured she was definitely making the bigger leap here, so I allowed it.

I'm not going to get into any of the details here—but what I will tell you is WOW! Thank God for my wife's persistence is all I have to say. For any of you who feel reluctant about doing this, all I have to tell you is to try it just once. If you don't like it, fine, don't do it again. But if you do, well, you are in for the orgasms of your life!"

Sexploration Exercise #12

1. When's the last time you gave your lover a full-body, head-to-toe, sensual massage?
   a. Our last vacation.
   b. When we were dating.
   c. Our wedding night.
   d. I never have.

2. When's the last time you received one from your lover?
   a. Last Saturday night.
   b. A few months ago.
   c. It has to be years now.
   d. I never have.

3. Do you think sensual massage is an important element of sexual expression?
   a. Absolutely—it's one of the most romantic ways to show your lover how much you care for them.
   b. If you can make the time for it, that's great—but who has the time?
   c. It's a bonus, but not a necessity.
   d. Nah—it's time-consuming and it really doesn't add anything to our sex life.

4. To me, a great massage is like:
   a. A luxurious, exotic vacation, with no expense spared.
   b. An unexpected getaway weekend.
   c. A romantic dinner.
   d. A torturous ordeal.

5. Do you think a sensual massage is a prelude to sex?
   a. Definitely—without a doubt.
   b. It should be—I mean, why else would you go through all that trouble?
   c. It doesn't have to be—sometimes it's just nice to give or receive that extra special bit of attention.
   d. By the time you're done, who has time for sex?

chapter 12

Erotic Massage

"What a day, eh, Milhouse? The sun is out, birds are singing, bees are trying to have sex with them— as is my understanding ..."
—*Bart Simpson,* The Simpsons

Everybody loves a massage, or at least everybody loves the *idea* of a massage. But tell the truth: When was the last time you actually treated yourself to one? Or, perhaps more rare still, gave your partner one?

The benefits of massage are numerous: It feels great; it provides a sense of being cared for when someone takes the time to do it to us; it makes us feel good that we can provide pleasure as the masseuse; and it helps our stressed-out, frazzled bodies to really relax. And it isn't just in your head. Scientifically speaking, the physical benefits of massage include improving circulation and easing muscle tension.

When a man and woman take time out of their lives to give each other sensual massages, a few other important benefits kick in: a reminder of the closeness or bond between the couple, a chance to engage in some loving fun, and an opportunity to usher in a period of sexual activity without rushing into intercourse.

So if massage is so wonderful, why do so few of us engage in it? We think the reasons come down to three: time constraints, fear of failure, and well, laziness. Our job in this is to rid you of all these excuses.

A Question of Time

Too many of us don't engage in massage simply because we are too time-pressed. Massage takes a while. A really great massage can take an hour to an hour and a half. Most of us feel that we don't have the time to spare.

We'd like to suggest that there's always time for a little massage in your life. Even five minutes of pre-bedtime massage is adequate to stimulate your partner in all sorts of exciting ways. First, your partner will thank you for your thoughtfulness. Second, your partner is likely to reciprocate. And third, who knows what those five minutes of massage that you offer your partner will lead to next? We don't know, but we'd bet you'd like to find out!

Attention, Overachievers

Sometimes we shy away from giving our partner a massage because we're afraid we won't do it well, so we end up not doing it at all. Perhaps you fall into the group of those who would rather not do something at all than risk doing it badly?

Fear of giving a bad massage should not keep us from giving any massage at all. Our solution: Instead of "taking the class" for a grade, take it pass-fail. In other words, reduce your expectations of how thorough and perfect the massage must be. Massages are like orgasms in that really there's no such thing as a bad one. Even an okay one is still fantastic. As we've tried to stress in this book, so much of sex is mental and emotional, so when it comes to giving or getting massages, it's the thought that counts. The main thing is simply to get in there and start touching. Of course, don't forget that like anything else, the more you practice, the better at it you will become.

That said, we implore you to release any fear you might have that you're not going to measure up to some sort of master masseur or masseuse. Your lover doesn't want a massage from a stranger; your lover wants five minutes or more of touching tenderness from you!

Lazybones, Get Off the Couch

If you are not inclined to give your lover a massage because you're too lazy, we suggest you head right back to the front of this book and start reading it all over again. Clearly, if you've gotten to this point and are still feeling you are too lazy to rub a little love into your partner's back and shoulders, then you haven't been paying attention. Exhaustion we can understand. Time pressure, sure. Even fear, if you're willing to deal with it and work through it, are all acceptable excuses. But laziness, not even close.

By saying you're too lazy to give your partner a massage, you're saying that you really can't muster enough motivation, or *care* to muster up enough motivation, to show your lover a little extra tenderness—and that kind of slacking off throws up a giant red flag up in your relationship. If you want to keep your relationship, we suggest you deal with your feelings right away, even seek counseling if necessary.

Stan, 48

"I'm a professional sports masseur by profession, so I know all about the benefits of massage—the physical benefits, that is. Players come to me with all kinds of injuries, pulling this, straining that, and report that after just a half hour to an hour of massage, they feel less pain and more relaxed.

Giving massages is my job: It never even occurred to me that there might be any emotional benefits to it. Does a baker think about how the dough he's kneading for bread is feeling? Of course, I care about my clients' injuries, but come on—you know what I mean.

So I always had this very at-a-distance, aloof, professional association with massage. That is, until my girlfriend actually surprised me with a massage one night!

I'd been dating Tina for only a few months. We had both been married before, so we knew a thing or two about the bodies of members of the opposite sex—how they liked to be played with, fondled, touched, that kind of thing. And we always made sure we knew exactly what the other wanted during sex. Physical contact without sex? We hadn't really explored that much ... not until that night at least.

When I got to Tina's apartment after work, all the lights were out. I called out to her and she didn't respond, so I figured I had just beaten her there. No big deal. It wasn't the first time. Tina has a pretty big and important job in banking. I'd come to get used to her hours. So I popped open a beer, sprawled out on the couch, and turned on the TV.

That's when I noticed there was light coming from the crack under the bedroom door. Was she home? Did she just forget to turn the light off that morning? Was she ill? I hoped not, but that last thought got me right off my butt and I raced into the bedroom.

When I threw the door open, there was Tina, sitting on the edge of the bed, which was surrounded by candles. She was sipping a glass of wine. 'What took you so long?' she cooed. I opened my mouth to speak, but she cut me off. 'Don't worry about it. I have a special surprise in store for you. Take off your clothes and lie down on the bed, on your stomach please.'

Okay, it wasn't a blowjob she had in mind, but I thought, no problem. Let's see what she's up to. So I followed her orders and lay on my stomach, awaiting her next instruction.

All of a sudden, all I could smell was sesame seeds. This was getting weird. When I heard Tina rubbing her hands together, I figured it out. Of course, I knew that sound—I made it myself several times a day. She was going to give me a massage.

This was great. The anticipation I felt while she rubbed her hands together was totally intense and I could feel myself starting to get aroused (and I was actually glad to be on my stomach then!).

Tina stroked my entire body with slow, deliberate strokes. Every now and then, she'd lean down and whisper in my ear—asking me how things she was doing felt; telling me how much she cared about me. I was so excited to feel all this love from her, coming out from her hands on me, I didn't know how long I was going to be able to hold out.

In her last maneuver, she straddled my back with her legs. I could feel that she was naked as she continued to rub me. She leaned over and began to rub my back with her magnificent breasts. That nearly forced me over the edge. When she finally bent close to my ear and whispered one word, 'Ready,' I was about to explode. She must have known because at that very moment, she told me to turn onto my back. We had the best sex of our relationship that night!"

"What is more obscene: Sex or war?"

—Larry Flynt (Woody Harrelson), The People vs. Larry Flynt

Setting the Mood

As we saw in the case of Stan and Tina, a great massage starts long before you begin even to undress or caress your partner. It starts when you take the steps to put the other person in the mood. If you can create a relaxing environment through light, music, a "do not disturb" sign and the like, then your recipient is going to feel relaxed already—without you even having lifted a finger.

Turn off the ringer on the phone. And while you're at it, if you have an answering machine, turn the volume all the way down. There's nothing like the ringing of a telephone to yank a person out of whatever pleasant mood they may find themselves in—and worse than that, the shrill voice of their boss, a creditor, or pesky telemarketer.

Turn out the lights. Got candles? Dig them out, set them up, and light them. The flickering of candlelight can relax even the most tightly wound among us. You can also try soft lighting, or even no lighting at all.

Set up a relaxing selection in your CD player. Music has a lot of inherent power. It can energize you when you're cleaning the house or getting ready for work, but it can also soothe you when played in the right setting under the right circumstances. A little light jazz may be something great to try in this situation.

Strip the bed. Clean sheets will give your partner a more soothing experience. The smell and feel of the clean sheets will put your partner's mind at ease with their crispness and fresh scent.

Once you're ready, go collect your partner. Lead him or her to the bed and instruct him or her to disrobe and lie down on the bed on his or her stomach. You may also decide you want to disrobe your partner, and that's fine, but be sure you don't get too excited by the prospect that you skip the massage and go right for the sex!

Now you and your partner are primed and ready; it's time to begin.

Full-Body Massage

If this is your first time, why not keep your approach to massage as simple as possible? As you begin to touch your partner, ask for guidance. Whispering questions like, "Do you like it like this?" and "Harder or softer?" will elicit the information you need without breaking the spell.

So where should you begin? There are no "shoulds" here. Begin wherever you like. Our only suggestion is that you avoid the genitals—at least at first. You can build up to that, if you go there at all. You've already made the time to do this for your partner. What's the rush?

The scalp is a wonderful place to begin a massage, simply because it is so unexpected. As we discovered earlier in the how to touch a man section, the scalp loves gentle rubbing, whether in a circular motion or just simply a gentle around-the-cranium caress.

Our faces are also repositories of tension. So many of us have lined faces due in part to the tension and frustration that manifest themselves in our facial expressions. Gently begin to touch your partner's face and ears. If your partner laughs because it tickles or because it is so unexpected, laugh along with your partner.

Move to the back of the neck and touch it only very gently, pressing small circles into the region around the spine and backbone.

Move from the nape of the neck to the shoulder blades. We hold so much of the tension we accumulate over the course of the day in our shoulder blades. Rub firmly with the heel of your hand, increasing or letting up on pressure as your partner dictates.

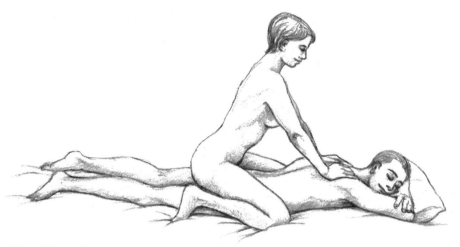

Move from the nape of the neck to his shoulders, keeping your own back straight.
(Hrana Janto)

As you move down the back, lessen the pressure as you approach the lower region. Press on the area on either side of the spine and backbone with your fingertips. Continue rubbing as you approach the coccyx and buttocks.

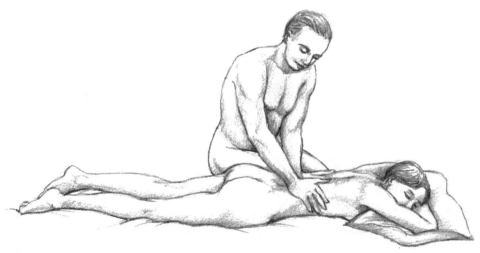

Lessen the pressure as you move down her back and try varying your own position.
(Hrana Janto)

If you don't think it will make you or your partner too excited, rub the buttocks with the heels of your hands. Remember, while there's nothing wrong with either of you getting aroused during this process—in fact, it's encouraged that you do—you don't want to get too aroused too soon. If you think you will, or start to, come back to this area later.

Move down to your partner's legs, rubbing them between your hands. Pay attention to the way your partner responds to your touch. Some sections of the legs are more sensitive than others. And here's a good thing to keep in mind about leg massages, especially if there's a history of varicose veins in the gene pool: Massaging the legs will improve the circulation, and thus, help prevent these from popping out.

Men can sometimes withstand rubbing with a pressure that may just be inconceivable to a woman. Women: Don't be afraid to really get in there and deeply knead his thighs and calves. And men, be sure to encourage your partner to rub you harder if it feels good—and if you think she has the physical strength. Of course, there's no reason for either of you to completely wear yourselves out giving—and receiving—massages. Gentle caresses also go a long way.

Massage Oils and Lotions

We are firm believers in massage oil. It's nice to have a variety of massage oils so that things don't smell the same way every time, unless, of course, you and your partner come to favor one particular oil over all others. Whatever oil you choose, be sure to read the directions on the bottle carefully. Some oils may actually irritate certain skin types. Here are a just a few the pros use to get you started:

- Almond. This oil is effective on most skin types, and especially appreciated by those who suffer from dry skin. It's also an excellent anti-inflammatory oil.
- Apricot Kernel. Good for skin that has aged prematurely, this oil relieves stress and creates a sense of balance.
- Borage. Helpful for psoriasis and eczema, this is also a regenerative and stimulating oil.

- Jojoba. An antibacterial that helps unclog pores (think pesky back acne, or "bacne" as it is sometimes playfully called), it also helps prevent the oxidation of essential oils.
- Sesame. A purifier that prevents premature aging of the skin, this is one of our favorites. It's also great for rheumatism and arthritis.

Never pour massage oil directly from a bottle onto your partner's body. Pouring liquid onto a person will generally cause that person to tense up, which is the exact opposite of the reaction you want. And there's also an interesting psychological benefit of not pouring that oil directly on to your partner: When he or she hears you pouring the massage oil out onto your hands, and then warming the oil in your hands as you rub it into a frothy lather, their anticipation at being touched by you builds with an incredible intensity.

Liza, 54

"I'll never forget the trip I took to St. Martin with my husband last year. Yes, it was a beautiful island, and we had such a wonderful time lazing around on the beach, gorging ourselves on food, drinking like sailors ... until the day I forgot to put on the sun block, that was.

When we got back to the hotel that night, I thought I was going to pass out. I felt so hot from the sunburn, I thought for sure I had a fever.

My husband of thirty years, George, was so understanding. He told me to go and take a shower and that he would order room service for us while I did.

The shower felt great and I felt better until I looked at myself in the bathroom mirror. I was red as a lobster. I'm not even kidding about this. I was so burned, I could swear I was swollen. I groaned so hard, my husband heard me. 'Don't worry, sweetie. Food's here. I ordered us up some lobster.' He wasn't kidding.

When I came into the room, something was different. The lights were dimmer somehow. I looked around and noticed he had thrown my sarong over one of the lamps. 'George, do you think that might be a fire hazard—' I started to ask him, but that's all I could get out. 'My poor darling,' he said to me, 'that looks really painful.' I was in no mood for niceness, and I snapped back at him: 'Ya think?' But George had a mission. I could see it in his eyes. He was up to something and, as usual, he wasn't going to let my sarcasm get in the way of his plans.

'Come here, love,' he said, as he led me to the bed. 'I've heard if you put aloe vera on a burn, it feels better. So go lie down on your stomach and let me cover you in it.' I thought, okay, and I followed his orders.

George covered every inch of me with sensual, determined strokes. He must have lathered me up for an hour or more—and even places where the bathing suit clearly covered and didn't require burn maintenance. As he rubbed, he whispered in my ear that he loved me and I was just transported to another place. It must have been heaven … No, scratch that. Heaven was the place he brought me to when he flipped me over on my back and rubbed the aloe into my front parts.

'I'm done … at least with Part One,' he said. And the he moved his head between my legs. With just a few flicks of his tongue, he brought me to the most amazing climax I had ever experienced in my life … Nope. I'll never forget that trip!"

part 3

Getting into the Act

Sexploration Exercise #13

1. What's your general feeling about the missionary position?
   a. It's the easiest way for both of us to get off.
   b. It's for amateurs who haven't learned to do anything more adventurous.
   c. It's the only natural way there is to have sex.
   d. It can be really exciting when you experiment with all the many variations of the positions.

2. On average, how frequently would you say you and your partner have sex in the missionary position?
   a. Every single time—there's no better way to go about it.
   b. Most times—it's really easy.
   c. Sometimes—it can get boring if we do it like this too often.
   d. Rarely—really like to shake it up!

3. How many variations of the position do you think there are?
   a. There's just the one—why complicate it?
   b. Less than five.
   c. More than five.
   d. There are so many variations, I don't think I could count them on all my fingers and toes!

4. Do you think the missionary position is sexist?
   a. Yes. It completely inhibits a woman's sexual power and puts her totally under the control of her partner.
   b. I suppose I could see where people might get that idea, but sometimes being controlled sexually adds to the fun.
   c. Anyone who knows anything about how to have sex in this position knows that women have a lot of ways to control their partners in it—just because you're on the bottom doesn't make you completely powerless!
   d. Honestly, I never thought about it.

5. If you perform the missionary position the same way all the time, are you ready to learn some new variations?
   a. Bring it on! I'm always ready to try something new.
   b. I guess so—as long as they don't overly complicate such an easy way to have sex.
   c. I have a bad back—I don't really want to do anything that might make it worse.
   d. No thanks.

chapter 13

The Missionary Positions

"There are a number of mechanical devices which increase sexual arousal, particularly in women. Chief among these is the Mercedes Benz 380 SL."
—*Lynn Lavner*

In the traditional version of the missionary position, the woman lies on her back. The man lies above the woman, facing her, his legs between hers. It's been referred to as the "meat-and-potatoes" of sex positions because it's generally the old standby—the default of sexual positions. But despite the perceived drawbacks of this position being a standard, "vanilla" way to make love, it can be a highly satisfying, exciting position with a wealth of opportunities for sexual enjoyment for many reasons.

For one, you can achieve exquisitely deep penetration in this position. It also affords a wonderful opportunity for intimacy, allowing partners to look into each other's faces and have maximum mobility of their arms and hands to tease and titillate each other's bodies. And if you're looking to get pregnant at this point in your life, the missionary position has proven to be one of the most effective positions for conception.

So put your old ideas about this old faithful of positions aside. What we're going to show you in this chapter is that the missionary is anything but typical. Variations on the basic theme can make this a regular in your bedroom—not just because it's easy, but because it is the position that sets you both on fire.

One thing we urge, as is the case with the whole of this book, is that you each read everything. Don't skip ahead to the parts you think pertain to you. You'll be sharing the experience of sex, and therefore it all pertains to you. Use this chapter—this book—as a forum for open communication between you and your partner.

Sarah, 43

"The first time I ever had sex was my wedding night with my husband, Joe. No, I'm not kidding about this! Even though I was coming of age years after the sexual revolution went into effect, I've always held close to my values. One just didn't have sex before marriage and that was that.

So, as you can well imagine, the first time my husband and I were together intimately, we made love in the missionary position. As far as I knew, this was the only way to do it.

As I got more sophisticated with sex, I began to learn that there were hundreds of other positions you could do it in—like animals in the zoo, even with me on top. Me on top? You mean there could come a time when I'd actually have to do the work? No, thank you, I thought. That didn't sound like me. It's not that I was lazy. Let's just say I felt less-than-confident about the whole thing. Needless to say, the first time my husband insisted we try it, I saw that I was right. It was less than fantastic, so we went back to missionary.

But what we learned over the years was that there were many, many ways we could have sex the way I preferred, with my husband on top. As we varied the routine, we were able to give our sex life enough diversity to make it interesting.

Another thing that was great was that all of this experimentation helped me become more confident in bed. Instead of just lying there, I learned that I could thrust with my husband, and that the sensation of sex became more enhanced and pleasurable when I did. And the more and more pretzels were learned to contort ourselves into, the less aware I became of who was on top, who was behind ... essentially, the less self-conscious I became.

Even though Joe and I have added many more positions to our sexual repertoire, I have to admit that I still like missionary the best. I love it when my husband's on top of me during sex. I just love that feeling of being dominated in bed. And I don't think there's anything wrong with that!"

Missionary Basics

No, Sarah. There certainly is nothing wrong with that. There is no right or wrong in sex, provided you and your partner are both enjoying youselves—and that one is not always compromising—or being compromised—for the other. And this is especially relevant when it comes to sexual positions.

With all the information out there these days, sex has almost become like an Olympic event, complete with grades handed out for "degree of difficulty" and increasingly complex positions. It doesn't necessarily have to be that way, however. While variation lends excitement, we can't emphasize enough that the most important part of sex is to have fun, to share intimacy with your partner, and bring each other pleasure in a zone in which you are both comfortable.

Most couples agree that as far as sex positions go, missionary is an extremely comfortable one for both men and women. Unfortunately, there has been backlash in the past against the missionary position because of the way it puts women in a submissive role to men. We'd like to think of this as forcing the issue. In the bedroom, we are always either dominant or submissive—and can be one or even both anytime we share intimacy. Guess what. It has no bearing on the rest of the world. What you do in the bedroom is your sacred territory. It's your time to explore fantasies and desires, to express affection. Man or woman, if you enjoy taking a passive role in bed, it does not

"Having sex is like playing bridge. If you don't have a good partner, you'd better have a good hand."

—*Woody Allen*

mean you are weak and passive in life. Besides, when you look at all the options a woman has at her disposal to control the action in this position, you see that missionary does not always mean complete submission. Let's look more closely at the dynamics of this position.

Women in Charge

As we previously stated, missionary-style sex can be not only satisfying for a woman, but also very pleasurable. Women, if you like the idea of being dominated by your lover in bed, you can enjoy the power your lover has over you, allowing him to take the lead in depth of penetration, speed, and intensity. And, you can easily take control for yourself, even in the missionary position, and work it to derive maximum satisfaction. How?

One way lies in the way you position your body, and especially your legs, while you are in this position. You can lay perfectly flat on the bed, your legs open around your lover's hips and thighs. The lower your legs are positioned during missionary-style sex, the harder his penis will work on the top of your vagina, thus stimulating your clitoris. But that's not the only way to enjoy this position. Even if you are not expressly working toward climax, the penetration it provides can be an extremely sexy sensation.

In that spirit, keep in mind that the higher you hold your legs, the deeper he will be able to penetrate. Therefore, you may opt to hold your legs in the air, bent at the knees, perhaps leaning against his sides or wrapped around his waist. And if you are particularly limber, you may also try resting your ankles on the shoulders of your lover for maximum penetration.

As you know, too much penetration can be painful. Pain in sex can be caused if he penetrates too deeply and roughly and his penis hits your cervix. He may also inadvertently hit an ovary. And, of course, if you have a bad back, this is a position you'll be most comfortable performing with your legs held up at a manageable level, if at all. Be sure to also keep in mind that it is not necessary to have *both* legs up to enjoy the penetration this position provides. Try keeping one leg flat on the bed or bent at the knee, with the foot of that leg flat on the bed. Raise the other leg up as high as is comfortable for you. You can hold this leg high, with your ankle locked on his shoulder; bent at the knee, with your calve and ankle resting comfortably at his side; or bent at the knee with your foot set firmly on the bed.

Be sure to be vocal about what feels good and what does not in this position. As exciting as this position is for you, you can just imagine how exciting it is for him; he might just get carried away with the moment, so it's up to you to let him know if what you are doing together is comfortable or not.

Missionary-style sex does not always mean you'll be holding your legs round him. You might try placing both of your legs between his for a change of pace. Squeeze your thighs together when he trusts into you, giving him incredible sensation in his penis—not to mention causing a wonderful friction that will stimulate your clitoris.

Another thing you can try is to place a small pillow underneath your buttocks to vary the angle of penetration. Instead of lying flat with your head on a pillow, you may also try propping yourself up on your elbows while your partner is inside of you to a position where you are in a half-sit. This position ensures that the tip of your partner's penis will be making direct contact with your G-spot. If you have exceptionally strong arms, consider sitting almost all the way up, leaning on your outstretched arms.

And did you know that you don't have to face your partner head-on during missionary-style sex? Try instead tilting your pelvis sideways when enters you, and be sure he keeps his hips positioned straight. By angling your pelvis, you can also derive clitoral stimulation when you and your partner thrust against one another. And thrusting is especially important to remember in this position. Just because he's on top doesn't mean you can't thrust back. Move in time with his thrusts or set a different pace. If you're feeling like you want to be orchestrating the action, clutch his buttocks and control the rhythm of his strokes.

A final note. Women, please do not be discouraged if you can't climax in this position. Even with all the G-spot and clitoral stimulation you may be receiving, this is reportedly the most difficult position for a woman to achieve orgasm. Enjoy the sensations this position affords, and if you want to try something different, indicate to your partner when you're ready to try a new position. More effective positions for clitoral and G-spot stimulation will follow in the coming chapters.

Missionary Men

Just as women can vary posture and positioning during missionary-style sex, so can men. The standard missionary position dictates that men prop themselves up on their elbows, arching their backs to position themselves for comfortable entry into the vagina. Another option for this position, however, if you have the upper-arm strength, is to raise yourself up so that you are leaning on your knuckles or the heels of your hands. Be advised that this angle will put more strain on your lower back than if you are propped on your elbows. If you have back problems, you may be better off sticking with alternative techniques.

A very intimate way to experience the missionary position is to rest on top of your partner, wrapping your body around hers in a cocoon-like embrace. Be sure, however, that you don't get so carried away that you forget that you (most likely) outweigh your partner by dozens of pounds. Try not to crush her. Remember to keep your weight carefully balanced if you opt to experience this position in this way.

Missionary is a very exciting position for men—certainly no one needs to be told that. But as carried away as you feel yourself becoming, you must also not forget to consider your partner's comfort. As you are enjoying her, you may feel inclined to move the position of her legs—perhaps bringing them up higher, bending them and holding her knees against your own body with your upper arms and elbows, or hooking them over your shoulders, even holding her feet in your hands, at the height of your own ears—as you enter her. Be sure to look to her to see how your actions are affecting her. Ask her if something you're doing feels good or not. Always be careful to follow her lead. While the female body has certainly been designed to endure a lot, too full penetration could actually hurt her.

> *"Women might be able to fake orgasms. But men can fake whole relationships."*
>
> —Sharon Stone

As we told the women, so we tell you. Missionary-style sex does not necessarily mean that the man enters the women with both his legs between hers, head on. There are several ways to vary the standard missionary position. Try entering her at a sideways angle by holding one of her legs down, one up, and crossing over her body—think perpendicular instead of parallel.

Try also altering the position of your own legs. You can move your legs completely outside of hers, which will cause her to squeeze her legs together and put more pressure on your penis. And you don't have to be completely between or wrapped around her legs. Another thing you might try is to place one of your legs over her, and one in between her legs. You can also try moving your legs one at a time while your own legs are placed around hers, all the while keeping your penis firmly inserted. Use your thigh muscles to create a slight degree of pressure on her thighs.

For an added thrill, hold her hips and buttocks, controlling the rhythm while you thrust into her. This can be very exciting for both partners.

Alter the position of your legs so that you and your partner are intertwined in a close embrace.

(Hrana Janto)

Taking It Up a Notch

Of course, these are not the only ways to enjoy the missionary position. Another variation of this position involves using a woman's breasts and not her vagina. If a woman is comfortable with this situation, it can be a highly erotic and extremely pleasurable situation for both. In this variation, the man straddles his partner's chest, and places his penis between her breasts. She holds her breasts together, and he then strokes his penis in her cleavage. For maximum pleasure, apply a water-based lubricant to both his penis and her cleavage.

One of the best things about the missionary position is that you don't have to be in your bed to enjoy all the luscious variations of the position. Furniture in your bedroom or elsewhere in your home can also be great locations for experimentation. We'll explore many of these—as well as enjoyable spots outside the home—in Chapter 28, but let's look at a couple of options now.

Do you have a footstool or ottoman? If so, the woman can lie across it on her back, with her knees bent and feet planted firmly on the floor. She can wrap her arms around the man's neck, and he can enter while she's in this position. As you get more involved in the act, the man can support one or both of her legs in his arms, or she can wrap them around his back. One of the great benefits of using one of these low pieces of furniture for men is that it can actually relieve back strain. When a man is flat on a bed with a woman, he must arch his back to angle himself properly to enter the woman. Here, he's at the level; no arching is required.

Another variation is for the woman to lie with her head and back on the seat of a large chair. Her head and back remain flat while the man pushes into her. He can hold her legs or buttocks for support, or she can wrap her legs around his back—or his shoulders if she is very limber.

A final variation of missionary that men and women can equally enjoy is to lie facing each other. In this position, he keeps his legs in between hers and each partner thrusts toward the other. One benefit of using this variation is longevity. Because he will have to work harder, taking longer strokes to complete his thrusts, he will not climax as quickly as he might on top of his partner. Also, lovers have the opportunity of facing each other on equal footing, so to speak.

As you sample the many pleasures of the missionary position, remember that your hands are just as important a component of the sex act as any other part of your body. In this position, one or two of them may be free at a time; use them. Women may stroke the penis as it enters and exits the vagina. Men, don't forget that in this position, you have great access to the clitoris. And neither of you have to go right for the "gold." Each partner can rub their lover's back, shoulders, chests—even tease the other's nipples. You can also run your hands across each other's faces, stroke each other's hair, and really just enjoy and appreciate your partner.

As with any position we look at in this book, many other variations we haven't looked at can be derived from the basic premise of the missionary position. Let your imaginations and comfort levels be your guide.

Sexploration Exercise #14

1. If you are a man, are you intimidated by the idea of a woman on top, calling all the shots, during sex?
   a. Hell, no! There's nothing sexier than watching my wife take me!
   b. If I feel weird about it or not, I just like to watch her beautiful breasts and this is the best position to watch them in!
   c. I like it, but I'm much more comfortable when I'm on top.
   d. I certainly wouldn't say I was intimidated; I just like being in control and that's that.

2. If you are a woman, do you like the feeling of being on top during sex?
   a. Hell, yes! I can move and thrust just the way I want to and get just the right friction I need to have an orgasm.
   b. I like it sometimes, but I also enjoy being dominated by my lover.
   c. I'm not really that comfortable being in control like that. I prefer him to be.
   d. My husband won't even think about trying it this way.

3. On average, how frequently would you say you and your partner have sex in the woman-on-top position?
   a. Always—I have a bad back and my wife isn't shy about taking over.
   b. Most times—I'm very sexually aggressive and I've rarely had any complaints from my male partner.
   c. Sometimes—we like to try lots of things, but it's definitely part of the rotation.
   d. Rarely—neither my wife nor I really like it very much.

4. Sexperts say that the woman-on-top-position is the easiest position for a woman to climax in. How do you feel about that?
   a. It's the only way my wife can have an orgasm.
   b. It's the most common way I know how to climax—though I've been lucky with other positions!
   c. I have a highly placed clitoris, so having an orgasm during basic intercourse is usually complicated—though when I have, it's usually been in this position.
   d. I never have an orgasm during intercourse, no matter what.

5. What's the best thing about woman-on-top sex?
   a. You get to stare at her full body and breasts while she pleasures herself on you—it's so hot!
   b. I love watching his face while I have my way with him.
   c. I get the night off!
   d. I don't like anything about it.

chapter 14

The Woman-on-Top Positions

*"There's a new medical crisis. Doctors are reporting
that many men are having allergic reactions to latex
condoms. They say they cause severe swelling.
So what's the problem?"*
—Dustin Hoffman

According to Dr. Alfred C. Kinsey, the woman-on-top position
was the main sexual position used in ancient Greece and
Rome. He further indicated that in the oldest known depic-
tions of sex on artifacts excavated from around the world,
many dating from 3200 and 3000 B.C.E., that woman-on-top
was the most common position.

But ancient wisdom aside, there's really only one reason to
share with your partner this position, or any position you'll
read about in this book, and that's pleasure—wonderful, life-
affirming pleasure.

In this chapter, we look at the myriad ways the woman-on-
top position can bring the utmost pleasure to women and men

alike. While this position essentially puts the woman in charge, that doesn't mean she's the only one in on the action. We'll find out why this position is not used as often as it could be in the bedrooms of our fellow Boomers, and we'll look at the various ways this basic position can be altered for maximum pleasure for men and women alike.

Christopher, 51

"I've been married nearly 30 years—and yes, to the same woman, my wonderful wife, Charlene. Just like most married couples, we've had some really good years—and really bad ones. It's just how it goes, you know? Ebbs and flows. But the year we had about two years ago was so remarkably bad, I didn't think we were going to make it.

You see, part of the secret of our success is that my wife and I have always enjoyed a very satisfying sex life together. Ever since we were in school together, we never could seem to keep our hands off one another—and even before we started having sex. Once we did—forget about it! All I can say is that if they handed out medals or trophies for that kind of thing, we'd probably fill a whole room in our house with awards! Even well into our thirties and forties, when most of our friends seemed to be slowing down, we were still as wild and active as ever.

In bed, I always played the dominating role. It's not like this was anything we'd ever talked about or anything. It was just what we fell into—what we were comfortable with. Believe me, in the other areas of our life, Charl is in charge of everything—from the household budget to where and when we take our vacations, even to where the kids went to school. Again, it was never an issue for us. Another reason I guess we may have fallen into our respective bedroom roles is that in terms of size, I guess you could say I tower over my wife—and outweigh her considerably at that. But again, my being the dominant sexual partner was never anything we planned. It was just what we fell into, and what we were used to.

And then one winter, everything changed.

Early in the year—I guess it was probably in late January or early February—I was involved in a pretty serious car accident. I didn't break bones or rupture anything. Nothing like that. But what I did manage to do was to throw out my back something awful.

Now, I'm not a young guy; I was already having some lower back trouble that I had been trying to work through. My doctor had given me some exercises to increase strength in my abs and stuff like that, you know, to take the strain off the back. But the recovery from the accident was so difficult, it seemed like there were no exercises in the world that could ever ease the pain I was in almost chronically—never mind making it go away.

Needless to say, this was terrible for our sex life. We couldn't really even have sex for months while I was in recovery. I mean, we could, but it was so tame—not what we were used to—so it wasn't all that satisfying for either of us. At first, all we could really do was oral sex and manual stimulation. Then we were able to move into this sideways thing, where we were both lying down, facing each other with our legs intertwined.

This was all very nice, but I can't lie to you: I wanted to dominate my wife sexually—just like before.

Don't get me wrong here. In our life together, Charlene and I had experimented with a number of positions. We really had tried everything. So don't think that just because we reverted to male-superior positions didn't mean we hadn't sampled other stuff or didn't like to do it other ways. Charlene had been on top of me before, and we both had fun. We both just liked having me on top the best.

The whole thing started to become extremely frustrating and I was getting pretty depressed. And, of course, it wasn't just the sex thing that was affecting me. I hadn't been able to work. For months, I couldn't even drive. I felt like an invalid and a loser. And I was starting to take my annoyance out on my family—especially on my wife. Honestly, I don't know how she put up with me all those horrible months. I know this will seem silly and kind of outdated to say, but part of it was like I just didn't feel like much of a man, because, crass as this is, I couldn't, um, give my wife 'the business' the way that I always had before—the way I wanted to.

Eventually, it looked like Charlene was also getting a little tired of me, and also of that side-by-side missionary we had reverted to. We were both starting to get distracted and detached from the sex act. I thought I even saw her yawn one night.

And then one weekday morning before she got up to get ready for work, Charlene apparently reached her limit. 'On your back. *Now!*' she commanded, and helped me into a flat-back position. At first I was a little wary of all this. I was not used to taking orders in bed from my wife. But I went along with it. 'Now, you are just going to lie there while I take this one home, understand?' I was pinned; I didn't really have a choice.

As Charlene went about the task of taking over, I watched her face and her hair. Her beautiful breasts. I watched her experience sex in a way I'd never seen before. She was confident and alive; she was in control. I reached up my hands and stroked her beautiful breasts while she rose up and down. She was magnificent. I wanted to thrust back—even tried to—but she stopped me. She knew that for the time being, we would both be better off if I didn't strain my back unnecessarily and allowed myself to heal. And you know what, I have to admit that it was actually kind of sexy being 'taken' by my wife like that.

My back's almost one hundred percent back to normal now, so I can finally 'take' my wife again. But nowadays, I kind of like it when she 'takes' me, too!"

Don't Be Afraid to Take a Chance

In Christopher and Charlene's relationship, there wasn't so much a reluctance to let Charlene take the lead during sex as there was a reluctance to swing away from their routine. When circumstances beyond their control stepped in, however, they were forced to break out of their routine and try and find something new. Now, there's no reason to wait for a car accident or anything like that to shake you out of your routine. We urge you to try new things everyday. And do yourself a favor; don't judge how you think you're going to feel before you do something new. You may be cutting yourself off from some incredible fun that way!

Naturally, and we can't stress this enough, in any sexual situation, pleasure should never come at the cost of comfort. When all is said and done, a female-dominant position may not be comfortable for a man or woman involved in a sexual relationship together. For her, it might be too intimidating to be so in control of the situation and have to play such a large role. For him, as it was with Christopher, he might feel as though if he's not orchestrating the action, he's not living up to his manly responsibilities.

The best favor you can do for yourself and each other is to talk through your feelings with your partner and get over any worries you may have about your sexual actions being misconstrued as something entirely different than what they are. Always remember that unless you are trying to conceive—and still even then—the main objective of sex is to share pleasure, trust, and intimacy. Sometimes—even mostly—taking a sexually subservient role in bed by no means makes a man less of a man, nor does it make a woman less of a woman.

Another point we'd like to make before going further is that just like with the missionary position, there are many variations of the woman-on-top position that we will not cover in this book. For one, there are just too many options to deal with properly. Also, at this point in our lives, we simply might not have the same limberness and flexibility that we might once have had, and therefore some of these variations will just be words wasted on paper that no one will ever use. We'll talk a bit about more daring sexual positions in Chapter 17; for now, let's learn about all the fun there can be had with "her" on top.

"My girlfriend always laughs during sex—no matter what she's reading."

—Steve Jobs (Founder, Apple Computers)

The Basics

During the act of intercourse, there are many advantages for the woman to be on top. The main reason is that this is the position that best allows a woman to control the action. She decides how quickly or deeply she wants to thrust, whether or not she wants to rock, and how deeply she will be penetrated, among a variety of other things. Some women find this level of depth and range of stimulation so exciting that it is the best, or in some cases, the only method to achieve orgasm during intercourse.

In the typical woman-on-top posture, the woman straddles the man, sitting up at a right angle. Naturally, as with any position we'll cover in this book, sex can—and should—be anything but typical. Variations on the basic woman-on-top position are as limitless as they are with any other position. We'll start with the basic, woman-facing-forward techniques, and move into more advanced poses.

In the most basic variation of this position, the woman sits atop her partner with her knees tucked to the side of her partner's hips. In this position, a woman has maximum control over her thrusts, degree of penetration, and friction. If she leans forward, she will experience more clitoral stimulation as the man's pubic bone rubs up against her, which can trigger a clitoral orgasm. If she leans back, the tip of the man's penis will rub up against her G-spot, helping to trigger a vaginal orgasm.

Many opportunities for true intimacy abound in this female-superior position. While she's thrusting against her lover, the woman may lean all the way forward, splaying her upper body across his chest, with most of her weight falling on her elbows. In this position, generally known as "the butterfly," lovers can kiss one another on the lips, plant small kisses on each other's neck and ears, whisper to each other. Also in this variation, the man supports his lover's torso in his hands, which means he can have more control of the action. For highly intense clitoral and G-spot stimulation, the woman may also try leaning all the way forward, with legs laid out behind her—as flat as her partner.

In a variation of the woman-on-top position known as "the cowgirl," the woman sits astride the man, leaning back, with her legs bent at the knee and both feet planted on the bed. When you try this position, you'll see why it's called the cowgirl: from the waist up, the woman gives the appearance of riding a horse. In this position, she can lean forward or back, each affording an entirely different sensation of penetration.

When she's on top, a woman's legs don't always have to be open around the man. She can move one or both of her legs between his, changing the angle of penetration until she gets a comfortable angle of penetration for clitoral and G-spot stimulation. He can keep his legs down with his feet firmly planted on the bed or raise them.

If a woman is exceptionally limber, she can try sitting over him with her legs over his chest and shoulders. In this position, she will have to lean all her weight on her upper arms in order to move, and it's more likely than not that he will be the one moving into her in this variation of the position. She might also sit facing him, her legs around him, while he sits as well. Here, she can either lean back on her arms or hook them around his neck. Again, depending on her upper-arm strength and flexibility, he might be the one doing most of the thrusting in this position.

Turn It Around

Instead of facing the man, another alternative is for the woman to straddle the man while she's facing away from him. This can be an exceptionally pleasurable alternative for both partners. For the woman, the angle of penetration created by this position means maximum G-spot stimulation. For him, on top of the way this changes the sensation on his penis, allowing him to hold out longer, it also affords him a wonderful view of his lover's behind—for many men, a huge visual stimulant.

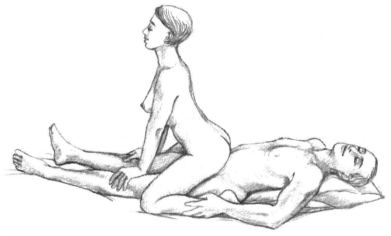

This variation of woman-on-top increases stimulation of her G-spot and his staying power.

(Hrana Janto)

While the woman faces away from the man, she can lean all the way forward, all the way back, and in several positions in between. When she leans all the way forward, he can place his body in a half- or full-sit, making the positioning of his penis more comfortable. When she's leaning forward, she can grab his ankles. This, too, will have very positive effects. For one, she'll give herself better balance and leverage for thrusting. But also, either or both partners might get a charge about the bondage-type implications of her holding his ankles, making it nearly impossible for him to move. But we'll talk more about bondage in Chapter 30.

Frieda, 41

"The first time I ever tried the woman-on-top position, it became my immediate favorite position. I just love how it feels to be on top like that, to take control of the movements during sex, to find my own way to orgasm. But why is it that when a woman gets on top, a man thinks his contribution to the sex act is to lie still and wait for it to be his turn again?

Okay, I guess that's not fair to say about *all* men. I think I might just be bitter right now. I recently came out of a long-term relationship with this guy, Larry, which lasted just about my entire thirties. Why I allowed it to go on for so long, I can't tell you for the life of me now. But while it was going on, I guess I was hooked, and for so many of the wrong reasons.

Larry was a successful financial planner. He was good-looking, wealthy, drove a great car, knew all the best restaurants, dressed like he lived at Armani—but he was dead wood in bed.

Don't get me wrong. It's not like he was always like this. Not when he was in charge—just when it was my turn to take the reins. I can't even tell you how many times we would be all worked up in this incredibly heated sexual fervor, with him towering over me, pounding away at a mile a minute, vocal, sweating, you name it.

And then it would be time for me to take over. Still in the crazed frame of mind he got me to just moments before, I'd push him down on the bed, straddle my legs around him, and then all of a sudden it was like he died or went to sleep or something.

I would move myself over him. Around him. He'd just lie there. Sometimes look away. Sometimes smile dumbly. I might as well have been getting busy with one of those giant sex dolls. I'd grind myself to orgasm, and once I came, he'd flip me over and work his way to his own orgasm. We were totally unconnected.

On several occasions, I tried to address this issue with him. I asked him why he never seemed involved, why he didn't even so much as touch me while I was on top of him. But he could never see what I was 'getting all upset about.' He thought I should be happy for having gotten off and that I should stop over-thinking everything.

Eventually, I saw the light and decided that all the trappings that made Larry look like a good match on paper were just not going to be enough if we couldn't ever really connect together sexually."

Don't Just Lay There

As we've already shown in this chapter, the woman-on-top position can be an exciting, fulfilling, satisfying position for both women and men. And, as we learned in the case of Charlene and Christopher, it's an especially good position to perform when the male is suffering from back trouble.

But as we saw in the case of Frieda and her boyfriend Larry, there's something men need to remember when it comes to this position: Just because you are not in the driver's seat does not mean it's time to slack off. Even though your female partner will be playing the dominant role, there are many ways you can get in on the action and not simply lay back taking an entirely passive approach.

In this position, gentlemen, you don't necessarily need your hands and arms to hold you up. If you are lying flat on your back, your hands will be free. Why not take advantage of this and use your hands to explore and stimulate your partner's body. Cup her breasts. Stroke her nipples. Trace the features of her face with your fingertips. If you can reach, run your fingers through her hair.

While you're underneath your partner, thrust your hips with her movements. Change the angle of your pelvis to give her more leverage with which to stimulate her clitoris. You can put a small pillow under your bottom to completely change the angle of entry. A few degrees either way can rock her whole universe. And, only if you do not have lower back problems, try raising your torso to deepen penetration.

Sexploration Exercise #15

1. On average, how frequently do you and your partner have rear-entry sex—doggie style or in spoons?
   a. Always—how else can we get that great penetration!
   b. Most times—we like it a lot, but facing each other so we can kiss throughout is also fun and not that easy in doggie style.
   c. Sometimes—it's a nice break from the standard positions we usually try.
   d. Rarely—I can't stand it when my husband wants to have sex in this position as it makes me feel really dirty.

2. If you are a woman, how often would you say you've had a G-spot orgasm in this position?
   a. All the time. It's the only way to go.
   b. It's hit or miss. I can usually have more powerful orgasms if he manually stimulates me.
   c. I had an orgasm a couple of times this way—and we're always trying.
   d. I've never had a G-spot orgasm.

3. What's the best thing about rear-entry sex?
   a. It's so animal!
   b. It's kind of sleazy in a really good way.
   c. My partner can easily stimulate my clitoris in this position so it's more likely that I'll have an orgasm.
   d. Definitely the depth of penetration!

4. What's the worst thing?
   a. Sometimes my partner goes too deep and it gets painful.
   b. I don't like that I can't see my partner's face—unless we're facing a mirror, that is!
   c. It's too much like anal sex, which I don't like at all.
   d. There's nothing bad about rear-entry sex as far as I'm concerned!

5. What's your favorite way to perform rear-entry sex?
   a. Doggie style—definitely doggie style!
   b. Spooning—it's much more intimate.
   c. We like to do it with my wife laying flat on her stomach.
   d. With me bent over a chair and all decked out in high heels.

15

The Rear-Entry Positions

"There's very little advice in men's magazines,
because men think, I know what I'm doing.
Just show me somebody naked."
—Jerry Seinfeld

While there are many euphemisms for rear-entry sex, it is most often referred to with two terms—either "doggie-style" or "spooning." This highly provocative position, in which the man enters the woman from behind, is extremely primal, and may appeal to both men and women for that reason. Also, the angle of entry this position affords is the most effective for the penis to make contact with the G-spot. In men, for several different factors, it is also the position that typically produces the quickest, most powerful orgasms.

In this chapter, we look at many variations of rear-entry sex and the reasons people like it, love it, can't live without it, or just can't stand it.

Alex, 42

"I love having sex doggie style. I know there are many other ways to have sex—as my wife, Karla, is usually pretty quick to point out—but there's something just so erotic about entering her like that. I can't really explain it.

Believe it or not, I've known Karla since high school. Back then, she was totally untouchable, but man, I wanted to touch her so badly. I was just a geek who used to worship her from afar in advanced algebra; she was a goddess in tight designer jeans with a butt that just wouldn't quit. My God, she had a sexy rear!

After graduation, I didn't see Karla for about fifteen years. When I ran into her one day at the video store in my neighborhood, there was no question in my mind who she was. A striking woman had accidentally dropped something behind a display counter and was bending over to try and retrieve it. I went immediately to her rescue. There was something about that behind I just couldn't resist.

Just as I might have guessed, she had no idea who I was. Finally, I was able to drop a few names that she recognized. We went out for coffee from the store and started to date from that very day. Within a year, we were married.

That was nearly nine years ago, and even today, after having three children, Karla still has an incredible body. Sure, it's changed over the years, but that's just what happens, you know? And that beautiful rear end … I guess it's gotten bigger, but what do I know. She'll tell you it's as big as a house, and she's very sensitive about it. I have no idea why.

Honestly, I just go nuts when I can bend her over and have my way with her, and just admire how beautiful she is. Even at my age, I can hardly control myself. I feel like I'm seventeen all over again—just as attracted to her and just as excitable. If there's any problem with having sex with my wife in this position, it's that I just can't last as long as I want to."

Listening to Your Inner Animal

Saying that a man likes sex doggie-style is like saying that a little boy likes candy. Most men would agree with Alex that this is the most exciting way for a man to have sex with a woman—but it can't be denied that this is also an extremely arousing position for a woman as well.

The fact of the matter is that doggie-style sex really brings out the animal in all of us. There's something so feral about the way it happens. That partners don't look into each other's eyes—unless they're in front of a mirror, that is. There's no inherent romance in this position. No intimate kisses or cuddles. Doggie-style means raw, wild sex, and when you're in the mood for it, there's simply no kind of position that satisfies more.

Aside from the animal element, one of the reasons that this position is so satisfying for the man is that the angle of entry permits a deeper level of stimulation and deeper physical entry into the woman. But be warned: Especially well-endowed men need to be careful here, as a very large penis can push up against the cervix, causing discomfort and even pain for the woman.

For the woman, the angle of entry presents the best opportunity for stimulating the G-spot. Also, while the head of the penis works at the front of the inner vaginal wall, the man or woman can stimulate the woman's clitoris. Depending on what variation of this position is being used, however, it will probably be easier for him to do it. (Likely, she'll be relying on both arms for balance.) Provided her partner can hold out for her, the kind of orgasm a woman can have in this position, a combination of clitoral and vaginal, is like nothing else.

On the downside, sometimes rear-entry sex can be so stimulating for a man, it can lead to early orgasm, thus cutting short what might otherwise have been a lengthy and delightful session of lovemaking. Therefore, many experts agree that rear entry should be saved for "dessert"; the final course on the sexual menu. However, if a man has a lot of staying power, or you're both looking for a quickie, there's no reason not to go directly to rear entry.

Another drawback for some is the lack of intimacy inherent in this position and the physical and emotional distance it may create. Some women may also be turned off by what can certainly be understood as a submissive posture, but as we learned in the previous chapter, sex is sex and life is life, and the dynamics of one do not necessarily reflect the other. Sex is about fun. About tossing inhibitions to the curb. It's not about political strife.

There are many positives for women in this position, which is why many women truly enjoy it. A woman may enjoy doggie-style sex because of the deeper penetration it affords, and that there's something wild about a man they cannot see thrusting deeper and deeper, harder and harder into them. And sex laced with a little safe mystery can be a very sensual experience indeed.

Other Approaches

The basic approach of rear-entry, doggie-style sex involves a woman leaning on her hands and knees, whether on the bed, floor, or a low sofa. The man kneels behind her and enters her. It's not the only way to enjoy this naughtiest of all sexual positions, however.

Another approach involves the woman bending over the edge of the bed or in front of a waist-high object (preferably secured to the floor) such as a sink. Again, the man enters her from behind. The position will not necessarily work if one partner's legs are considerably longer than the other's. A man can stand on something like a phone book or footstool if he needs the height; if it's her, there's nothing like a pair of high-heeled shoes to do the trick. Which brings us to a great tip for enjoying sex in this position: Leave your clothes on, removing only select articles, or, even better, pushing them to the side if they get in the way. We'll look at more alternatives for stand-up sex in the next chapter.

> *"According to a new survey, women say they feel more comfortable undressing in front of men than they do undressing in front of other women. They say that women are too judgmental, where, of course, men are just grateful."*
>
> —*Robert De Niro*

One very sexy way to enjoy rear entry sex is like a woman-on-top position. The man sits on a bed or chair, facing outward.

The woman sits on him as she would sit down on the bed or chair if he were not there. Still in a rear-entry situation, in this position it is the *woman* who is responsible for the majority of movement. Be advised that working this position may be a lot like doing squats at the gym, depending on how high the surface is upon which the man sits. In other words, if a woman has bad knees, this might not be a very comfortable position for her.

The Lowdown on Backside Entry

Are you wondering if doggie-style sex should serve as a prelude to anal sex? Let's make this easy for you: Stop wondering. Even though the positions you and your partner will find yourselves in are essentially the same for both, vaginal intercourse and anal sex are not at all the same thing. Sure, you're in the same general neighborhood, but you might as well be operating in parallel universes as far as these two methods are concerned. So the answer to the above question: absolutely not.

Vaginal sex and anal sex should never take place in the same lovemaking session, and for more than one reason. In terms of physical health, the vagina and the anus are homes to different types of bacteria. While you could conceivably make contact with the anus after the vagina, you should never, under any circumstances, make contact with the vagina after the anus—and this includes fingers, lips, tongues, sex toys, and penises. If these do come in contact with the anus, be sure to wash them thoroughly and carefully with soap and warm water (and brush your teeth and tongue) before they find their way back to the vagina.

Another reason that you might not want to follow up vaginal sex with anal sex is entirely emotional. While both acts are exciting and not wrong by any stretch of the imagination if both partners are willing and comfortable performing them, they are very different, psychologically speaking, and really don't belong together in the same session. We'll look more closely at anal sex in Chapter 23.

Regina, 54

"I know how slutty this is going to sound, but I really love it when my husband, Julian, has sex with me doggie-style. Or, I should say, I really *used* to love it. In fact, there was a time in the early part of our marriage when that was the only way I wanted to have sex!

I can't help it. There's just something so primal, so incredibly sexual about being entered by a man while you're all bent over and vulnerable. But that's only part of the excitement of it for me.

What I learned to do in this position, and which has always been hard for me in other sexual positions, is to have an orgasm. Now, I'm not talking about the kind of orgasm that tickles your belly …. Those come fairly easily, especially at this point in my life when I know just about everything there is to know about my sex parts. What I'm talking about is the kind of orgasm that shudders through your entire being. That makes your entire body shake. You know—the kind you feel in little aftershocks for hours even after you have it!

In talking with friends about sex one day, I couldn't help but tell them about this incredible kind of orgasm I found I could have in that position. It was my friend Peggy who let me in on exactly what was happening. It seems the tip of my husband's, um, apparatus, was hitting something called my G-spot, and when this area gets stimulated, apparently, you can have the most incredible orgasms ever. Well, no there was no 'apparently' about it—it just was!

And you can imagine there were no complaints from Julian doing it just this way.

But most unfortunately for me, over the past few years, I've developed osteoarthritis in my knees. That means getting down on all fours just isn't as much fun as it used to be. In fact, it's horribly uncomfortable these days.

When the symptoms first started to develop, I couldn't believe it was happening to me. I wasn't going to be able to do that much anymore because of my bad knees, like running and playing tennis, my doggie-style and mind-blowing orgasms days were also going to be behind me now.

But don't worry: There is a happy ending here …. When I shared with Peg what was going on with me, she told me that yes, perhaps my running and tennis days were going to be behind me, but what didn't have to be were my fabulous G-spot orgasms.

Peg asked me if Julian and I had even tried rear-entry sex when we were both lying down on our sides—like spoons. I told her we hadn't but we'd certainly give it a shot that very night!

Well, you can guess that Julian was into it and soon enough that night, we found ourselves totally enjoying this new position—almost more than we had enjoyed doggie-style. It took longer for us both to climax, but it was really nice just being there in each other's arms. And when my climax finally came .... Oh yeah! It was the good kind!"

Spooning

The sexual position that Regina and Julian learned and mastered is what's commonly known as "spooning." Spooning is another variation of rear-entry sex, which many feel is not as raw as doggie-style sex—for better or worse, depending how you happen to like the elements of doggie-style sex. In spooning, a woman lays on her side, typically with her knees bent slightly, and the man tucks himself in behind her, facing her back as if they were two spoons in a drawer, and enters her vagina.

Spooning brings more intimacy to the excitement of rear-entry sex.
(Hrana Janto)

Spooning shares many characteristics with doggie-style sex, but there are some marked differences. Spooning is considerably more intimate than doggie-style sex because in this position, lovers are generally touching in more places than just the genital region. The man embraces the woman, either holding on to her legs or even cuddling up to her back, perhaps with his head right next to hers or nuzzled in her neck. Spooning allows easy access to one another's genitalia, but also allows the man the added pleasure of kissing the hair, face, neck, and shoulders of his partner, which, in most variations of doggie-style sex, is impossible due to the laws of simple physics. Another benefit of spooning is that it permits the man to have plenty of access to his lover's breasts and clitoris.

Spooning is exceedingly different from doggie-style sex in especially the following respect: In spooning, there is limited freedom of movement for the man to thrust into his partner. Because he is essentially wrapped around her, and because his buttocks remain in contact with the bed, couch, or floor, his movements are inhibited—but most men would agree that this is not in a bad way. The less thrusting a man can do, the slower his and his partner's excitement builds; and for the man, the slower the excitement builds, the gentler the push toward orgasm.

The angle of entry in spooning has plusses and minuses. The good news is that just like in doggie-style sex, this form of rear-entry sex provides direct stimulation of the G-spot. The bad news, however, is that since the thrusts are shorter in duration, penetration is also compromised. In other words, the man does not go in as deep, hard, or rapidly as in standing or kneeling rear-entry sex.

Once you start spooning in any given lovemaking session, it's awfully hard to move to something else. But why would you want to? Spooning is so comfortable and easy—on both the back and the libido. It's soft, intimate, and doesn't require a lot of work. It's the perfect position for Boomers who've had particularly long and difficult days in the big bad world—where job exhaustion, household demands, and more are par for the course. You can easily slip from spooning into sleep.

Spooning Techniques

As we've pretty much already covered, the basic spoon technique involves the man lying behind his lover, like spoons in a drawer. The effort is minimal; the reward is bliss. But as with other sexual positions we cover in this book, you can bet there are lots of ways to alter the traditional method, depending on desire, need, and preference.

One thing to note is that if starting off in the sideways position is a little too challenging—and many couples find this to be the case for reasons of inadequate vaginal lubrication and awkward angle of entry—you and your lover can always start off in the standard missionary position. Once insertion has been successful, the man then places one leg outside his lover's legs, rolls himself to a spoon position and guides her onto her side, all the while being careful not to slip out of her.

Advanced spooners can try this variation. After the man has inserted his penis, he can shift his legs, placing his top leg between both of hers. This increases the intimacy and slightly changes the angle in a positive way.

To change the angle of entry, the woman can set a small pillow under her hip. In another variation, the man can move his body away from hers, so that he is approaching her at a perpendicular rather than parallel angle. If she is limber enough, and if she does not suffer from any back problems, he can also lift her leg as high as it will go, thus increasing penetration.

Sexploration Exercise #16

1. When's the last time you and your partner tried having sex in a stand-up position?
   a. Maybe when we were first married—like 25 years ago?
   b. We've tried it a few times through the years, but it seems like the older we get, the more comfortable we are having sex as horizontally as possible.
   c. Within the past six months.
   d. Last night.

2. On average, how frequently would you say you and your partner have sex standing up?
   a. Always—there's no better way.
   b. Most times—especially when we're pressed for time.
   c. Sometimes—it's a great way to do something a little different and shake things up.
   d. Never—it's really not for us.

3. What's the thing you like most about having sex in this position?
   a. It's raw. It's the kind of sex you have when you're having sex someplace you really aren't supposed to and that's very exciting—even if we're doing it in this position in our own bedroom!
   b. It definitely puts our athletic abilities to the test. If we can't pull it off, that means more time at the gym.
   c. I love it when my husband holds me up against a wall and I can watch the bulge of his arms as he glides me up and down.
   d. I love the way it feels to penetrate my wife so deeply and to be so in control of our movements because sometimes it's just impossible for her to thrust back. It's extremely erotic.

4. What's the worst?
   a. Definitely the back pain! One crooked thrust and I'm uncomfortable for days.
   b. I get scared that he might not be able to hold on to me when he gets really excited—that he'll drop me or something—and that takes away from the excitement.
   c. My wife has gained a little weight since we were first married, which is not really a problem with me at all, except it makes it more difficult for me to maneuver her when she wants to have sex in this position.
   d. My husband has developed really weak knees, so if we have stand-up sex that I need to lean on him for, we can only have it as a novelty—for only a couple of minutes at a time.

5. Where's the craziest place you ever had stand-up sex?
   a. The backyard one night when the kids—and we hope the neighbors—were asleep.
   b. The bathroom at a friend's dinner party.
   c. The elevator in my office building.
   d. A secluded alleyway when we were in New Orleans for our anniversary!

chapter 16

The Standing Positions

"Hockey is a sport for white men. Basketball is a sport for black men. Golf is a sport for white men dressed like black pimps."
—Tiger Woods

When was the last time you and your partner made love standing up? We're guessing it's probably been quite a while—at least that's the response we got from all the Boomers we talked to when we were compiling research for this book. Many felt that stand-up sex was for kids. Or it was something you did only in the beginning of a relationship, when the desire to have sex with each other knew no bounds, limits, or even regard for anyone else who might be around at the time. Many even admitted avoiding it entirely because they believed that at their age, they might actually hurt themselves—their legs and backs especially—by having stand-up sex.

Is that what you think? That by the time you've reached your forties or fifties, having sex standing up just isn't worth the trouble anymore? Well, then we must insist that you think again.

We're not saying that the physics of stand-up sex isn't challenging. If he tries to be heroic and picks her up, straddling her around his waist, chances are, he may be too concerned about the strength of his upper arms and even his back to have a satisfying orgasm. And what if he drops her? What if he pulls a muscle or strains his lower back and has to be out of work for a week or so? What if it lasts longer than that? Will the mortgage go unpaid? And what about her? Certainly if he has a reason to panic, so does she. If he drops her, what about her job? Or if she's not working, who's going to look after the house if she's stuck, incapacitated and flat on her back for a week? Their teenaged kids? Too may of us shudder at that thought!

So with all the risk there is to worry about, it's no wonder this position isn't as popular with the over-forty set as the surefire horizontal, *not* defying gravity missionary or woman-on-top positions.

However, great risk can sometimes produce delicious rewards, and for that reason, we urge you to reconsider having sex in this position. It isn't just for the young. It isn't just something people do in porn films.

Now we're not suggesting you do it standing up all the time—and if you have back and leg problems, you're probably best off just fantasizing about it—but every now and then, adding a little danger to your desire might be just what the doctor ordered.

In this chapter we look at all kinds of ways you can have earth-shattering, wonderfully orgasmic stand-up sex, and we'll show you techniques to modify the way you might remember having stand-up sex so you can savor every naughty moment of it—even now!

Ned, 47

"I have a question for all the men out there who may be reading this. Have you ever known a woman who was into yoga? If you haven't, I can't recommend more that you get to know one right away—or get your woman to get acquainted with it!

I am dating this woman right now, Joan. She's older than me by a few years—I think she's about fifty-four or something like that. Anyway, this woman is the most incredibly limber, flexible woman I have ever met in my life. When I asked her what her secret was, she answered me with one word: yoga.

Now I've known all kinds of women. Ever since I started dating, I always liked to date women of every race, religion, background, age— you name it. So I know what kind of flexibility a twenty-five-year-old has. I know what a forty-year-old woman can typically do in terms of range of motion. And I know how stiff the body can get after fifty. But not Joan. She's like a pretzel!

My favorite way to have sex with Joan? Definitely standing up! There are a couple of ways we usually do it. I work out a lot, so I'm pretty strong in my upper body. That means I can support Joan in my arms and I don't even need to lean her up against a wall or anything. But the way I like having sex with Joan the most is when Joan bends over in front of me and grabs her ankles. I penetrate her from behind and it's just Wow! Holy cow! It's like nothing else in the world. Those Kama Sutra guys definitely knew what they were talking about!"

Standing and Delivering

There are essentially two basic ways to perform stand-up sex. You can either stand face to face, or you can do it rear-entry style, with man standing behind woman. And just like in any sexual position, there are many variations on these basic themes, as we will see in this chapter.

We all know that face-to-face sex is incredibly fun. Pressed up against your partner, grinding against one another is just erotic bliss. And let's not forget how fantastic it is to look into your partner's eyes while making love. To watch his face change as new levels of pleasure overtake him; to watch her reaction to every glorious thrust—the passion, the surprise, the desire, the love. That's what intimacy is all about.

One of the complaints some people have about making love standing up is that movement can be inhibited. When you are having sex, stand-up style, gravity plays quite a significant role in the scheme of things. The need to balance may overcome creative positioning of limbs and the like, which may mean more difficulty for partners to get the right parts to hit the right way.

However, while having sex in this position can be inhibiting, it isn't always necessarily in a bad way. While there won't be a lot of leverage in thrusting, this can actually add to the powerful sensation. More intensity must go into the thrusting that can be done.

In addition, being in a standing position may limit a couple's ability to get into a good rhythm. And yet, even a bad rhythm is fun when you're standing up and facing the other person. Couples report that they feel loose, uninhibited, free, and really, well, connected—emotionally, that is. And isn't that what great sex is all about?

The other way couples can perform stand-up sex is with the man standing behind his partner. He can press her up against a wall and grind his chest against her back, entering her while he kisses her neck or ears—maybe even whispering a few choice dirty sentiments. Or, he may decide to bend her over a chair or other choice piece of furniture.

One of the problems some couples encounter in stand-up sex is incompatible proportions. Maybe he's much taller than his partner. Or perhaps both partners are essentially the same height—but her legs are longer, making it difficult for him to reach her properly when standing. How can you deal with this? Be creative. Men can compensate by standing on a book or whatever it takes to get the right height; women can don a sexy pair of high heels—which will probably push both partners right over the edge.

We'll learn more specific techniques for having sex these ways a little later in this chapter.

Making It Work

Just as real estate is about location, location, location, stand-up sex is all about lubrication, lubrication, lubrication. Men, remember—just because you've got visual proof of your own excitement, namely, your erection, she may not quite be onboard with you right away. Keep in mind that it takes a woman a considerably longer period of time than a man to get into the swing of things sexually and especially if she's not completely convinced that what's about to take place is going to work out the way it's supposed to.

Just as in any sexual act, most women need more warming up with men. That's just that way it is. They cannot be expected to ready-wet-go at the drop of a hat—or a pair of pants—even if their male counterparts are. Therefore, men, you have to help her catch up.

When you're about to perform any variation of the horizontal mambo, penetration, even when the woman is just barely wet, is much easier to pull off. In a laying down position, the penis can be gently eased into the vagina, which will begin to lubricate with every try. When standing, entering this way is impossible, thanks to gravity. Therefore, and we can't stress this enough, it is essential that the man help his lover reach maximum lubrication before even considering going anywhere near her vagina with his penis. If he tries to enter her in this position when she is not properly lubricated, scorching pain for both partners may be the result.

Fortunately, we have a fail-safe solution. Before having stand-up sex, do whatever you can to bring her to the place you are. You can kiss and caress her, press yourself against her, fondle her, manually stimulate her, or what have you.

The best way to get a woman ready is for the man to drop to his knees and orally pleasure his partner before proceeding on to the main event. (Look for great tips on performing oral sex on a woman in Chapter 20.) Not only will this relax her, it will make her natural lubrication process begin, and mixed with saliva, she will be properly lubricated to comfortably accept his penis in this position.

> "You know 'that look' women get when they want sex? Me neither."
>
> — Steve Martin

Serena, 41

"I've only recently started having sex with my boyfriend, Charlie—sex standing up, that is. I know that may seem weird—especially because we've been together nearly four years now—but it's true.

Don't get the wrong idea. It's not really that I had no interest in trying it out all those years. It's not like I'm a kid; I've had plenty of lovers before—and have had lots of exciting stand-up sex in my life. It's just that with Charlie, I don't know, with Charlie, it just always seemed kind of dangerous.

Okay, I know how crazy that sounds, but if you knew my boyfriend, Charlie, you might think differently. Standing in my bare feet, I'm 5 feet, 3 inches tall. Charlie—no socks or shoes—is 6 feet, 4 inches tall. So it doesn't take a lot of imagination to see why positions sitting and laying down are probably best for us! Or so I thought.

One night, when we were flipping through the channels on television, we tapped into what looked like a dirty movie. It's not like we're porn addicts or anything—don't get the wrong idea about that—but sometimes it's fun to catch one of these cheesy movies in the middle. This one was there, in our faces, so we thought. Why not watch at least for a laugh?

Well, I'll tell you this—it's amazing how much stand-up sex there is in dirty movies. I guess it's because the characters are generally doing things—and people—they ought not to be doing, and sometimes in places that in reality, they would likely be arrested for. Anyway, not to get off the subject here, there was this one couple that I guess you could say resembled me and Charlie. Now that was kind of weird, because typically, they use actors who are pretty equal in size, but these two looked really mismatched.

Well, they got down into it, you know, and they actually managed to have sex standing up. I'm not going to say exactly how, but what I will tell you is that there were a few carefully placed pieces of furniture involved. I was intrigued.

I grabbed the remote and turned the TV off. I said to Charlie. 'I think that's something we should try, right this minute!' Of course there was no reluctance on his side. That did it. Since that night, we've worked stand-up sex into our sexual menu—not all the time, but enough—and our sex life has never been hotter!"

Standing Ovation

As Serena and Charlie quickly learned, there are lots of ways to compensate for unequal proportions in stand-up sex. All you need is a little creativity, ingenuity, and imagination, and you'll be surprised where you'll get!

So now that you're geared up and ready to have the stand-up sex of your life, here are a few ways you might decide to try it out for the first time—or revisit it!

In the most basic variation of the stand-up sex position, the woman and man face each other. The man's feet are firmly planted on the ground; the woman will need to lift one of her legs in order to create an angle for penetration. How high she lifts her leg will determine how deeply he can penetrate her. She can rest her bended knee against his hips or waist—or even rest her ankle on his shoulder—if she is exceptionally agile, like Joan from earlier in this chapter. Man and woman can face each other, freestanding, or one—and more likely, the woman, can lean back against a wall.

Here's a challenging variation to the basic stand-up technique that you can try if both your backs are in really good shape and you have the utmost faith in the strength of the male partner's upper arms. In this posture, the man presses his partner up against a wall and wraps his arms under her buttocks. He lifts her, so that her legs are up over his hips, and inserts into her. She locks her legs around his waist, and he moves the action away from the wall. With his arms securely locked around her, he lifts her up and down over his penis.

If you think this method is perhaps a bit too ambitious for you, another alternative is to keep the female partner pressed up against the wall. This will take some of the strain off the man's arms and back as well as alleviate the stress on her legs and lower back. Also, she will have the wall to leverage against, actually making it possible for her to thrust back.

For rear-entry stand-up sex, the man and woman can both stand upright, but this will only work if they have the same length legs—or hers are slightly longer than his. Essentially, he comes up from behind her and may slightly bend his knees in order to enter her. This

Standing in embrace, she raises one leg to let him penetrate.

(Hrana Janto)

posture can be performed freestanding, if both partners have incredible strength and balance, but it is more likely that she will be leaning her front against a wall or other immobile vertical surface. And make sure that surface doesn't move; otherwise you're both likely going to fall forward when the passion hits peak intensity.

In this rear-entry position, it is not as essential for the woman to raise one of her legs for the man to penetrate her. However, bending one knee and leaning it into the wall will ensure deeper penetration.

It's not necessary for the couple to both be entirely vertical during rear-entry, stand-up sex. A very sexy variation can be enjoyed if the woman bends at the waist, almost in an L-shape or right angle, over the back of a chair or like piece of furniture. Just like in typical rear-entry laying-down sex, in this position, not only will deeper penetration be enjoyed by both, but she will likely be getting more stimulation to her G-spot. The woman can further vary this alternative by bending one of her legs and resting her foot on the seat of the chair.

Sexploration Exercise #17

1. Are you and your partner open to experimenting with more advanced positions?
   a. I am, but my husband is a very conservative meat-and-potatoes type of guy.
   b. I am, but my wife would be totally scandalized if I told her I wanted to break up the routine with something really risqué.
   c. Both of us are willing to try any position we can still contort our bodies into.
   d. We like the basics and no extra frills.

2. What's the most daring position you ever tried?
   a. Something called the "wheelbarrow."
   b. It was from the Kama Sutra, believe it or not. I think it was called the "Butterfly" or the "Locust"—something nature-oriented.
   c. We love the Slide!
   d. The most daring position we've ever tried was woman on top! Are there more daring positions than that one?

3. If you could try any new advanced position, which would it be?
   a. Scissors
   b. Starfish
   c. Interlock
   d. Slide

4. When was the last time you and your partner had sex in a position—any position—more daring than missionary style?
   a. Within the past week.
   b. Within the past month.
   c. Within the past year.
   d. It was too long ago to remember.

5. What's the most exciting thing about having sex in a daring new position?
   a. You get to find new ways to please your lover.
   b. You learn more ways for you to get off.
   c. It makes sex more exhilarating.
   d. It breaks up the monotony.

chapter 17

Positions to Try at Your Own Risk

*Marie Barone: "Another sex game? Didn't you have
enough with that other sex game you and Robert
used to play all the time when you were kids? ...
You know, the one with all the colored squares ..."*

Ray Barone: "Twister?!"
—Everybody Loves Raymond

In this short chapter, we look at some of the more daring sexual positions there are to try. A word of warning: These positions are *not* for everyone. There may be some positions in here that will put unnecessary strain on bad backs, or knees, or what have you. If something you're doing feels uncomfortable for either party, cease the activity right away and move on to something else. The best sex is satisfying and enjoyable for both parties; if only one partner is having fun, the sex will simply not be worth having.

Another thing you should keep in mind is that in sex, and this is especially as we get older, there are physical limitations. In addition to not being as young or agile—or even as thin—as we used to be, there are some positions even the strongest, most limber twenty-year-old will have trouble contorting him- or herself into. We are not all yoga experts, naturally.

However, there's at least one way to enjoy these positions, which involves few to no limits. Just as in the other chapters in this section, you may start out trying to get into or actually sampling a position we suggest, maybe even work off the variation provided; then you can vary it even further to maximize your comfort quotient. And of course, there's a simple way to enjoy any of these positions, no matter what your physical limitations: Use your imagination.

Just because you and your partner may not be able to physically perform any given position in this chapter doesn't mean you can't have a ton of fun experimenting—and, yes, fantasizing. Again, the only real limits you're ever going to run into are those your own imagination imposes on you.

As a final note, one of the best manuals you'll want to look at for getting ideas about new sex positions is one of the oldest sex manuals there is: the Kama Sutra. We'll delve further into the delights of that ancient practice of sexual expression in the next chapter. For now, let's investigate modern methods for bawdy boomers.

Jill, 48

"Last year, my husband, Jason, and I started ourselves on a 'take-no-prisoners' exercise regime. We jog together just about every morning for cardio. For strength, we each enrolled in weight-training classes at the gym. And, as a special treat two days a week, we take a power yoga class together. Needless to say, we've never felt better. And holy cow—I can't even begin to tell you what it's done for our libidos!

Throughout our relationship, we've always engaged in the standard sex positions—him on top, me on top, him behind. It's always been satisfying, don't get me wrong about that, but lately, now that I have the energy—and I'm thinking, flexibility—of a thirty-year-old, I'm ready to try some of the zanier things we used to do in the beginning. I just wonder if he's ready.

A few years ago, Jason had some pretty serious surgery done on his knee, which is at least part of the reason we got into exercising in the first place. He's much stronger now, but I'm still afraid that some of the positions I've seen in books and on the Internet may still be too strenuous for him. I'd still like to try at least some of them out, though! I know if we use our heads, that surely we can find a way to do most of them. I mean, you don't have to do them exactly the way the kids do, right?

This weekend, I'm going to show him some really hot pictures in one of the books I found and see how it turns out!"

The Gymnast

In this wacky position, it would certainly be a very good idea if the woman was a gymnast—and him, too, for that matter, at least in his upper body, and, um, the prized member of his lower half! There must also be absolute trust in the strength and flexibility of each partner.

Man and woman stand facing one another. He lifts her up by the buttocks, and she straddles his waist with her legs and wraps her arms around his neck. Slowly and gently, he guides her onto his penis. And now for the fun part: While still impaled on his penis, he carefully—and let's stress this one again, CAREFULLY—helps her lower the top portion of her body into a kind of backbend, holding on with all his might to her waist and buttocks. When her arms reach the floor, she orchestrates the movement of the thrusts by pushing up from her arms and abs.

Baby Boomer Variation: In a word, think "brevity." Kudos to the two of you for having the strength and flexibility to even get yourselves into this position—let alone hold yourselves in it for even a few minutes. It's a fun one to sample, but chances are, you're going to be moving to a different position to climax. If she's enjoying the sensation of blood rushing to her head, you can vary this simply by enacting a simple missionary posture, with her hanging her head and upper body off the side of the bed. Be sure to put a pillow on the floor under where her head hangs—just in case!

Wheelbarrow

This position gives new meaning to the term "role play." In it, he acts like a working man with cargo to transport in a wheelbarrow. She is that cargo. Strong upper bodies are the most important requirement of this rear-entry position.

She and he stand, with him facing her back. She kneels on the floor in front of him, and bends forward, placing her arms on a comfortable stack of pillows. She spreads her ankles apart as far as they can go. He kneels behind her, and inserts his penis into her. Then, he grabs her ankles and holds them at his sides, and rises to a standing position.

Baby Boomer Variation: If the position becomes too uncomfortable for her, if she has trouble holding the top part of her body up on her elbows, this can always be morphed into a standard rear-entry position, with all her limbs set safely and securely on the floor.

Scissors

Sure, you like spooning, but there are so many other tools and utensils you can simulate for maximum erotic impact. In this position, both man and woman part their legs and connect like two pairs of scissors locking into one another.

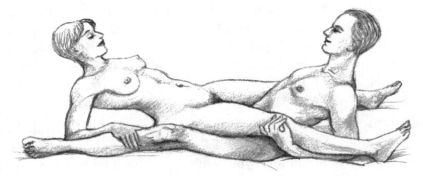

With the scissors position, he and she both open and close their legs to pull and thrust.

(Hrana Janto)

To perform this position, he lays on the bed, his head at either end, flat on his back and with his legs open. She climbs up on the bed and mounts her partner. Then, with his help, she lowers herself also to a position of lying on her back, with her head at the opposite end of the bed. By each party opening and closing their legs, the other party gets pushed away and pulled in, creating the necessary thrust movement. Backs should be arched, if possible, to allow for maximum flexibility.

Baby Boomer Variation: If either of you has lower back problems, no doubt visualizing the last part of the directions for this position may have caused a twinge of pain in that region. Vary it in this way: She lies like an open scissors and he kneels in front of her, entering her missionary style. She can continue opening and closing her legs, scissoring, while he thrusts into her head-on. To put less strain on his back, position her buttocks and hips on a small pillow.

Jason, 52

"They say that in the best marriages, your spouse never seems to stop amazing you. Okay, maybe it's me who says that, but to know my wife of twenty years, Jill, is to live in a constant state of awe!

A few years ago, I had surgery on my knee. I had aggravated an old hockey injury—get this—running up a flight of stairs to catch a train. What was it that Mick said? 'What a drag it is getting older?' That about sums it up all right.

Anyway, I was in a lot of pain for a long time. The rehab lasted a lot longer than I thought it would, and I thought I'd never get full use of the old knee back. Then Jill decided it was high time we got into shape—and that we'd do it together. So we started an exercise regime, slowly at first and then built it up over the years, and now I feel like I have more strength and stamina than I did in my twenties. It was last weekend that Jill decided to put what I felt in my own head and body to the test.

Saturday morning, after we had taken a nice hot, naughty shower together, she sat next to me on the bed, still all naked and wet, and dropped this book on my lap. It wasn't just a regular book—it was like a hardcover, respectable porn magazine, which she said was called a 'sex guide.' Right. Anyway, she flipped through the pages and showed me pictures of things she wanted to try.

I looked at the pictures. These people were maybe just barely legal, they were so young. And their bodies so firm and strong-looking. 'Come on, sweetie,' I chuckled when she pointed to a picture in which I couldn't tell if anyone's feet were actually touching the ground—and they were supposedly standing. 'Do you really think a couple of near-old-timers like us are going to be able to pull that one off?' I laughed, but it seems I had underestimated my wife.

'Put the book down and shut your trap,' she said, and proceeded to rip my robe off of me. 'I've been thinking about this one for a while, and I think I've been able to figure out just how to pull it off—even without putting any pressure on that knee of yours.'

I'm not an idiot; I learned many years ago in our marriage who the boss is. So I let her twist me around and marveled at her agility when she completed the pose by wrapping herself around me. She was right. I looked down at the picture, and I'll be damned—we were doing just what those kids were doing, and I felt no strain on my knee whatsoever.

Apparently, she had studied that book pretty thoroughly, as we spent the remainder of the afternoon contorted into one pretzel maneuver or another. Just like I said—she is amazing, that wife of mine!"

Froggie Style

If you love doggie style, you're going to love froggie style—just remember that the anatomy of the two so-named animals is drastically different. You'll see what we mean! This position works best when the woman has very long legs.

In this position, the man sits on the bed with his legs out straight in front of him. She lies on her back, over his outstretched legs, and moves her hips and buttocks toward his. When he is inside of her, she puts her legs over his shoulders, and pulls her feet down as far as they'll go. Ideally, and this is where those long legs are important, she will tuck her feet—even just her toes—under his buttocks.

Baby Boomer Variation: Even if her legs are long enough to reach all the way to his buttocks, this position involves a certain degree of back-arching on her part, and may be more comfortably enjoyed with her simply putting her legs over his shoulders—even just her calves if need be.

Accordion

You'll feel like you're riding through the canals of Venice on a gondola—in the capable hands of the driver's accordion-playing friend, that is—when you try out this sexy position. In it, man and woman thrust together, using their arms to do most of the work.

Start this position out in missionary fashion—with his legs on the outside of hers. When he's in, she puts her legs over his shoulders, resting just her ankles on them. Then, he moves his positioning from kneeling to sitting back on his buttocks and she also raises herself to a sitting position. Both rest their weight on their arms, pushing their pelvises together and pulling apart.

Baby Boomer Variation: You can enjoy this position as half an accordion just as well as a full-on one when either he remains in his kneeling posture, or she continues to rest on her back instead of sitting while he sits.

Wall Sit

Remember in phys ed class when you had to do those grueling callisthenic exercises—and how good it felt when you finally had them mastered? In this case, we're talking about the notorious wall sit, an exercise you were timed doing over the course of the year, whereby you leaned against a wall with your back and pretended to be sitting in a chair that wasn't there. You didn't even realize then all the strength you were building in your upper legs and buttocks! In this variation, the wall is a lot more compelling to lean against, and there's even a real and rather enjoyable place to sit!

To get into this position, the man kneels on the floor, with his knees apart to give him maximum balance. Still standing, the woman leans her back against his chest and slides down to penetration. There's nothing for her to grab onto; she can continue to lean her back on his chest, but she must control all the motion from her legs, mainly her knees, as she raises and lowers herself on him.

Baby Boomer Variation: If you and your partner have questionable leg strength, bad knees, or a dubious sense of balance, we'll tell you right now that this position will not work for you. To vary it to a more manageable level, two chairs of the same height can be placed on either side of the man and woman. She can push herself up and down, now also using her arms, by putting most of her weight, through her arms, on the seats of the chairs. Be sure if you try this, however, to use very well-built, solid chairs. The fold-up variety could mean a catastrophe waiting to happen!

> *"That's the bedroom, but nothing ever happened in there."*
> —Dana Barrett (Sigourney Weaver), Ghostbusters

Upside-Down Squat

In a variation of the Wall Sit, the man, instead of on his knees, rests on his back with his legs folded up in the air. She sits on the backs of his legs and he penetrates her. This one can get pretty uncomfortable for the guys. For one, he's going to have to keep his lower back lifted off the floor for most of the time in order to properly balance her and support her weight. But that's not where the most discomfort can stem from. In this position, his penis must bend almost straight downward in order to maintain his penetration of her.

Baby Boomer Variation: The aforementioned chair maneuver will also work here. Not at all recommended for bad backs, bad knees, or non-bendy penises.

Catapult

One of the most complicated compromising positions you can ever find yourself in with a partner, this position actually works best in an armchair. In it, the woman straddles the man in a position that is almost birdlike as she, well, becomes catapulted into ecstasy.

The man sits in a chair, his arms extended out to the side—and close to behind him. The woman takes a rear-entry approach to penetration as she sits on top of him. And then comes the hard part. From the sitting position, she bends forward from the waist. He pulls her legs up over his shoulders. Then she arches her back up, reaching her fully extended arms behind him, and locks her hands on his shoulders at the base of his neck. Boomer females who are not yoga experts need not apply.

Baby Boomer Variation: Boomers can vary this position for maximum comfort and to their ability. One variation has her still sitting on him, rear-entry style, and bent over from the waist. However, instead of her legs being pulled up to God knows where, she can rest her feet comfortably on the ground. True, she won't feel like she's flying in the same way, but at least she won't have to worry about throwing her back out. And, she can also get in on the thrusting action, pushing up and down with her now well-grounded legs.

Sexploration Exercise #18

1. When you hear the term *Kama Sutra*, it calls to mind:
   a. The passion of the ancients. A tradition of lovemaking that's held through the centuries.
   b. Being in traction. I've seen some of those positions and they don't look like they'd be good for my back.
   c. Something trendy I heard about at a party that I don't particularly have any interest in, but if others are doing it right now ...
   d. A new way booksellers have found to complicate sex for the rest of us.

2. Have you ever tried out any of the positions or practices taught in the *Kama Sutra*?
   a. No way. No one would be able to get into some of those crazy positions!
   b. I might consider it, but I don't think my wife would be comfortable looking at all those dirty pictures.
   c. If my husband would ever get off the couch, put down the remote, and actually read something, I'd try and get him interested in it.
   d. We've tried some of them—the ones that are just like the ones we do today. Leave the more difficult ones for the younger folks!

3. If your lover came to you tonight with a *Kama Sutra* video and massage kit, would you give it a try?
   a. Sure. If they went through that much trouble to try something new, why wouldn't I go along with it?
   b. Maybe. It would depend on how tired I was from the day.

   c. I don't think so. I'm not all that interested in trying new things.
   d. Absolutely not! I'm a modern, Western sexual being myself!

4. If you have practiced *Kama Sutra*, what's your favorite thing about it?
   a. The variety. If you and your partner play with *Kama Sutra*, you can do something new every night!
   b. The certainty. There's just something so exciting about doing it in ways that have been tried and true throughout the ages.
   c. The element of kinkiness. There's a lot of watching of naughty videos and dirty pictures that are meant to be "instructive."
   d. The time it takes. When you do *Kama Sutra*, you can't just roll over on top of your lover and get things over within a couple of minutes or so. You need to take the extra time to really pay attention to each other and focus on what you're doing, and that really makes you closer to one another.

5. Your least favorite?
   a. There's not enough spontaneity. We do it strictly by the book, so where's the imagination in that?
   b. When I'm open to experimenting with him, it seems like he takes things too far. He gets really serious about doing everything just right and it seems like we're missing the point somewhere.
   c. The lack of comfort. Some of those positions can be really taxing.
   d. The results. After all that work, the results don't always live up to their promises.

chapter 18

Kama Sutra

"Good to see you Mr. Bond. Things have been awfully dull around here. I hope we're going to see some gratuitous sex and violence."
—Q *(Alec McCowen),* Never Say Never Again

Written in India somewhere between 400 and 100 B.C.E., the *Kama Sutra* is one of the world's earliest sex manuals and the most famous guide to sexuality ever. Ironically, the author, Vatsayayana, reputedly lived a life of abstinence.

So what is it about this ancient text—penned by a person who didn't even have sex—that makes it so compelling to modern lovers?

Most people associate the *Kama Sutra* with sexual positions that require the nimbleness and athletic grace of the most flexible yogi combined with the physical strength of a linebacker. However, most of the positions in the *Kama Sutra* are much tamer than most people would expect.

Essentially, the positions featured in the *Kama Sutra* are very similar to the ones we've covered in this section, from missionary to standing—and yes, even some of the more adventurous combinations in the previous chapter. But while the positions are the same, the names are wonderfully different—in some ways, a lot more clever than the names we have. For instance, a version of our "woman on top" is Vatsayayana's "soaring butterfly." We'll get into more of these as we move along.

In this chapter, we briefly touch on the principals of the *Kama Sutra,* and we find ways to perform some of the more exciting ancient positions in more modern ways.

Phyllis, 53

"For the past few years, ever since he hit fifty is my estimate, my husband, Tom, has been working longer and harder hours. He says it's because he's worried that if he doesn't show his bosses that he can keep up with the 'kids' as he calls them—the ambitious and energetic twenty- and thirty-somethings—that his company will 'put the old cow out to pasture,' or, force him into early retirement.

I used to take it personally. I used to believe that the reason he was working so much was that he was sick of our marriage, sick of our sex life—just sick of me. Working so hard had made him tired, and his libido just didn't have the same oomph it once had. So instead of being rational and believing that this was because of his job, I turned it around in my head and made it be about me, which began to put a strain on our marriage—more so than the sex we weren't having.

One day I finally woke up and realized that if I was inventing all this stuff in my head—which maybe I was and maybe I wasn't—the reason may have been that I probably wasn't getting enough intellectual stimulation. The idleness of my brain was creating a whirlpool into which all kinds of destructive irrational thoughts could circulate.

That's when I—got acquainted with the *Kama Sutra.* Well, not exactly. You see, I first learned about the *Kama Sutra* in a Continuing Ed evening class I enrolled in at the local high school in an effort to offset my boredom and frustration over being left alone so much by my husband. And no—it wasn't a human sexuality class. It was a seminar on ancient cultures. The *Kama Sutra* just happened to come up because it was one of the most important texts to come out of ancient India.

We didn't get into too much detail about the *Kama Sutra* in the class. I guess the lecturer realized he was dealing with a bunch of middle-aged suburban types who probably weren't interested—or, more likely, would be offended—by what they probably would have decided was blatant pornography.

The concepts he did cover, however, intrigued me. He explained that according to ancient Indian religious belief, life was composed of three responsibilities that people had to fulfill. One was *artha*, earning one's living in the world and not being dependent on others. The second was *dharma*, which means meeting one's daily responsibilities and expectations. The third leg of the stool was *kama*, or sexual pleasure. A person was not a complete and respectable person if he or she didn't have good sex? That was something that begged looking into!

That weekend, I went to the library and, deciding to pretend to anyone who asked me that I was a student (not a lie) with a paper to work on (big lie), I checked out every book I could get my hands on about the *Kama Sutra*. Talk about steamy reading!

I was curled up in our bed with one of the books when Tom came home from work late yet again. 'What have you got there?' he asked me. And for whatever silly reason, I could feel myself blushing. This is a man I had been married to for more than twenty-five years. There wasn't much I was ever embarrassed about in front of him. But I still felt like a schoolgirl who'd been caught doing something naughty. Not that this was necessarily a bad thing, mind you!

Tom took the book from my barely clenched grasp. 'Good God, Phyl! There's all kinds of dirty things going on in here!' he gasped. 'I know,' I blushed. I looked up at him to see that a crooked smile had passed over his face. 'See something you like?'

With that, we had a pretty hilarious time balancing against and wrapping around each other, trying to do some of the positions in the book. It truly was one of the most fun nights of sex we had had in a long time!"

Ardent Ancients; Wanton Wisdom

The *Kama Sutra* is much more than a book with dirty pictures and sizzling sex tips. As Phyllis learned—which was what had initially attracted her to learn more about the ancient practice—the *Kama Sutra* is a guidebook to help users to become more complete human beings.

In the ancient world, a distinction wasn't made between sex and spirituality (and we'll look more closely at this in Chapter 19). Rather, sex was a way by which you could become more spiritual and, instead of making God angry with your salacious activities, you would actually be bringing yourself closer to the divine with each sexual experience you had.

In the ancient Orient, sex was an art—and one of sixty-four arts a person should master. The other arts included singing and dancing, sculpture and painting, flower arranging and cooking, architecture and design, etiquette and languages, sports and household management, and many others. A person who was accomplished in all sixty-four arts, whether man or woman, was generally regarded with honor.

> "Had my dream again where I'm making love, and the Olympic judges are watching. I'd nailed the compulsories, so this is it, the finals. I got a 9.8 from the Canadians, a perfect 10 from the Americans, and my mother, disguised as an East German judge, gave me a 5.6. Must have been the dismount."
>
> —Harry Burns (Billy Crystal), When Harry Met Sally

Now this certainly doesn't mean that you need to become a master in all of these arts to have better sex. However, as it always goes, the more you know about something, and the more time you put into perfecting it, the better at it you will be!

For the rest of this chapter, we look at some of the positions featured in the *Kama Sutra* and see how they translate to modern times.

Trying It Out for Yourself

So you are intrigued by the ancient teachings of the *Kama Sutra,* and you think you are ready to sample a little spiritual celebration of your own? In this section, we'll show you some of these almost doable positions—try them out for yourself!

The *Kama Sutra* was originally written in Sanskrit and in verse form. For that reason, we've taken the liberty of providing further translation for the mostly esoteric language it's been written in. (These positions were taken from Indra Sinha's *The Love Teachings of Kama Sutra,* as featured on Tantra.com.)

If you're tempted after reading this chapter to head right to the bookstore to pick up a book with all the techniques of the *Kama Sutra,* and you find yourself getting lost in the lingo when you bring it home and read it, here are the two most important terms: linga, which is "penis," and yoni, which means "vagina." Enjoy!

Missionary Themes

The ancients didn't think this basic sex position was boring, and they had lots of interpretations of it. Here are just a couple.

The Flower in Bloom

She cups and lifts her buttocks with her palms,
spreads wide her thighs,
and digs in her heels besides her hips,
while you caress her breasts:
this is "Utphallaka."

Translation: The woman lies on her back, with her knees bent and feet secured firmly at her sides, instead of holding her legs in the air. To get a good position for penetration, she holds her buttocks upward while he enters her.

Aphrodite's Delight

Catch hold of her two feet,
raising them till they press upon her breasts
and her legs form a rough circle.
Clasp her neck and make love to her:
this is "Ratisundara."

Translation: In this difficult position, the woman lies on her back with her legs, this time, in the air. Once the man enters her, he grabs her ankles, and, pretzel-like, bends them in toward her chest so her legs appear to make a circle. Only the most limber woman should even think about this one!

Woman on Top

As we stated in Chapter 14, ancient civilizations were especially fond of this position!

Lovely Lady in Control

Catching your penis, the lady
with dark eyes like upturned lotus petals
guides it into her yoni,
clings to you and shakes her buttocks:
this is "Charunarikshita."

Translation: He lies on his back; she straddles his hips and sits herself on top of his erect penis, her back upright, and she orchestrates the thrusts and movement.

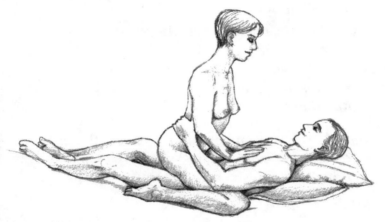

Lovely Lady in Control lets her set the pace.

(Hrana Janto)

Swan Sport

If she strides you,
facing your feet,
brings both her feet up to your thighs,
and works her hips frantically,
it is known as "Hansa-lila."

Translation: In this position, the man lies on his back; the woman sits astride him, but this time, she faces away from him. Then, she folds her feet over his thighs and leans forward. In this position, she also takes control of thrusting and movement. Not recommended for women with bad knees.

Rear Entry

These positions give new meaning to the term "animal sex!"

The Dog

If you mount her like a dog,
gripping her waist,
and she twists round to gaze into your face,
experts in the art of love say
it is "Svanaka."

Translation: In this position, she rests on her hands and knees, with her ankles spread apart; he kneels behind her and enters her from behind. Instead of leaning forward, she arches her back up and watches him as he thrusts into her.

The Cat

If she lies on her stomach
and you seize her ankles in one hand,
lift them high and make love,
tilting her chin back with your other hand,
it is "Marjara."

Translation: In this position, she rests on her elbows instead of her knees, with her ankles spread apart; he kneels behind her and enters her from behind, grabbing her ankles and lifting them up in one hand as he thrusts into her.

Standing

If you thought stand-up sex was already a challenge, these may not be positions you want to try; however, if you're looking for new ways to "bond on the vertical," see if you can master these!

Suspended

When the woman sits in her lover's
cradled hands, her arms around his neck,
thighs gripping his waist,
her feet pushing back and forth against a wall,
it is "Avalambitaka."

Suspended requires strength and trust. The reward is worth the effort.

(Hrana Janto)

Translation: In this position, man and woman stand facing each other, him with his back against a non-movable wall. She locks her arms around his neck, and he lifts her and holds her up by the buttocks. She keeps her legs at the level of his thighs and presses her feet against the wall, extending and bending her legs to thrust him in and out of her.

The Knee Elbow

If you lift your lover
by passing your elbows under her knees
and gripping her buttocks
while she hangs fearfully from your neck,
it is "Janukurpara."

Translation: In a more daring execution of the previous position, man and woman face each other. This time, he holds her up from under the knees, while she holds on tight to his neck. In this situation, it is he who will be controlling the thrusting and movement as he lifts and lowers her onto himself.

Oral Pleasure for Her

Contrary to what many may think, moderns did not invent oral sex. Here are some ways a man can get started in pleasuring his female lover.

The Quivering Kiss

With delicate fingertips,
pinch the arched lips of her house of love
very very slowly together,
and kiss them as though you kissed her lower lip:
this is "Adhara-sphuritam."

"People don't just bump into each other and have sex. This isn't Cinemax."

—*Jerry Seinfeld*

Translation: As we urge you in Chapter 20, so does Vatsyayana: Don't go right for the kill! This technique encourages the male to tease the female by closing her up, and kissing the outer labia before even thinking about what's inside.

The Circling Tongue

Now spread, indeed cleave asunder,
that archway with your nose and let your tongue
gently probe her yoni,
with your nose, lips and chin slowly circling:
it becomes "Jihva-bhramanaka."

Translation: Again, the teachings of the *Kama Sutra* recommend starting slowly and gently, paying attention to the vagina as a whole and not zeroing right in on the clitoris.

Oral Pleasure for Him

And now, ancient techniques for her to use on him.

Touching

When your lover catches your penis
in her hand and, shaping
her lips to an 'O', lays them lightly to its tip,
moving her head in tiny circles,
this first step is called "Nimitta."

Translation: Before accepting the penis into her mouth, the woman should first fondle it with her hand or hands. She begins playing first with the tip of the penis to make her lover aroused.

Biting at the Sides

Next, grasping its head in her hand,
she clamps her lips tightly about the shaft,
first on one side then the other,
taking great care that her teeth don't hurt you:
this is "Parshvatoddashta."

Translation: After concentrating on the tip, she moves up and down the shaft with her mouth, paying attention to all sides, and paying specially close attention that she does not use her teeth.

If you are intrigued by ancient practices of lovemaking, you're not done yet—at least not in this book. In the next chapter, we'll forge all-new ground with tantalizing tantric techniques!

Sexploration Exercise #19

1. What does the term "tantric sex," mean to you?
   a. Some boring, old-fashioned way to have sex that no one in the twenty-first century really cares about.
   b. An exciting way to make orgasms go on forever.
   c. A way to really take your time and savor each other.
   d. An activity you partake in after eating Indian food?

2. Have you ever dabbled in tantric sex?
   a. We like to take one weekend every month if we can to try out tantric practices and strengthen our bond.
   b. We've talked about it but never really got our acts together on it.
   c. Tantric, schmatric. Who wants to spend that much time working towards one little orgasm. Please!
   d. No—but we've "dabbled" in raising kids, working full time, and running a household, with hardly a moment left over for regular sex!

3. If your lover asked you to take a few hours this weekend to try tantric sex, what would you do?
   a. I would respect that they are looking to broaden our sexual horizons and set apart a big chunk of time to fit it in between chores.
   b. I'd be willing to devote an hour or so to trying it out, but who has six or more hours—even on the weekend—for sex?
   c. I would hand my husband a mop and tell him that he clearly doesn't have enough to do around the house and has too much time on his hands.
   d. I think I'd pretend I had to work overtime on the weekend and try and catch the game with some friends. Tantric sex sounds a little too floofy for me!

4. If you have practiced tantric sex, what's your favorite thing about it?
   a. I love that when we are involved in tantric sex together, it's like there's no one else in the world but us.
   b. I appreciate the time my lover takes to appreciate me—and I try to be very conscious to reciprocate all that special attention.
   c. It's fun to pretend that you're Sting—cool and rich and have a lot of time to spend having sex to inspire you to write your next hit song.
   d. I keep doing it because I can't wait to have that eight-hour orgasm I've heard about!

5. Your least favorite?
   a. That we can't have tantric sex all the time.
   b. That my wife only pretends to be into it, but she's off paying bills or writing a big business proposal in her head when we do.
   c. That it takes so much time and energy that's really hard to come by these days.
   d. That sometimes you don't even get to the orgasm—I mean, come on! If you don't make the goal, what's the point of the game?

chapter **19**

Tantric Sex

*"Let's fool around. Let's do it some strange
way that you've always wanted to, but nobody
would do with you."*
—*Tracy (Mariel Hemingway)*, Manhattan

Tantra is a 6,000-year-old Indian movement. When it was
first introduced, it went against the established teachings of
organized religion at the time—that individuals needed to
separate themselves from their sexuality in order to reach
their highest level of spiritual fulfillment. (Keep in mind that
the *Kama Sutra* came almost 4,000 years after the tantric
rebellion.) Today, even though this separation still exists in
western cultures, more and more people are embracing the
tenets of this movement for the potential it has as one of the
most romantic ways of expressing love and passion there is.

But while tantric sex, which is also sometimes known as
"sexual yoga," can be a wonderful, freeing experience for many
couples, our society's ever-puritanical approach to sex—even
40 years after the sexual revolution we started—still causes
people to shy away from this practice. Not letting go of our

stubborn notion that there should be a split between spirituality and sexuality, however, deprives us of experiencing sex on a spiritual level, and nearly diminishes what sex can really be like.

For the most part, Western sex, at least sex in the United States, is goal-oriented, and the big O is the target. A lovemaking session that fails to result in a climax for either party is often an embarrassment, a trigger for guilt, and a perceived failure. Getting it on is reduced to little more than getting off.

Tantric sex, on the other hand, is incredibly romantic, and since it removes the stress and pressure to bring the other person to orgasm as quickly as possible, it offers a wonderful chance for long-time lovers who may have grown a bit bored with each other to reconnect on a very deep level.

The goal of tantric sex is total surrender. The experience makes you become one with the universe as you let go of all your external emotional, mental, and cultural baggage. There is no "thinking" in tantric sex; just blissful sensation and feeling. Also in tantric sex, when—and if—orgasm is achieved, it belongs not only to the lovers, but to the universe. It is in that way that sex transcends the physical and enters the realm of the divine.

So, as you can probably imagine, tantric sex also takes a lot more time to properly experience than the down-and-dirty variety we generally enjoy, and therefore, many don't get involved in it because they are always so pressed for time. But we feel this is a mistake. Tantric sex does not have to be the be-all-and-end-all of your sex life. Savor it in small doses, incorporating elements of it into your sex play from time to time; by allowing yourselves time to appreciate each other this way, you will enrich your sex life and your overall relationship.

In this chapter, we learn some of the principles of tantric sex, and how to incorporate at least some of them into our hyperbusy daily routines.

Emily, 45

"When my husband, Joe, and I first heard Sting go on and on about the wonders of tantric sex all those years ago, we thought: 'Jeez. It must be great to be a famous rock star and have all that money to be able to waste all that time!' ... And then to not even actually have the orgasm, but to just enjoy building up to it? That's just crazy.

Joe and I work hard enough for barely nothing as it is! He heads out sometimes at six in the morning—even six days a week—to his plumber job. I clock in my time at the phone company. My job isn't exactly stimulating and it isn't exactly easy either. We both come home pretty tired and with plenty of aches and pains.

And then there are the kids: We've got five of them—and all under eighteen. So there's always a soccer practice to run off to, helping them with their homework, heck, even making dinner for all those mouths after a long day dealing with phone customer complaints wipes me out.

So if you ask me if I have five hours to wait for an orgasm I might not even ever actually have, Mr. Sting, I'd tell you absolutely not! Some days, that orgasm is the only thing I have to look forward to, and I don't want to work for it!

On the other hand, I do have to admit that the 'closeness' aspect of tantric sex makes me wonder if it isn't worth trying. With all the directions Joe and I get pulled in the course of a day, I feel like sometimes we really don't have enough time for each other .... Who knows—maybe it might be worth looking into. I mean, maybe there's a quickie way to do it or something. Heck—you never know ...."

Getting Started

Good news, Emily: You don't have to be a constant practitioner of tantric sex to enjoy at least some of its benefits. You can take the time to appreciate your lover and bring your sex life into a more spiritual domain even if you only practice tantric sex some of the time. Of course, if you don't embrace the teachings of the tantra with full enthusiasm, you might never reach your erotic nirvana—or experience the "hands off" orgasm .... You'll see what we mean later!

The most important thing to remember about tantric sex is that due to the nature of the soul connection you and your lover will be working to forge and firmly establish, there's really no point in sampling this particular sex practice with someone you don't or hardly know. The best tantric experiences occur between two people involved in a deeply committed long-term relationship who are seeking to cement their bond.

Before you get into any kind of serious tantric play, you should work up to the experience. Tantric sex can be a rewarding, enriching, but sometimes emotionally overwhelming experience that you and your partner will more satisfactorily enjoy if you build toward it.

Be sure to build gradually. You and your partner may start out setting apart fifteen minutes a day, several times a week, just to spend with one another. And you can begin these sessions by simply talking to one another.

The sexier part comes later.

Forging the Connection

Yes, you're probably all hyped up to see if the rumors about tantric sex—the extended orgasms, the "hands-free" orgasms—are all true. But that doesn't mean you are to jump right into it.

Also, you might want to try just getting to know each other again—on a more spiritual level—and hold off having sex for a while. Make these sessions you share at least fifteen minutes long, and a few times a week, please. Work up to the sex like you're working up to the whole experience.

First and foremost, before you do any kind of bonding whatsoever, take the time and care to set a proper mood. Remember the section in Chapter 12 when we made all kinds of suggestions for creating a sensual ambience? Here's a good time to flip back to that section to get some good hints. Don't underestimate the power of the warm glow of candlelight, of soft sensual music playing low, of the sound of children's laughter—far away at a friend's or neighbor's house perhaps.

One exercise you can try together is to synchronize your breathing. We'll get more into breathing exercises in the next section; but for our purposes now, let's do some rudimentary breath work.

You can do this sitting across from each other, standing opposite one another, or, in the sweetest way, lying down together, either facing each other. While spooning would also be an extremely intimate way to do work together, it's important in this exercise to be able to see your partner's face.

Look deeply into each other's eyes and do not speak to each other—except through your eyes. Hold hands while you hold your partner's gaze, and concentrate on your love for each other. It's important not to giggle—though we can't promise you that you aren't going to, at least initially. Now, harmonize breathing, synchronizing inhalations and exhalations. You should try and do this exercise for fifteen to thirty minutes—or even more, if time allows. You'll soon see that the power of two breathing as one is undeniable.

Another exercise you can practice together is meditation. Meditation clears the mind, helping to push out all stress and negative energy, and ushers in thoughts of the moment, sharpening focus and concentration. Meditate together the same way you harmonize your breathing. Just concentrate on your love and your passion—the both of you. The kids' homework and the score of the game can wait!

Becoming One—With One Another and the Universe

You are just about ready to physically consummate the bond of your love. However, here's another exercise that Tantramagic.com recommends you try, again, for fifteen minutes a day, several days a week, before moving into more sexually charged activities.

Called "Two Bodies as One," it does not mean having sex—so don't get the wrong idea! In this exercise, man and woman lie flat on the floor, with feet touching the other's feet—so as to make one straight line. Next, pressing your feet together, bend your knees and raise your legs together. Continue to push your feet together and remain in that position for at least fifteen minutes, as you reflect upon the love you feel for each other and how to make your bond together only stronger.

If lying on the floor with your feet pressed together isn't your cup of tea, don't worry, there's a variation. You

Use this exercise everyday to realize spiritual unity before coming together sexually.

(Hrana Janto)

can sit facing each other, each partner placing his or her hands on the other's knees, palms facing upward. Press your foreheads together and relax for at least fifteen minutes in this position, keeping the thoughts of the love you feel for your partner and your bond as the only thoughts you have for that fifteen minutes.

Also, Keep in Mind ...

Tantric sex suggests that we give sex at least the same amount of specialness that we give other areas of our lives and that we make a division between the way we were acting, thinking, and feeling prior to a lovemaking session and the way we act, think, and feel once a lovemaking session has begun. The meditation and breathing exercises we just covered can help put you in that state of mind, but you need to work a bit to maintain your focus.

Remember to take the time to make your appearance appealing to your mate. Zig Ziglar, in his book *Courtship after Marriage,* points out that many dress up beautifully for the office; however, the moment they come home to their beloved, they can't wait to strip out of all that finery and retreat to the sweat suits and T-shirts that are the typical domestic uniform. Sure, they're comfortable as hell, but there's nothing sexy about them. If we dress nicely at the office to make our clients feel special, certainly our lovers deserve as much, if not more, regard.

Taking the time to look good for each other isn't the only way to show one another our appreciation and devotion. Other ways to bond abound, and, just like with most anything else in this book, the limits on the activities you can enjoy together are set only by your own imaginations.

Consider taking a shower together at least once a week. Chances are, with all the hustling and bustling you do just to get out the door in the morning during the week, this might be a special Sunday ritual. If you have kids, and you don't want the young ones invading your privacy, this makes for a great reason to skip sleeping in on a Sunday.

In the shower, lather each other up, taking careful precautions not to miss a single inch. The feeling of rubbing soap all over the skin of your lover will be sensual, but also nurturing. Wash each other's hair. Comb through conditioner. Even shave each other. The time that you spend looking after each other in this way will only increase the bond you share—and may even make you more than a little frisky at the same time …. But we'll talk all about tub and shower sex in Chapter 28.

Another seemingly mundane ritual you can perform together is to feed one another. Perhaps one night, when you've sent the kids off to stay with family and friends, you can have a special dinner for two, in bed. Naked. After all, everything tastes better when you're naked. And when you're being fed at the hand of the person you love most in the world, whose fingers—hopefully running with some kind of succulent juice from a ripe piece of fruit or the like—you'll enjoy licking clean. In this instance, be sure to opt for an expensive delicacy—perhaps oysters—something that you both enjoy and that you don't normally buy for yourselves. And we'll also be getting into food and sex later in this book, so we aren't going to spoil your appetites with it now.

Tantric Orgasms

Just because it isn't the ultimate goal of tantric sex doesn't mean you don't get to have an orgasm! As we stated earlier, in tantric sex, there are different kinds of orgasms—and not necessarily those that have been included in the ones we've already looked at in this book! What do we mean by that? Read on!

By this point—in this book and in our lives—it's safe to assume that we're all acquainted with the physical variety of orgasm. Whether clitoral or vaginal for women; sparked by intercourse, oral or anal sex or manual stimulation for men; thunderous and torrential or merely a pleasant tingling sensation—we've all been there. But how many of us have had a purely spiritual orgasm?

If you are a practitioner of tantric sex, perhaps you have been lucky enough to have one of these.

According to an article entitled "The Spirit of Western Tantra," posted on Tantra.com, the Pure Heart Orgasm or Energy Orgasm occurs when you get deeper into the practice of tantric sex.

> "An artist may paint a thousand canvases before achieving one work of art. Would you deny a lover the same practice?"
>
> —Don Juan (Errol Flynn), Adventures of Don Juan

As you get more involved with the exercises, and with your involvement in working on the connection you are building with your lover, it is believed that you will reach a point in your spiritual consciousness whereby you can have an orgasm with no physical touching or stimulation at all. You simply need to breathe them, and they will, and please pardon the term, come. That certainly seems like incentive to try something new to us!

Peter, 45

"The most amazing thing my girlfriend and I ever did together was to discover tantric sex. I know that sounds kind of flaky, maybe, and an unusual activity for a couple of hard-boiled investment bankers to get into, let alone even come across. But what can I say—it happens!

Actually what did happen was that Sandy was called away for a week-long banking seminar, and when she found out it was going to be held at a spa we had been dying to try out, she immediately made arrangements to smuggle me in.

I was thinking the whole time we'd be getting seaweed wraps and massages—that kind of thing. And we did get plenty of those. But one evening, when we were coming out of the sauna, we saw a posting for a class on tantric sex, inviting adventurous couples to join.

I was skeptical. I like my sex like I like my steak: an old standby, but on the raw side. I wasn't into cymbals or chimes or flowers in pubic hair or any of the other things I imagined when I saw the picture that went along with the flyer—some ancient India print or something like that. But Sandy had other ideas.

'I've heard about this,' she said to me, tapping the poster with a long, sexy, impeccably manicured finger. 'This is what Sting does … and he says he can last all night long. Can you imagine that?'

Sadly, I could not. I certainly don't have the endurance now that I had when I was a kid—and even then I couldn't hope to last the whole night. But I was afraid Sandy was trying to tell me something. Was I too quick for her? Did she need something more? Was she not satisfied?

'Let's sign up. It'll be fun!' she insisted, to which I gave up a meek 'Okay.' The class was a lot more interesting than I thought it was going to be, and it really taught us a lot about being in our relationship—and not even in the sexual way. And no, there were no cymbals or chimes or pubic buds—nothing like that. I will say that even though we don't get into even a quarter of what we learned on that trip—both in that class and practicing afterwards—I have to admit that the tantric techniques definitely gave our sex life a boost!"

> "[I'm] trying to get my wife into tantric shopping. That's when you go shopping for five hours and not buy anything."
>
> —*Sting, on* Conan O'Brien

To recap what we have covered in this chapter, tantric sex, modern style, is, in its most basic essence, all about building the bond you share with your lover in the limited time the modern world affords for you to be together. Now, you have a new way to relate to your partner, someone with whom you enjoy these intriguing practices. If anything, this is a middle ground between the asexual relationships of our mundane activities and the act of sex.

Sexploration Exercise #20

1. How often do you orally pleasure your female partner?
   a. Every time we have sex.
   b. About once every couple of weeks.
   c. Rarely—she doesn't seem to care for it that much.
   d. Never if I can help it. I don't like it at all.

2. If you don't like to do it, why not?
   a. I get turned off by the scent.
   b. Sometimes my wife tastes funny down there.
   c. When I was growing up, this was not something a guy had to do, but now if he doesn't do it, he's like the devil or something.
   d. All kinds of other weird things happen down there. It's just not sanitary.

3. If there were ways to compensate for some of these deterrents, would you give it another try?
   a. Of course. If it's something that makes her happy, and I live to make her happy, then I'll try whatever I can to be able to do it as often as I can.
   b. I don't think so. If you don't like something, you shouldn't be forced to do it.
   c. I guess I could try, so long as it doesn't involve anything too weird.
   d. Why should I have to go out of my way to do something I hate to do in the first place?

4. What's the first thing you need to do when orally pleasuring a woman?
   a. Take her whole body into account—not just where the panties cover.
   b. Take her into the shower and give her a good scrubbing down.
   c. Just dive right in and get to it.
   d. Be sure to get yours first. You never know how long it's going to take her!

5. Is your female partner able to climax in other ways aside from receiving oral sex?
   a. Yes, she can pretty much have an orgasm doing anything.
   b. Usually if I manually stimulate her, that will do the trick.
   c. Not really, which is the only reason I do it, even if I don't like to all that much.
   d. Why is that my problem?

20

Oral Pleasure Tips for Men

*"I don't exactly know what I am required to say
in order for you to have intercourse with me.
But could we assume that I said all that. I mean
essentially we are talking about fluid exchange
right? So could we go just straight to the sex?"*
—John Nash (Russell Crowe), A Beautiful Mind

Oral sex is one of the most intimate experiences a couple can share—no matter who's giving or who's receiving. In this chapter, we'll talk to the guys about how to give your lovers an experience they'll want to tell all their friends about; and don't worry, ladies, in the next chapter, it's your turn.

For a woman, being on the receiving end of this special act can produce an orgasm like no other. The sensations that a warm, moist tongue and lips can provide are the ones that build into the most mind-blowing, toe-curling—the most unforgettable orgasms ever. But the receiver isn't the only one in a position to enjoy this delicious expression of love. When performing oral sex on his lover, a man has ultimate control over the movement and motion of his tongue, and the pressure and intensity he applies to her pleasure regions like nothing else. The satisfaction of bringing your lover to orgasm in such an intimate fashion is very exciting for many men; providing a lover with so much pleasure has been known to bring more than one man to the near brink of his own climax.

If this is something you may not have tried with your partner, or even if it's a skill you've been looking for tips on how to perfect, now's your chance to learn to become an oral sex master. One thing we always strongly encourage: Read this chapter together. Ladies, please disagree with us when you need to—and by all means, please let your lover know when we've got it right and there's something you've been just aching to try. Take advantage of us, please. It's what we're here for. And remember, guys—the next chapter will give your woman lots of tips in returning the favor.

Of course, this method of showing affection and giving pleasure is not for everyone, but if you're reading this, we like to think you're at least open to it—if not a frequent, enthusiastic practitioner looking for some new tips.

Scott, 51

"Go down on a woman? What, are you kidding me? I would never do that and any woman I've ever been with knows it. No self-respecting guy in his right mind would. Just ask them. Oral sex is for men to enjoy and women to give and that's that.

So maybe you think I'm being pig-headed? Yeah, well, I've heard that one before. I've had some girlfriends even leave me because they didn't think it was fair that they gave me oral sex and I didn't reciprocate. Well, good riddance to them.

Of course I've tried it. I would never just say no way to something I've never tried before. There's just nothing about it that I like. The vagina is for penetration as far as I'm concerned. I don't like the way it looks, smells, or tastes for that matter. And think about where that thing has been and what it's used for? At least with a guy, you can wash it off easy—it's not like it's all inside or anything with us.

I especially don't like the way my tongue gets all tired from it. I mean, come on—if it's really supposed to feel all that good for her, then why does it take forever for her to come? When a woman goes down on me, it doesn't matter how good or bad she is at it—all she has to do is put it in her mouth and I explode in no time.

Hey, if a woman I'm seeing doesn't like that I won't do it, let her find someone who will!"

Behind the Resistance

It's sad but true: Some men just won't perform oral sex on their lovers. In the tragic case of Scott, well, this guy just refused to get out of his own way with it. It's no wonder he was single when we talked to him. In our opinion, this guy needs more than a lesson in understanding women, he needs some serious reconditioning.

Of course, Scott is an extreme example of the aversion some men may have to giving oral sex to their partners. Actually, the fact of the matter is that most men who give cunnilingus a chance learn that they actually really like it.

There are, of course, a few more reasons that going down is a big taboo in the bedroom—and it has nothing to do with being a guy like Scott.

If you are not against performing oral sex on your female lover and are ready to learn red-hot tips, skip right over this section. You don't need any coaxing from us. However, if you are in the other group, stay right here. In this section, we're going to address the reasons you feel reluctant, and hopefully, for the sake of nurturing the intimacy of your relationship, get you to reevaluate your reasons.

Do you oppose performing oral sex on religious grounds? If that's the case, know that we would never try and force you to go against your religious beliefs. Stop reading this chapter right now and advance right to section four of this book.

Is it a generational thing—maybe when you were coming of age sexually, this was something frowned upon by your peers? It's certainly not a topic you covered in sex ed class, but outside of school, talking about sex with your friends. Today, it's likely that the friends you have and who you may bounce this kind of thing off on are close in age to you, and share your same ingrained hang-ups and misgivings. If that's the case, it's time to look past your friends and open your minds. There are so many worlds in the sexual realm to explore. It's time to think for yourself and forge new sexual ground.

It takes a woman on average about twenty minutes to reach orgasm through sexual stimulation—which certainly makes a great point for starting out slowly and pacing yourself! Also, remember that the more worked-up a woman is beforehand, through kisses and caresses that don't come even remotely near the clitoris, the quicker she will climax.

Another reason you may have for not wanting to perform oral sex on your lover is because of the genital area's association with the expulsion of waste material—that you feel the area just isn't clean, no matter how hygienically pristine she is. If that's the case, why not try it when you're both shower fresh. If going down on her is part of your evening plans, start things off in the shower. Showers are sexy and relaxing, and they will do a lot to put your woman in the mood.

One of the most painfully common reasons that people avoid this type of sexual activity—and all kinds of other activity—is that they simply don't feel comfortable and confident with their own skills. Do you avoid this act simply on the grounds that you just don't think you know how to do it? If you haven't gone down on your female partner—either all that often or even ever—because you're afraid of doing it wrong, that's the easiest reason we can deal with. Keep reading this chapter and we'll spell it out for you—literally. You'll see what we mean!

Total Bliss in a Different Kind of Kiss

We've stated this before—and we will, again and again: The center of a woman's sexuality is her clitoris. But never confuse the word "center" with "only." A woman's body is one total sex organ. Everything can potentially be—and generally is—sexy for a woman.

That said, when it comes time to perform oral sex on your significant other, never go right for the clitoris. In fact, don't even go near that area at all—not right off the bat. The key is to work up to it. To build up to it. When you play golf, you don't whap at the ball with all your might in the hopes it will magically somehow land at its destination. You line up your shot, watch your form, and carefully take your stroke, putting proper care and concentration into the execution. You know this is the only way to get the best results; the same is true with effectively pleasuring a woman.

For best results, start when your partner is still dressed—or at least partially dressed. You can work her up by removing articles of clothing, piece by piece, maybe even with your teeth.

Give your lover soft kisses and caresses all over her body. Work your mouth over her face and neck. Softy nibble her ears. Run your tongue over her shoulders and arms. The area just where her arms meet her sides, just next to where her bra strap covers, is exceptionally sensitive. With one languorous lick with the tip of your tongue, move to her breasts, delicately teasing her nipples. Draw a line with your tongue between her breasts and naval. Play with her naval for a while. Dart your tongue in and out, and circle around it.

With the tip of your tongue, trace a line from her naval to the top of her pelvis. This is where you're going to get the maximum effect if she is still wearing her underwear. Without removing them, run your mouth over the area that her underwear covers. Lick the sides. To make her really nuts, press your open mouth over the front of her underwear. Now breath out. That hot breath will make her mad with lust. Lick her over her underwear and continue to administer long, hot breaths.

At this point, you can either remove her underwear—or continue to tease and tantalize her by leaving them on, pulling them to one side or another to make direct contact with her vaginal region. Now remove her underwear, slowly, teasingly—and don't forget that teeth maneuver if you're feeling particularly frisky.

Even though you may think she's ready, do not go for the clitoris just yet. Lick around her labia, looking to her or listening for her moans to see what feels the best for her.

Are We There Yet?

By now, she should be just about ready to burst. It's finally time to go for the prize, but as much as you want to, don't rush it. Pace yourself.

Move slowly, as if there's nothing else you'll ever need to be doing in the world and no other place you'll ever need to be.

Lightly brush her clitoris with your open lips. With some women, one side of the clitoris will actually be more sensitive than the other. Find that spot by trial. When you find it, don't go right for it. Lick around the area, paying attention to what gives her the most "charge."

At this point, there are many easy and advanced tongue techniques you can try out. Tease the area by lightly dabbing at it with the tip of your tongue. Or, swirl your tongue around the area, like you're licking an ice cream cone.

With your tongue, trace the letters of the alphabet on that special spot, from A to Z and back again. Or, count from one to one hundred—or however long it takes. Be creative. Draw out a diagram of the winning play of the football game you watched that afternoon or the plans you have in your head for the new shed you want to build. Whatever you do, it will all feel good.

While you're down there, don't forget about the rest of her body. Reach up and stroke her breasts or lightly pinch her nipples. Manually stroke the rest of the area while licking. Insert a finger or two into her vagina, even search out her G-spot to build her to a double whammy of an orgasm!

Add caresses to oral stimulation to bring her to exquisite climax.

(Hrana Janto)

Be your own porn star. While you are giving her oral sex, make a lot of noise. (Well, not *a lot* of noise. Just make some "mmmmm" sounds to go along with what you're doing.) The more excited you sound, the more excited she will be. Also, the vibrations that come from your making sounds with your mouth will be stimulating to her as well.

Does she like it? The easiest way to find out is to ask. Just because the two of you may have been going to bed with each other for a few decades doesn't mean it's too late for you to ask these questions. Don't presuppose that you know everything about her sexuality. Things change. Asking what she does like every time will get you everywhere. Also, what feels good to her can vary, which keeps it interesting—especially if you like a challenge.

Our last suggestion: Do not stop what you're doing when she reaches orgasm. Unlike you, if you stop what you're doing at the crux of her climax, she may lose her orgasm. When she's had enough, she'll let you know.

> "Al, do you know I cooked four hours for that five minutes of sex we had? It just isn't worth it."
>
> —Peggy Bundy (Katy Segal), Married ... With Children

Hilary, 48

"I've been with my husband, Jay, for twenty-three years, and do you know that he's never, you know, gone south on me? It's not that I'm complaining or anything. It's never really bothered me before so I never felt the need to talk to him about it. Besides, I've never had to do it to him either, and I'm kind of grateful for that. I'm not sure I'd even do it right. I hear lots of men insist that their wives do it, but not Jay. It's not like we're missing anything. For the most part, our sex life has been satisfying. Or at least that's what I used to think.

Recently, Jay's job offered to promote him, but only if he agreed to relocate to Charlotte—miles away from where our families and friends lived in New Jersey. I had a very active social life and didn't want him to take it, but it was too good an offer for him to pass up, so we packed up and left our lives behind us. It would be months before I found a job, though.

Soon enough, I was feeling lonely. Sure, I could talk to my friends from home on the phone and even email and instant message them. But it just wasn't enough. I've always been very interested in sewing, and at home, I was a member of a quilters' group that met one or two Saturdays a month, and I had made lots of friends from it. So I fished around on the Internet for a local quilters' group to join.

I finally located what seemed like a great one and called the leader up. She said I was in luck—that they were going to meet that Saturday at one of the homes of the group members and she gave me the address and the time.

The women were very nice in the circle. What actually had really surprised me at first, but then I started not only to get used to but to look forward to, was they were all extremely candid about their sex lives. This wasn't so much a sewing circle as it was a forum for giving and receiving advice about sex.

The first few sessions, I was pretty buttoned up. I appreciated listening to the banter and collecting new tips. It sure beat exchanging recipes. Then one day, the talk turned to oral sex. One of the women, Stacy, had a new boyfriend who was opposed to doing it to her, and although she liked him for so many other reasons, she was considering dumping him because of it.

Having done without it my entire sex life, I was pretty confused. I don't know why I chose that as the time I was going to contribute to the group, but I couldn't stop the 'So I don't understand. Why can't you just do without it?' as it innocently slipped from my lips.

I was greeted with a pensive silence and lots of stares. Stacy looked at me blankly. 'Well, Hil, that's because when a guy does that to me— that's the only way I can climax.'

Some of the other women agreed, and many who could climax in other ways, like me, said that the orgasm you get from oral stimulation is like no other kind of orgasm. Now it was my turn to be shocked. 'Is it really that much better?' I asked. The women erupted in a fit of giggles. 'Are you telling me you've never had this done to you before?' one of them asked. I started to feel embarrassed. 'Well, actually … no.' Then Stacy said to me that it was high time I did something about it.

Since that afternoon, I've made lots of hints to Jay, but he hasn't really gotten it yet. Last week, Stacy suggested there was only one way: I had to do it to him. And then tell him it was my turn. So I think I'm gonna try it out tonight. Why not? And maybe the next time the group meets, I'll have a few tips to share with them!"

Positioning

Just because you've got the technique down doesn't mean you need to stop there. Just as intercourse can be enjoyed in many delightful positions, so can oral sex. In this section, we'll look at a few.

In the most common position, the woman lies on her back, likely on the bed, and the man kneels before her. She may have her legs bent at the knee, with her feet comfortably resting on the bed, or, if she has the leg strength, can hold them up in the air as she lays flat on her back.

The man can vary this position by kneeling on the floor in front of her as she hangs off the side of the bed. Many men who have neck and shoulder problems consider this a comfortable alternative because it alleviates neck strain. Another position to consider if you suffer from neck or shoulder pain is for both of you to lie on your sides, almost in a 69 position. He can rest his head on her inner thigh, which creates a kind of pillow for him, while he pleasures her.

In a very sexy position, the man lays on his back, with his head supported by a pillow. The woman straddles his face. Like the woman-on-top sexual position, she will be completely in control of pressure and movement; all he need worry about are the flicks of his tongue.

Another alternative to this position involves him coming at her from behind. This position is not for everyone; some contact with the anus may be inevitable, and so it should be avoided for those who are squeamish about face-to-anus contact.

Sexploration Exercise #21

1. How often do you orally pleasure your male partner?
   a. At least once a week if possible.
   b. Only sometimes—mostly for special occasions or if he's been especially helpful around the house.
   c. Not as often as he'd like me to, that's for sure. If it were up to him, I'd be attached to him that way at all times!
   d. I'd never put that thing in my mouth—are you kidding?

2. If you don't like to do it, why not?
   a. Because it expels waste and it enters the part of me that expels waste. Can you say "germ factory"!
   b. Because sometimes he gets so excited with his thrusting into my mouth that I feel like I'm going to choke.
   c. Because he's so hairy down there, I always get tickles in the back of my throat when I do it to him.
   d. Because sometimes he gets too excited and he forgets to pull away in time.

3. If there were ways to compensate for some of these deterrents, would you give it another try?
   a. Of course. If it makes him happy, it makes me happy.
   b. I'd definitely do it for him more if I could ensure he did it for me more.
   c. I'd rather just use my hand on him or do it the old-fashioned way, if you know what I mean.
   d. How can you compensate for all those germs? Cover him in Lysol? That's certainly not an improvement!

4. What's the first rule in orally pleasuring a man?
   a. Pretend you have no teeth!
   b. Be sure to lick and rub him everywhere down there.
   c. Don't be too rough, but don't be too gentle either.
   d. Pay attention to the signs of his climax and pull away from him before it's too late!

5. Do you swallow his ejaculate?
   a. All the time. It doesn't bother me.
   b. Sometimes. It all depends on the mood I'm in.
   c. Rarely. I know they say it's not supposed to taste like anything, but they've never met my husband.
   d. Never. It's bad enough I have to put that thing in my mouth to begin with. What would he want next? To urinate in my mouth? Forget it!

chapter 21

Oral Pleasure Tips for Women

"Jocks only think about sports, nerds only think about sex."
—*Lewis (Robert Carradine),* Revenge of the Nerds

We said this in the last chapter, but it's well worth repeating: Oral sex is one of the most intimate experiences a couple can share. When he gives and she receives, for her, the result is an orgasm without rival. In this chapter, it's his turn—so to speak. Now, it's the women's turn to get the inside story on how to perform mind-blowing oral sex—and the man's turn to concur, disagree, beg, or what have you—but essentially to just communicate to his partner all the things about this act that will really get him going.

There are few things more arousing to a man than receiving oral sex. Some may even prefer it to vaginal sex. Why? It's very much for the same reasons a woman likes oral sex. The sensations that a warm, moist tongue and lips on his penis provide are like nothing else—including those he feels from the vagina. The latter, while the ultimate pleasure chest, essentially, well, let's say "grips" the penis with similar pressure all the time—changed only by her inner contractions. Oral stimulation, however, can vary all the time—and several times within the span of the act itself.

And just like it is when a man bestows upon his lover an oral caress, the receiver isn't the only one who can enjoy this highly erotic act. When a woman performs oral sex on her lover, pressure, speed, and penetration are essentially in her control—taking her cues from him, naturally. In that way, the satisfaction of bringing a lover to orgasm can be very exciting for women, and bring them closer to their own climax.

If oral sex is not something you and your partner have tried, or if you're just looking to sharpen your already well-used skills, this chapter will give you tips on delivering a blow-job he may just want to brag about. In the next chapter, we'll give you tips on sensational simultaneous oral stimulation ... but let's not think about that just yet!

As in the last chapter, what's good or not good for the gander applies equally to the goose. We realize this highly intimate expression of affection isn't for everyone, but if you've read up to this point, we're guessing you're at least open to it—if not a frequent, enthusiastic practitioner looking for some new tips.

Robert, 40

"I love when a woman goes down on me. It doesn't really matter what she's doing—as long as she's using her mouth and tongue, and definitely not using her teeth!

The thing is, right now, I'm with this terrific woman. Sharon is perfect in every way, and in most ways, sex with Sharon is the best it's ever been. By that I mean actual intercourse. The only problem I have is that she doesn't like oral sex—giving it, that is. She's maybe done it for me once or twice, but every time I ask her, she begs off it. I don't know why she won't do it for me.

Believe me, even if she isn't doing exactly what I want her to do, it just feels so incredible. One time, actually the last time she performed oral sex on me, I started to tell her exactly what I wanted and what I didn't like. She got really upset, thinking she wasn't doing it right at all, and she stopped, cold, and just when I was all turned on and ready to explode. Then she got dressed and went home. It was very confusing.

After that, I've been very cautious about how I communicate with her sexually and almost a little inhibited. I'm afraid to talk to her about anything she does—even though I always ask her if she likes what I'm doing to her. She's never headed south again since that time she took off and went home—though I've gone down on her and she seems to enjoy it.

I'm not really sure how to handle this. I guess I could live without oral sex. But to be perfectly honest here, and I know how bad this sounds, believe me, I'm not sure I really want to."

You Want Me To Do What?!?

The issue between Robert and Sharon seems less an aversion to oral sex and more an inability to communicate. It's time for them to read Chapter 5 of this book! But in all seriousness, the problem could go deeper. Sharon may not have been eager to orally please Robert in the first place, and may have just gone along with it to make him happy or in fear of losing him. It might just be that she's hiding behind the fear of doing it incorrectly in order to avoid telling him that she may have other issues.

Certainly, if other issues exist, there's nothing to be ashamed of. Just like it was with the guys, so it is with the women. There are many reasons to avoid going down on a lover, from basic religious tenets and beyond. If it's not an issue for you, skip to the next part of this chapter. However, if you are in the other group, stay right here. In this section, we're going to look at those reasons why you may feel inhibited about performing fellatio, and hopefully get you to change your mind if we can.

As we already mentioned, and will mention over and over again in this book, if you oppose oral sex—both giving and receiving—on religious grounds, we're not going to push you into ignoring the doctrines of your faith or do anything like that. If this describes your particular situation, stop reading this chapter right now and skip right over the rest that follow in this particular section as, we're warning you now, it just gets naughtier from here. Go ahead—we'll catch up with you in Part 4.

Maybe the reason you're reluctant to perform oral sex on your male lover is that when you were growing up, nice girls didn't—and you still don't. All we can say to that is that times are different now; nice girls don't do it to everyone, but when it comes to being in an intimate relationship with someone special, nice girls do—and, actually, have been known to really like *doing* at that.

Perhaps you don't want to go down on your lover because you feel the genital area just isn't clean. The penis, after all, is the same tool with which a man urinates. Also, you might find the musky scent of his genitals by the end of the day to be too strong to breathe in. What goes for the guys goes for you as well: If oral lovemaking is on the menu that night, why not start off with a sensual shower? The hot water, your loving hands, and a bar of soap will go a long way to arousing him—not to mention, you'll be in control of making sure he's squeaky clean down there!

Another common reason many women don't want to fellate their lovers is that they're afraid they'll be forced to swallow. Guess what? You don't have to. Unlike with women, the male orgasm is essentially completed before ejaculation occurs. If you pull away before actual ejaculation, you won't be ruining his orgasm. Later in this chapter, though, we'll talk to you about swallowing and hopefully make you see that it's not as bad as you might think.

The top reason, however, that women avoid performing oral sex on their lovers is that they're afraid they won't be doing it right. Let's admit it right now: Men aren't the only ones who suffer from performance anxiety. In some cases, women may be so concerned with their ability, or lack thereof, to perform oral sex on their partners that they prefer not even to try. We say: try. If you haven't gone down on your partner—either all that often or maybe even ever—because you're afraid of doing it wrong, that's the easiest reason we can deal with.

Before we make recommendations for the right way to do it, we're going to share some very good news for you: Ladies, there is no such thing as a "bad" blowjob. Just better. Practice makes perfect. The more you perform oral sex on your partner, the better you're going to be at it. And men, if you're reading this—and you should be reading this—that goes for you, too!

Be sure to remember that just like every woman is different, so is every man. That means what really works for one will not necessarily work for others. Also, just like women, what feels amazingly great one session may not have the same umph in another—and what got yawns one time may get raves another. The secret is to always pay attention to your partner and what makes him feel great right at that moment. But we'll get into this more as we move along.

Start Simple—and Take It From There

One of the biggest favors men and women can do for each other sexually is to *not* go about pleasing their lovers the way they themselves like to be pleased. Here's the biggest lesson of Sex 101: Men and women are different and do not respond to various types of sexual stimulation in the same way. If the key words for pleasing a woman are "gentle," "build," and "sensual," for a man they are "urgent," "fast," and "rough." This doesn't mean that you need to treat your man with brute force, yanking, pulling, and sucking on his penis nearly to the point of trying to detach it from his pelvic region; but it does mean that the light, feather-like tapping sensation you may enjoy sometimes when he's going down on you is probably out of the question for performing really successful oral sex on him.

There really isn't much that's complicated about oral sex. Essentially, you can put your mind to rest. After all, as we said before and will say again, what men like most about oral sex is simply getting it in the first place.

One of the ways to get really great results with your man is to warm him up before heading south. Kiss his neck and ears. Run your mouth all over his body—everywhere but just there. Tease and torment him. This is at least one commonality in male and female sexuality.

Be sure to keep in the back of your mind that for the most electrifying effect, work your hands and your mouth in tandem. Using both ways to stimulate him will produce the most powerful orgasms.

Softly rub your lips over his nipples. Men's nipples are extremely sensitive and will become evermore so if while you're doting on them, you lightly scratch his belly with the backs of your fingernails. Move across his belly—and even to the top of his underwear—but don't go under the underwear.

Trace the line that runs between his chest and belly with the very tip of your tongue, edging also toward the underwear line—but not past it. While your mouth is moving down his torso, your hands—and especially those fingernails—can be lightly scratching the area around your lover's pelvic region. His inner thighs are especially sensitive, and so are the backs of his knees.

Once you've made it to the region with your mouth, you don't have to get right down to business. Continue your tease-and-tantalize game. He may be begging you at this point to just do it—but don't. If he still has his underwear on, press your open mouth up against his package and breathe over his penis and testicles with slow hot breaths. While you're doing this, cup his testicles with one hand while you slide one finger up and down his shaft with the other.

> *Perform sex? Uh, uh, I don't think I'm up to a performance, but I'll rehearse with you, if you like.*
>
> —Miles Monroe (Woody Allen), Sleeper

Once he is completely disrobed and about to explode, then it's time to go all the way. So don't stop reading now!

Give Piece a Chance

Remembering always that the hands work in tandem with the mouth when you pleasure a man orally, begin to massage the shaft of his penis with your hand before you go anywhere near his penis with your mouth. If he's not circumcised, firmly rub the foreskin between your thumb and fingers over the head of his penis. If he is, simply grasp the shaft and move the skin up and down. As we stated earlier, a man requires a firmer grasp. Hold him firmly, but whatever you do, be extremely careful not to hold him too hard or pinch the skin. If you do, he will let you know. Be patient and concentrate on your touch.

It's now time to go down. Don't take all of him in the first oral stroke. Tease him. Lick the head of his penis, paying special attention to the corona, or the area just under the spongy tip. Start slowly. Then lick and kiss the entire region. Be very, very mindful of your teeth. Wrap your lips around your teeth. (If you are not working with your own teeth, this is not a time to be vain. Just take 'em out. Believe us, he will appreciate the gesture.)

With your mouth, move up and down the shaft of his penis. While your mouth moves up and down, lick around the shaft with your tongue. Dart your tongue teasingly around the tip of his penis and all around.

Keep his perineum in mind. He will be very pleased if you kiss or lick that area before you get too deeply involved with the end game of orgasm.

While you don't need to have a thousand different techniques for oral foreplay, vary the order and intensity of the ones that you use in each new oral-sex session. Make it a little bit different for him every time.

Also, here's a surefire trick to bring him to the brink: Look up at him while you are fellating him. Don't hesitate to brush your hair out of the way so that he can see what you're doing. Men's sexuality is very visual. The more in-and-out action he sees, the more aroused he will become.

Some men are very fond of deep-throating, or taking all of a man's penis into your mouth. We don't recommend this for the novice practitioner, however. Get comfortable with the basics first. Especially if you have a tendency to gag, you might want to save this for when you have more experience, or maybe never even do it at all. Never let anyone tell you it's a deal breaker. Just as a man will derive maximum pleasure by having his penis in your vagina, so will he enjoy being in your mouth; deeper may provide a more intense sensation, but in most cases, it won't be absolutely necessary for him to get off. And here's a trick if you are a gagger: Don't breathe through your mouth—at least don't inhale. Take breaths in through your nose and exhale through your mouth. The hot breath you produce this way will also add to the sensation.

You can definitely learn more about what he wants by asking him directly. You'll learn a lot by watching him and listening to his moans, but don't be afraid to ask if something feels good or doesn't. And remember that just because he may not be making any noise at all doesn't mean he isn't enjoying himself. You may just have rendered him speechless!

When he's about to ejaculate, you will feel his penis engorge and tense up like it hasn't before. It may even begin to twitch before the spasms of orgasm begin. Also, a drop of pre-ejaculate will form at the tip of his penis. It's now that you have a decision to make. You can allow him to ejaculate in your mouth, and either spit it into a towel or even, yes, swallow. Semen has almost no taste. Some have compared it to liquefied alfalfa sprouts.

Here's a tip that will make fellatio more pleasant for both of you: Before you go down on him, pop a couple of strong mints in your mouth. The tingling sensation it gives him will drive him over the edge—and will make the taste in your mouth minty fresh.

There are factors that will affect the taste—just as there are factors that affect yours, but it's an instant sensation, like doing a shot of tequila or taking a dose of medicine. And semen has almost no calories at all. Those on the Atkin's Diet and other high-protein plans will be glad to know it is essentially all protein—no carbs. Take a chance: If you don't like it, you'll never have to do it again. The decision is ultimately yours.

Positions

To turn up the heat on this incredibly erotic act—or, let's face it, at our age, to avoid getting a stiff neck, sore jaw, or any of the other physical ailments you might develop from being in a particular position too long—fear not: options abound.

In the standard position, the man lays on his back with the woman in front of him, bent over on her knees—either facing him, or with her back turned toward him, affording him a sexy view of her buttocks. Being in this position too long may cause discomfort to her neck or knees, so both partners can be positioned on their sides for maximum comfort. She can also take advantage of the "pillow" provided by his inner thighs.

Take him in gradually, paying special attention to the area just under the tip of his penis.

(Hrana Janto)

Another alternative is for the woman to kneel in front of him on the floor with a pillow under her knees. He can sit with his legs over the side of the bed, or kneel if it makes for better height.

An especially sexy alternative involves him standing, with her either kneeling on the floor before him or sitting on the bed. For a really kinky thrill, he can stand next to a mirror, and the both of you can check out the action!

Another alternative that is comfortable for some reasons and almost scary for others is for the woman to lay on her back, her head on a pillow. He straddles her head and inserts his penis into her mouth, controlling the movement. If she has a tendency to gag, you might be better trying another position. Remember, as always, let your imagination and your own degrees of personal comfort guide you.

Sexploration Exercise #22

1. When's the last time you and your partner did a 69?
   a. A week.
   b. A month.
   c. A year.
   d. Several years.

2. If it's been longer than a year, why haven't you done it?
   a. I want what's coming to me and I don't want to share!
   b. Sadly, it never really comes up any more.
   c. My partner isn't interested in trying it again, no matter how often I ask for it.
   d. We really never liked it to begin with.

3. If you enjoy 69, what's your favorite thing about it?
   a. It doesn't happen all the time, but when we can climax at the same time, it's just bliss!
   b. The more excited my partner gets, the more she takes it out on me—and vice versa.
   c. I love the shared intimacy of it all—you're never more intimate with one another than when you're in a 69.
   d. I love so many things about it. It's hard to name a favorite!

4. If you don't like 69, what turns you off about it?
   a. My wife and I can never time ourselves just right, and if I come before her, she gets bent out of shape.
   b. When my husband gets too excited, he forgets all about pleasuring me and just thinks of himself.
   c. I prefer each of us to have our own special treatment instead of having to share the time.
   d. If my partner's on top of me and gets really excited, I get afraid of being smothered to death.

5. Do you think 69 is only for the young?
   a. No way. It's a hot position that everyone should get reacquainted with at least once in a while.
   b. Not especially. Sure, at our age, you can't do it as often as you may have when you were just learning about each other, but a good, healthy 69 once in a while can be a real boon to your sex life!
   c. Mostly. Lust fades—that's just what happens. You can't bring that same sexual hunger with you into your middle years. You'll starve to death!
   d. Absolutely. They have so much yet to learn!

chapter 22

69

*"That was the most fun I've ever had
without laughing."*
—Alvy Singer (Woody Allen), of having sex,
Annie Hall

Most sex manuals espouse the glories of the 69 position, a position in which man and woman perform oral sex on each other at the same time. They talk about the extreme delight that the sensation of kissing and orally caressing your partner's genitalia brings when he or she is doing the same to you. They speak of the utter excitement that arises when a couple can time their orgasms to occur simultaneously.

This is one of those sex manuals.

Although most people agree that the 69 position can be fantastic, many Boomer couples we spoke to in our research admit that this is a position they have not tried, in some cases, for more than twenty years. But there's good news. After speaking with us, many have tried it again, happily reporting back to us that they had no idea what they were missing.

In this brief chapter, we'll explore the many wonders of this position, and hopefully provide you with the impetus—and maybe a few great tips—to reincorporate it into your sexual repertoire.

Henry, 51

"When we were first married, my wife, Sue, and I used to have sex all the time. We couldn't keep our hands off each other. We tried everything there was to do—and I'm sure we invented a thing or two as well. We were on fire.

Within the first ten years, the monsoon of sexual activity we used to have trickled into an occasional drizzle—with all the many outlandish, outrageous, and exciting components disappearing one by one. 69 was probably the first to go.

I'm not sure what happened. It's like one day, she just lost interest, and that was that. For good. From what I could tell, it was never her favorite activity anyway, but she used to be up for it at least once in a while.

Then, blam! Right out of the blue, it was nothing. After 69, the constant oral sex we used to enjoy winded down to occasional mouthplay—and so on. Anyway, it's really just too depressing to dwell on.

But you know, I just can't help myself. So it's like this: I know we're not as young as we used to be and we're never going to get back up to the level of sex we had when we were kids, but I'd like to try to bring at least a little of it back.

And actually, I have tried little by little to introduce the oldies and goodies back into our routine—although I haven't been that successful with it.

It was just the other day that I got it into my head to go down on Sue. Much to my surprise and total delight, she responded—and quite positively at that. I was feeling great. I thought at last we were getting somewhere. I got ahead of myself.

Because I perceived—or misperceived is more like it—myself to be on such a great roll, I decided why not try and turn it into a 69—you know, take advantage of the situation while it presented itself. Boy, was I wrong about that.

As soon as I pulled off my shorts and put myself into position, Sue got very upset and pulled away from me. 'This was supposed to be about me,' she scowled, 'why do you always have to make it about you?' I was confused. 'I was just doing it for us,' I told her, but she would not budge from her opinion that my actions were self-serving and nothing more. 'I don't even like 69,' she said. 'I never did. Didn't you know that? Why do you think we never do it anymore!'

I'm ashamed to admit that I must have been asleep at the wheel all these years as the fact that she just didn't like it was pretty much news to me. I tried to get her to tell me what she didn't like about it, but it seemed that door was already closed—actually, more like slammed as she left the bedroom in a huff.

Later that night, Sue came back to bed to talk. She explained that she didn't really like the 69 position because it took most of her concentration to focus on having her own orgasm. When it was time for hers, she wanted it to be all about her. She reminded me that I never had any issue with coming. She certainly had me dead to rights on that one. Also, Sue confessed that sometimes she just couldn't get comfortable enough in the position we generally did 69 in—on our sides—for her to focus on climaxing.

Taking all this in, I put my arm around her and told her we never had to do 69 ever again, but that I wasn't a mind-reader, and I don't know what she's thinking if she doesn't tell me. The resentment she must have been building over the years over this made my stomach start to knot. I also told her that if she ever wanted to try it again, that there were many ways we could vary the basic theme to ensure she'd be totally comfortable.

Once we talked it through, Sue openly told me that she wouldn't necessarily be totally against trying out 69 again in the future, just so long as I kept in my mind the things she told me. And she also made me promise that if we tried it again that I would at least make sure to give her a healthy head start …."

The Flipside

While 69 can be a wonderfully exciting, highly gratifying position, there are many, like Henry's wife, Sue, who simply don't like it for their own reasons. There's nothing wrong with that. The only time it's wrong not to like any given sex technique is to decide not to like it without even having tried it!

So what are some of the main reasons people get turned off of 69?

We all know that part of the fun of receiving oral sex is watching it—for men and women alike. Rare is the man who does not enjoy the sight of a woman going down on him; and many women get an extra-special thrill when they observe as well. So people with this particular preference may not be great fans of the 69 position, because essentially, while it's going on, you're pretty much limited to looking at what's right in front of you; what's going on "below" is generally a mystery. You only know it feels good. For some, just feeling the sensation of a warm mouth stimulating them while they return the favor just isn't enough.

Another complication some may have with the 69 position is that one party may be so incredibly stimulated that he or she may forget that there's also someone else involved in the same sex act with them, waiting to be stimulated. This sudden halt in the mutuality of the act can lead to a sense of frustration on the part of the partner who is still giving—and resentment if this kind of thing continually happens between them.

Another favorite complaint of the nay-sayers: lack of mobility. In the 69 position, man and woman are typically twisted into tight pretzels, without a lot of freedom of movement. However, no matter what position you and your partner are enjoying 69 in, you at least have a slight ability to do some light hip thrusting if desired. And really, what's the big need to move around a lot? Surely it's just as nice to simply lie there and enjoy it—isn't it? Some say no.

One of the most fun aspects of 69 is the one that causes the most frustration if it doesn't occur and that's the simultaneous orgasm. Some people put so much pressure on themselves to time this just right that if they fail to climax at the same time, they feel the whole experience has been a waste.

May we make a suggestion here? Let the label "wasted sexual experience" fall right out of your sexual vernacular right this very minute. Also, the word "pressure" must also fall out of your perception of all things sexual, and quickly at that. Sharing intimacy with a partner is not your job or a class. You are not being graded on your performance, nor will there be any raises for making an imagined sexual quota. Relax. Everything will fall into place, and if it doesn't, so what? Just enjoy yourselves. If one partner gets too excited too soon and can't wait for the other to catch up, we say that's show business. Better luck next time. And the one who couldn't hold out can always finish the other off right afterward.

> "I arrived last night. Right in time for English Department cocktails. The cock was mine. The tail belonged to a lovely young thing with a passion for D. H. Lawrence."
>
> —Charles Herman (Paul Bettany), A Beautiful Mind

The Rest of the Story

And now for the yay-sayers! You know that 69 is a treat to be savored and enjoyed—and we're going to try and show you how to enjoy it to its full potential!

You took your oral sex lessons in the previous two chapters, so by now, you should be well-practiced, geared up, and ready to take it to the next level.

First, the biggie: Many couples find it very exciting to time their orgasms to coincide. But this is not a perfect world, and because of that, more often than not, one member of the couple (normally the male—what a surprise!) may have a tendency to climax much more quickly than the other. We're not saying it's always like that: sometimes it's the woman who comes first—or who comes more than once in the time it takes her male partner to come once.

Of course, it's fun to at least try to come together, and for that reason, before you and your partner assume the 69 position, be honest with yourselves if one of you is more, um, trigger-happy than the other. If one of you—male or female—tends to get there first, even way ahead of the other one, start off with one-way oral sex. The quicker partner warms up the one who typically takes longer. A "head" start, if you will. When the slower partner has been brought to the appropriate boil, Speedy can then pivot his or her body into the 69 position and finish off their partner while getting finished off him- or herself. Now, once you're both at it, you can either lick and suck without giving it a second thought—and may the best man or woman win—or you can continue to pace yourselves till you both reach your climaxes.

To slow her down, take your mouth away repeatedly. Instead of tracing a steady rhythm of A through Z, sporadically skip a few letters and continue to randomly break rhythm. Don't do this too much, however. You certainly don't want her to slow down to a stop. To speed her up, take your cue about what feels best to her from what she's doing to you. Chances are, when she gets really enthusiastic with your member, you're probably doing something right. Keep doing it.

> "My mother never saw the irony in calling me a son-of-a-bitch."
>
> —Jack Nicholson

To slow him down, simply stop stimulating him, or, as is the case for slowing a woman down, sporadically break the rhythm of what you're doing. On the other hand, to speed him up, pull hard but not rough, and use massive amounts of tongue action—especially on the tip of his penis.

Positions

There are a few different ways to enjoy 69. Couples may have a tendency to use one of the positions to the exclusion of all others, which is just like having intercourse in the same position all the time. Boring. To really spice up your oral antics, you've got to switch it up at least every now and again.

The standard position—the old reliable of 69 positions—features man and woman lying on their sides, facing each other. As we learned in Chapters 20 and 21, on orally stimulating men and women, this is a very comfortable position as it alleviates neck and shoulder strain for both partners by providing those pillows—the insides of each other's thighs—on which to comfortably rest your heads.

Simultaneous and mutual oral stimulation is highly erotic.

(Hrana Janto)

The woman-on-top is the second most common position for reasons that will become obvious. In this position, each partner works from a comfortable vantage point of straight necks and backs. The woman rests on top, which is typically a good idea—especially if her partner significantly out weighs her. Also, when she is on top, she can control the pressure and movement on her clitoris by easily lifting or raising her hips over him.

The man-on-top 69 position is highly erotic and can be very dangerous for a couple if the man typically gets carried away in the heat of the moment. Initially when he's on top of her, he will remember to displace his weight on the bed or the floor so as not to crush her. However, the sheer mind-blowing excitement of stimulating his partner at the same time he's being stimulated may cause him to get a little carried away and forget about the weight he's supposed to be displacing. Ladies, if this happens to you, a surefire way not to get crushed is to stop what you're doing immediately. For obvious reasons, this position is not recommended if she is typically prone to gagging.

Sexploration Exercise #23

1. If you've never had anal sex, why not?
   a. I'm terrified of the pain.
   b. That's how people get AIDS.
   c. It's much too dirty for me.
   d. I've thought about it, but how would I ever bring that up with my partner?

2. If you've considered having anal sex but haven't yet, what is it that's holding you back from trying it?
   a. I just don't know how to go about asking for it.
   b. I asked for it and my partner was not receptive to the idea.
   c. My partner thinks it's too risky, even though I've explained all about how to keep this "dirty" act "clean."

3. If you and your partner do engage in anal sex, how frequently would you say that you have it this way?
   a. Every time almost. It's the best birth control method ever!
   b. About once a month. Just enough to shake things up a bit.
   c. Maybe just for special occasions, like his birthday.
   d. We've honestly only tried it a handful of times.

4. Aside from the obvious, how is having anal intercourse different than having vaginal intercourse?
   a. It's really hot because it seems really wrong, which makes it very exciting.
   b. My wife is much tighter there, which is very arousing.
   c. My husband really hits my G-spot during anal sex, which really gets me going. He doesn't have to go anywhere near my clitoris and I'll usually have an orgasm.
   d. There's really very little difference.

5. Do you use sex toys in anal sex?
   a. No. It doesn't seem like you can ever get them clean enough to use anywhere else.
   b. We usually use a butt plug as it enhances orgasms.
   c. Anal beads for her; a dildo for me.
   d. You name it, we've tried it!

chapter 23

Anal Sex

*"I just don't want to be known as the
'up-the-butt girl.'"*
—Charlotte York (Kristin Thomas), Sex and the City

The anus is an extremely sensitive, extremely intimate part of the body, and not something that interests everyone sexually. However, men and women alike have been known to experience wonderful pleasure by employing this most unlikely tool to sensuality.

In the most basic act of anal sex, the man's penis is inserted into the woman's anus, instead of into her vagina. However, many couples are known to engage in anal play that doesn't involve actual intercourse at all. We'll look at the various ways the anus can be used in sexual play throughout this chapter.

Alexis, 52

"My husband, Jack, and I tried anal sex exactly one time. I'm not even sure what possessed us to try it, but we learned pretty quickly that we are strictly front-door folks.

Actually, we know what got into us. One night, over coffee after a particularly wine-soaked dinner party we threw, someone started to talk about sex. And you know how it is—once someone sparks the conversation by bringing up the topic in a room full of drunks, everyone gets in on it, and without reservations or hang-ups or anything like that.

Our friends Philip and Louise had just started to have frequent anal sex. Louise admitted they had tried it long ago when they were kids, but never really took to it. But recently, they tried it again and actually really liked it. Amazingly, out of the four other couples we had invited to dine with us that night, three were actively and happily engaging in at least occasional anal sex—and they weren't me and Jack—that was for sure.

Later that night, when everyone finally left and we made a half-assed attempt at cleaning up, Jack asked me if I'd be interested in trying it out. Clearly, he pointed out, that if other of our middle-aged, well-respected-in-the-community friends were dabbling in it, it couldn't be that bad. With the same drunken logic, I couldn't help but agree. So we staggered up to the bedroom to see what all the hoopla was about.

We fell out of our clothes and onto the bed. Honestly, we were so turned-on by the prospect of trying something new after more than twenty-five years of marriage, we were like kids again.

And then we tried for what was supposed to be the grand finale and we just couldn't make it work. My body simply would not accept Jack. But we kept trying. When he finally made it in, I was in so much pain, he had to pull out again almost immediately.

I had spotted bleeding for a couple of days after the incident. Jack and I still scratch our heads at our friends and wonder why anyone could like that way to have sex!"

The Downside

Such as was the case with Alexis and Jack, anal sex is not for everyone. That they didn't approach the situation in the right frame of mind—they were drunk—and neglected to use proper lubrication may only have been part of the reason why it was something they did not enjoy, and would not ever consider trying again.

There are many factors that can make feelings about anal sex negative. For the very religious, the idea of anal sex may put into mind the prohibition against homosexuality. And even in our highly secular society, anal sex often violates the laws and mores against sodomy. Another problem with anal sex is that it can be very painful, especially if the anus is not properly lubricated when entered or entry is forced and happens too quickly.

There's a third problem with anal sex for individuals who are not in a long-term, committed relationship: the possibility of spreading HIV. Because the anus is not designed for the insertion of a penis, anal sex is the easiest way for a man to pass the HIV virus to a woman. The penis is likely to break tissue within the anus, and thus the HIV virus can pass easily from sperm into broken blood vessels. Therefore, it's recommended that couples who don't really know each other all that well or who are not monogamous with each other should abstain from anal sex.

The Upside

For all the negatives that people may feel about anal sex, those who love it and practice it often cannot necessarily be labeled sexual deviants. Especially in recent years, anal sex has a huge following. The thought of anal sex is dirty; when it comes to great sex, this is a plus for some and a minus for others.

Why does anal sex feel so good and why does it appeal to both women and men? Unlike the vagina, the anus wasn't designed for taking in a man's penis. For that reason, the walls of the anus and walls of the rectum are a much tighter fit than the walls of the vagina. Many men who practice anal sex love the sensation of total constriction that their penises experience inside a woman's anus.

On top of the physical, there's also an emotional aspect to anal intercourse. Men who enjoy playing a dominant role between the sheets may be especially attracted to the more intensified sense of domination anal sex brings them. On top of that, there's a sense of mystery, of forging unknown territory, of breaking away from the tried and the true. Additionally, men who enjoy anal sex may also get an extra erotic charge from the breaking of taboo associated with anal sex.

Women who enjoy anal sex have their own reasons. Especially after childbirth, the elasticity of a woman's vagina can be compromised, diminishing the sensation of the feeling of her lover's penis inside her. And even if she can adequately enjoy her lover's penis in her vagina, a woman can also enjoy the unusual sensation of a man's penis in her anus, for the same reasons a man may like it—including the sense of mystery, of breaking taboo, of the ultimate feeling of submission that comes with being penetrated anally.

Another aspect of anal sex that a woman may find especially attractive is that during anal penetration, the penis comes in fantastic contact with the woman's G-spot, even better than during vaginal intercourse, which, with every other physical and emotional thing going on, can produce one heck of an orgasm—especially if her lover reaches around and massages her clitoris while he penetrates her anally.

As we'll get into a little bit later in this chapter, and especially in more detail in Chapter 33, a penis is not the only thing that can be used in anal play. A tongue, a well-lubricated finger, or a specially designed sex toy are all contenders for exciting anal play—and also open up the playing ground for men and women alike.

The most important thing to remember with this variety of sex—and any for that matter—is that if your partner expresses discomfort about parts of your body or other objects being inserted into his or her anus, don't press the issue. There are so many other wonderful expressions of intimacy for you to share and enjoy with each other. If it's not good for both of you, relegate anal play to your fantasy life and leave it at that!

Getting to the, Um, Bottom of It

Before we get into the various ways to experience and enjoy anal sex, we must re-stress a point we made earlier in this book because it is very important that you never forget it. As we have seen throughout this section, there are several sexual positions that can offer very tempting, easy shifts from rear-entry vaginal sex to anal sex. However, that's not such a great idea, primarily for health-related reasons. Remember that certain bacteria that live in the anus simply do not belong in the vagina and will undoubtedly cause infection if transported there on a humid

penis. If you are going to engage in anal intercourse, be sure the penis—
or any other object that comes in contact with the vagina—and mouth—
are properly cleaned before used elsewhere. And that means soap and
water—a quick wipe on a nearby towel or tissue from a box on a night
stand simply won't do the trick.

Want to give your lover the orgasm of his or her life? Just as you are bringing your
lover to climax, insert your clean (nail neatly trimmed) index finger into your
lover's anus just as he or she is about to come. Your partner will find this a truly
electrifying experience. If you're performing oral sex on your partner, sticking
your tongue into your partner's anus will give your partner the same electrifying
sensation.

Also, and just as important, you must never, under any circumstances,
try and force a non-lubricated penis or other object into the anus. Anal
sex requires a huge degree of lubrication, for one, because the anus does
not secrete any natural lubrication like the vagina does. Also, because the
anus will typically be smaller and more constricting, with little to no
elasticity, it will not allow objects larger than it itself appears to penetrate. Only with proper, adequate lubrication will the anus comfortably
permit entry.

Forcing objects—from fingers to penises to what have you—into the
anus without proper lubrication will cause problems for women and men
alike. Unwarranted friction may cause the delicate tissue of the rectal
opening to tear. The tiny tears may very well escalate to painful anal fissures, which can wreak all kinds of havoc, including colitis, if the fissures
go untreated.

Be careful. And remember: You don't have to be having full-on anal sex
to enjoy milder elements of anal play. There are ways to capitalize on
anal stimulation in lovemaking, which threaten no harm to the anus at
all as penetration may not even be involved.

One thing we urge, as with any other sexual technique in this book, is
that if it doesn't violate any religious or moral tenets for you, that you
at least experiment with anal play. You may not like it at all; or, it may
intensify your sexual enjoyment so much that it becomes a staple of your

sex life. The point is that unless you try something at least once, you'll never know what you're missing.

Lubricants

Lubricants play an important role in sex, especially if it becomes useful or necessary to get some outside lubrication for vaginal sex—but especially for engaging in anal sex.

> "I don't like having anything inserted in my anus, even though it may come as a surprise."
>
> —Stanford Blatch (Willie Garson) Sex and the City

To find the one you like best, experiment with the various lubricants on the market. A word of caution: Whatever you choose, be sure that the lubricant does not contain nonyxodol-9. Nonyxodol-9 is derived from bleach, and while it is efficient at killing sperm, it has also recently been found to cause terribly painful damage to the delicate membranes and tissues inside the vagina and anus.

Assume the Position

The options for performing anal sex are more limited than for standard vaginal intercourse, but that doesn't mean, as is the case with any type of sex, that you can't spice it up with at least a little variety in positioning. In this section, we'll look at some of the positions in which you can enjoy anal sex. But don't let us limit you. Your sense of imagination and daring for experimentation may show you things we've never thought of in our wildest dreams! Of course, your mutual sense of comfort must always serve as your guide.

The most standard position for anal sex is rear-entry. Both partners can be kneeling on the bed—or even lying down, which is recommended at least for the first foray into this exotic erotic place. Or, for more advanced and experienced anal adventurers, both can be standing, perhaps with her bent over a chair.

If both partners will be lying down, she should be on her stomach with her legs fully extended toward the bottom of the bed and her ankles spread apart as far as they can go—like she's in the open position of a jumping jack—except, in this case, laying down. If kneeling or standing, it will also help for her to keep her ankles apart. When her legs are spread apart in this fashion, penetration is facilitated; when her ankles are together, penetration becomes more difficult. With a basically impenetrable space, this makes more than a little sense.

He kneels or stands between the backs of her legs, and with his fingers and a bottle or tube of water-based lube, he gently and thoroughly covers the outside and inside of her anus with the lubricant. Then, he makes sure to thoroughly lubricate his penis.

Gently, he should edge himself over her, until the tip of his penis is lined up with her anus. In vaginal sex, this is about the time when the man forgets what he's doing. As soon as the tip of his penis slips into the vagina, he generally pounds away happily into the night. This cannot and should not be the case with anal entry and penetration. He must remain gentle, careful, and cautious, until the whole of his shaft has been inserted into her—and even afterward. Essentially, until it becomes comfortable.

Men, start with the tip of your penis and gently ease it into her. You will feel resistance. This is totally normal, no matter how relaxed and comfortable she may be. Be patient; especially for the first time, it might take a while to fully immerse yourself. Stroke her hair and her back. If you are laying almost directly over her, whisper into her ear, kiss her face and head and back—whatever you can do to put her at ease. If she stops you, that means it's over. You won't be winning any points if you continue to try to force your way in if she calls the game over.

Women, you must also play an active role in what's going on. If you don't feel properly lubricated, speak up. If he's entering you too quickly, slow him down. This is not, we repeat, *not*, a way to have sex when you have limited time. If you feel like you're with someone who won't slow down for you, you're not with the right person. Do not get yourself in the position to try this type of sex if you feel like the person who will be having it with won't be able to stop if the need arises.

As he moves deeper and deeper inside of you in this way, a little discomfort will be normal. To alleviate some of the pressure if you are laying down, you might lift your hips off the bed, angling them in a more "welcoming" position—or even put a pillow under your belly to give your hips a better angle.

It is very important to remember that although he is in the position of domination in this act, you are ultimately in charge. If the penetration becomes too overwhelming or too uncomfortable for you, it's time to stop—picking up again at a later time or calling it off for good. It's your call.

More advanced participants in this sexual practice may opt to perform it missionary style. This is not recommended, however, if the woman has back or neck problems. The anus is lower than the vagina when a woman is on her back, and therefore, not as easily accessible.

To enter her anus from this position, no matter how low he positions his hips on the bed, it's more than likely that her hips will not be able to rest comfortably on the bed. She can put a small pillow underneath them to give them enough lift, but this may still result in strain on the lower back and especially on the neck. She can throw her ankles over his shoulders, but still, she might likely still cause herself some neck strain. It is recommended that unless both partners are exceptionally limber—which is more than likely not nearly as limber as we may have been twenty years ago—if this sexual technique is practiced, it be limited to rear-entry style.

Variations on Anal Stimulation

Penile penetration is one way to enjoy anal sex, but it isn't the only way. There are many ways you can bring this body part into the sexual arena—and some more daring and intimate than others.

One of the ways is to massage the anus with a finger—without entering it at all. When you are stimulating your male or female partner either manually or orally, take your thumb and line it up on your partner's anus. Gently rub in a clockwise or counterclockwise motion while you stimulate your partner in other ways.

Or, if you're feeling more daring, take it a step further. Instead of coasting around the outside of the anus while you're stimulating your lover in another way, insert a well-lubricated finger into your lover's anus just as he or she is about to come—a surefire way to intensify his or her orgasm.

If you're performing oral sex on your lover, and you've both just emerged from the shower or swimming pool, why not take the action a little further south. Orally stimulating your partner's anus is known as a "rim job" or a "smoothie," and can be very pleasurable if both parties are up to it. It is certainly not an option for the most sexually squeamish. However, the feeling is indescribably pleasurable, and it may be something the anally adventurous might want to try.

Finally, you can use any number of sex toys for anal play. The main word here—as with all anal play—applies and then some: lubrication. Men and women both have been known to enjoy being stimulated anally by sex toys, from vibrators to butt plugs to anal beads and beyond. For men, sex toys can be used anally to stimulate the prostate gland, making for more intense orgasms; for women, sex toys used anally can work to stimulate the G-spot.

Most sex toys are made from resilient plastic or other harder substances—including, remarkably, glass—and are in no way as malleable as a human penis or finger, no matter how soft and pliable they are made to be. In that case, using lots and lots of lube for anal play with sex toys is highly recommended. We'll learn more about sex toys in Chapter 33 where you learn why batteries were really invented!

Sexploration Exercise #24

1. When's the last time you and your partner had a good old-fashioned "quickie"—not a quick roll in the hay because you were tired and felt obligated, but a sexual experience you just had to have at a random moment because you just couldn't control yourselves?
   a. I'd say not since we were dating. We have quickies now just because we're too tired for much else.
   b. At least once a month if not more, my partner does something I find so crazily sexy, I can't help but jump on her—no matter where we are.
   c. I don't think we've ever done that.
   d. We just started seeing each other after we each had a significantly long dry spell—so our answer would be all the time.

2. When you do have "quickie" sex, who usually initiates it?
   a. He does.
   b. She does.
   c. It can go either way.
   d. Neither of us initiates quickie sex.

3. Do you feel like "quickie" sex has replaced "quality" sex in your relationship?
   a. Yes. We never seem to have long love-making sessions anymore. It's always "wham, bam, thank you ma'am."
   b. Sometimes I do. I think because we've been having so much quickie sex, my husband's gotten lazy and won't work for the good stuff these days.
   c. Not "replaced," more like "enhanced!"
   d. Not really. Every now and then, if we want to have sex and we really don't have the time, we squeeze in a quickie—no sweat.

4. Where's the most exciting place you and your partner have ever shared a quickie?
   a. In the car before dropping my wife at the airport for a business trip.
   b. In the dressing room of a department store. The attendant must not have seen my husband sneak in!
   c. In the kitchen while we were throwing a dinner party.
   d. At the ninth hole of the golf course while we waited for our friends to catch up with us.

chapter 24

The Art of the Quickie

*"Sex and golf are the two things you can enjoy even
if you're not good at them."*
—Roy *"Tin Cup" McAvoy (Kevin Costner),* Tin Cup

When it comes to quickies, there's both good news and bad
news. Which would you like to hear first? The good news?
Naturally! The good news about having quickie sex is that it
can be the sign of a great sex life getting even better. When
things are good, quickie sex indicates that you've got two
people who can't keep their hands, or much else, off of each
other. They grab at each other every chance they get or, better still, they make chances to enjoy a brief interlude of sex,
often ten minutes or less, before returning to the other facets
of their lives. Quickie sex for happy couples occurs while getting dressed for work, in the shower, in the kitchen while
preparing dinner, and even in some intriguing public places.
We'll get more into that in Part 4.

And then there's the bad news: Quickie sex can also be the
sign of a declining sexual relationship. The nature of quickie
sex means that there is little romantic preparation, if any—
no bubble baths, no candles—making the quickie more like
junk food as opposed to an impeccably presented full-course

gourmet meal. It points to a relationship on the decline if it's pretty much the only kind of sex the couple has.

In this chapter, we'll look at when quickies are good—and when they're a sign of something really bad—and we'll give you tips for making the most of good, cheap, raw, quick sex with the one you lust after the most!

Fiona, 46

"When after three years of going together my boyfriend, Evan, started jumping me almost constantly—and in the weirdest places—I thought he was finally starting to realize that we were meant to be together and that he was going to be proposing marriage soon. I could not have been more wrong!

What was really going on was that he met someone else, this Ellen person, and that all the long, languorous lovemaking he used to do with me, he was now doing with her. He wasn't having all that mad, impetuous sex with me because he was unbelievably turned on, it was because he was (a) exhausted from being with her, and (b) feeling unbelievably guilty. I'm only sorry it took me so long to see the truth.

The signs were there. I'd fend him off sometimes, telling him I wasn't ready. He'd just trudge on without any regard to my even being wet enough to accept him—and forget about waiting for me to have my orgasm!

I've been in relationships before. And I've had quickies before—lots of them—but they always happened in the beginning of the relationship. I loved the feeling of not being able to keep my hands off the other person, and him not being able to control himself about being on top of me. I guess I was just hoping this was what was happening with me and Evan. I guess I should have been smarter—I should have kept my eyes open.

I'm still reeling from that breakup, so I'm not exactly ready to date anyone new yet, but one thing I promise myself is to not let my last experience tarnish the excitement of quickies. I'll just be smarter about it the next time!"

On Your Mark, Get Set—Is It Over Already?

We've said it many times, but especially in the case of the quickie, it begs repeating: Men, you may want to recognize that your partner's sexuality is not as easily or quickly as ignited as yours. John Gray suggests that men think about how many minutes it takes them to become sexually ravenous and then add a zero to that figure to understand a woman's sexual response.

Yes, a quickie can be both enjoyable and orgasmic for both parties, but brevity generally favors the man. A man should properly express his gratitude to a woman who offers him quickie sex by saving time and energy for the sort of longer, more deeply fulfilling lovemaking sessions that she might prefer.

Quickies are not about love notes, flowers, candy, and romantically inscribed helium balloons. This is sex at its most raw and compelling. Grrrrrrrr!

Are Quickies for Everyone?

Of course, quickie sex is not for everyone—just like oral and anal sex and other ways to express passion are not for everyone—but it's certainly not just for men. Far from it. A woman who initiates quickie sex is likely to get a positive reaction on an average of, say, 10 out of 10 times. And another advantage of the quickie: It is all too easy for couples, especially long-term couples, to fall out of the habit of making love, and the quickie can be a wonderful tool for bringing back sexual excitement into an otherwise sleepy romance.

Carole Pasahow, a sex and marital therapist, told *Redbook Magazine* that a couple should schedule a 30-minute fantasy encounter during which no touching is permitted. Instead, they simply tell each other all the things they would like to do to each other, or have done to them. This is followed up with two 10-minute physical encounters (we know them as "quickies"). Pasahow reports that both the quantity and quality of sex leaps upward when a couple

> "*Suzanne, if sex were fast food, there'd be an arch over your bed!*"
>
> —*Julia Sugarbaker (Dixie Carter),* Designing Women

conducts these three sessions. Pasahow urges, and we second the notion, that a couple try never to do the same thing twice in a row.

Ernest, 52

"This weekend, my new girlfriend, Cheryl, reminded me what is was like to be a college kid again, all full of lust and with no regard for rules, regulations, or respect for proper place and time of any kind all over again. And again. And again. Of course, it doesn't hurt that where she showed me was at my thirty-year college reunion—and that Cheryl just happened to have been a college girlfriend!

I guess a little background is in order here. You see, Cheryl and I met when I was a sophomore and she was a senior in college. We were in the same finance class together and man, was she beautiful! Still is, actually. Anyway, I thought she was totally untouchable. Not only was she breathtaking, she was an upperclassman—and taken. What was she going to want with a kid like me?

Yes, Cheryl had a boyfriend when I met her. Eric was a finance major, on the fast track to corporate wunderkind, and he was only taking this class we were in so he could coast through his last semester and use up some credits. He already had a job lined up and everything. Cheryl was taking the class to be with him. And me, well I was taking the class because I was still trying to find out what it was I wanted to be when I graduated. It turns out finance was not going to be for me, but that's another story.

Anyway, as the semester rolled on, I developed a stronger and deeper crush on Cheryl, and she seemed to be getting only closer to Eric. Word in the dorm was they were going to get married after graduation, so I kept my romance with Cheryl alive and well in my fantasy life—and nowhere else. Jeez, she even sat next to me and never even acknowledged me. Until one fateful day when she came in with a tear-streaked face and murder in her eyes, that is.

Apparently, Eric had cheated on her that weekend at one of the frat parties she hated going to. I watched her suffer that whole class, which, fortuitously, Eric did not happen to be present for. Around the end of the class, I guess Cheryl couldn't hold it in anymore and she started to cry, forcing herself, unsuccessfully, to keep it quiet. Because I sat right next to her, and because I always had my eyes on her, I noticed, and passed her a tissue. She thanked me and eventually she calmed down. After class, she found me in the library and thanked me for my kind gesture. I asked her if she wanted to talk about it, and I guess from that moment, we forged a friendship. I had no idea it was going to lead to more than that.

One night, during one of our many night-long talks, Cheryl jumped my bones. I didn't want to take advantage of her, but she insisted. She was so angry at Eric, so the sex was explosive. I knew she was probably using me, but I didn't care. I'd pick up the pieces of my broken heart later.

That one night eventually led to a crazy succession of sexcapades, which became the wildest sex I had ever had in my life. We did it everywhere—the laundry room, in the stairwell, in a phone booth late at night—it didn't matter. One day, we even did it in the classroom just before the other members of our finance class rolled in, including Eric. I think he was suspicious, but I didn't care. I was on top of the world.

And then came the crash.

Apparently, one weekend while I went home for a visit, Cheryl and Eric made up. I was sad that my days as her red-hot lover were over, but if she was happy, that's really all that mattered to me.

After graduation, Eric and Cheryl were married as planned. I went on with my life, eventually got married myself. By the time the reunion came up, I was already divorced.

Now you have to imagine that I was shocked to see Cheryl there. Remember, she was a couple of years older than me. When we met up, she told me she had crashed the reunion hoping to run into me. Apparently, she was also divorced. Years earlier, she had given up on Eric after what was probably his hundredth affair with a new secretary. So that was it. We were both free—and we were both feeling wild.

So that weekend, we reenacted our antics of that semester. Cheryl was still as quick to respond sexually as ever—even at fifty-four—and we banged our way through memory lane, from the laundry room to the phone booth, magically still standing, to our old classroom.

After the reunion, we exchanged phone numbers and she promised she wasn't going to screw things up again like she had all those years ago. In fact, I'm even going to see her tonight!"

Sally Albright: "Most women at one time or another have faked it."

Harry Burns: "Well, they haven't faked it with me."

Sally Albright: "How do you know?"

Harry Burns: "Because I know."

Sally Albright: "Oh. Right. That's right. I forgot. You're a man."

—Meg Ryan and Billy Crystal, *When Harry Met Sally*

---

part **4**

Have More Fun in Bed—
or Wherever!

Sexploration Exercise #25

1. Do you focus on your breathing when you're in bed with your partner?
   a. Sometimes I try, but I get so excited, breathing is the last thing I'm thinking about.
   b. Usually. I find that by controlling my breathing, I can sometimes pace myself to not climax too early and wait for my partner to catch up to me.
   c. Always. The best way for me to climax simultaneously with my partner is to breathe at the same pace at him.
   d. Why would I focus on something as automatic as breathing when there are so many other wonderful things going on in bed?

2. Have you and your partner ever tried to synchronize your breathing to perfect your performance?
   a. When we first tried tantric sex, we used to do those kinds of exercises all the time.
   b. Not really. Sometimes when we remember to do it, we can really connect—but we don't remember that often.
   c. All the time. I love the feeling of really being one with my partner, and breathing in sync really makes that possible.
   d. No. We're too busy having fun to think too much about something like breathing together.

3. Do you focus on your partner's breathing in bed?
   a. Oh yes. My husband is very quiet in bed, but I can tell by the pace of his breathing what he's really enjoying and what he isn't.
   b. The way my wife breathes in bed is very sexy. The more aroused she becomes and the closer to orgasm she gets, the more deep and heavy her breaths become.
   c. My partner's very vocal and loud, so I'd say that probably distracts me from the breathing thing.
   d. If I focus too much on too many elements, I get overly excited and much too soon, so I usually don't consider breathing—mine or my partner's—very much at all during sex.

4. Have you ever used breathing exercises to prolong an orgasm?
   a. The best day of my life was the day I learned a breathing exercise to stretch out the duration of an orgasm.
   b. That sounds like a lot of work to me. I like my orgasms just as they are.
   c. No, but it sure sounds like something I'd like to try!
   d. I've tried several of these exercises but nothing ever seems to work for me.

5. What's the likelihood that you and your partner are going to try out some of the sample breathing exercises in this chapter?
   a. Fairly good.
   b. I'd like for us to at least try one.
   c. I'd like for it to happen—but convincing my husband may be another story.
   d. We might as well stop reading here. I'm sure that my wife will never go for it.

chapter 25

Better Sex Through Breathing

"Okay, Robert, you want to know the advantages of marriage? Fine .... There's .... Uh .... Okay! Here! Got it! You know when you fall asleep and you stop breathing? When you're married, there's always somebody there to nudge you back to life .... That's not a good example ...."

—Ray Barone (Ray Romano), Everybody Loves Raymond

The simple act of breathing actually says much about who we are and how we live. When we are breathing in the manner most conducive to health and wellness, we are breathing deeply, from the diaphragm, like yoga students or opera stars. When our breath is shallow, it's because we are tense. Shallow breathing means less oxygen to the brain. The less oxygen the brain gets, the tenser we feel.

The ultimate end of this vicious cycle is the panic attack, when we get so little oxygen into our system that we actually think we are dying of a heart attack. That's no fun. And yet, the way we live produces so much tension that we may find ourselves breathing in a tight, tense manner all day long. And even during sex.

But that shouldn't be, which is why we're here to make some changes. In this chapter, we offer suggestions and solutions for breathing differently, which will hopefully improve the quality of your sex life—and your life in general, for that matter!

Lillian, 44

"I know this is hard to believe, but I have to attribute my divorce last year as the reason I now have the most incredible, life-affirming, powerful, and long-lasting orgasms I've ever had in my life. Okay—so maybe it's not as cut and dried as that. Let me explain.

You see, I was devastated when Deck told me he was leaving me. We had been together since school. He was the only man I had ever loved. Well, apparently, I wasn't the only woman he had ever loved. … Though I didn't find out right away, I would soon be in for the shock of my life when I learned he had left me for Judy—twenty-nine years old, petite and firm, and sleeping with my husband.

Everything happened so fast, my head was spinning. I was so broken and so shaken that I was having dizzy spells and nearly fainting every single day. One night he was sharing our bed with me, even having sex with me; the next night, he was gone, along with most of his stuff. I was in pieces.

A concerned friend finally suggested I see someone—a psychologist or social worker, just to get me back on track, and maybe prescribe something to take the edge off the anxiety. My work was starting to suffer, after all, and if I was going to be relying on one income and probably needing to pay a lawyer and God knows what else was going to come up, there was just no way I could lose my job and survive.

I ended up going to a bunch of different therapists, and I didn't like any of them. There was one woman who tried to blame me for what had happened. Another guy suggested that Deck just needed to sow some wild oats with a fresh partner for a while—a mid-life crisis thing—and that he'd be back. Another put me on antidepressants that made me so depressed, I nearly lost the will to live. And worse yet, this bounce from shrink to shrink went on for months. I was fit to be tied.

Then I started seeing Sharon, who seemed more sympathetic to my plight—and who really listened without passing judgment on me. Best of all, she didn't prescribe any medication for me. She said that my condition was being brought on by stress, and if I could take measures to help myself eliminate stress, then the dizziness and near-fainting would probably stop.

Sharon recommended I take some classes on breathing ... and then I thought she was as nuts as the rest of them. I asked her: 'Breathing, right. That involuntary process my body conducts to keep me alive from one wretched day to the next?' Sharon laughed. 'No,' she replied. 'What I meant was a class on using breathing exercises to help you to eliminate stress.' She had lost me. 'You know, like new age therapy?' But I still had no idea what she was talking about.

Eventually, the ever-patient Sharon whipped out a brochure. 'Here,' she said as she handed it to me. 'Go through this and tell me what you think when you come back this Thursday.'

The brochure was for a wellness center, which actually offered classes in breathing. I decided to take a chance on it and I enrolled in the class.

Within a couple of weeks, I was starting to feel better again. Sharon noted the change in my condition and congratulated me for moving forward. She then asked me if I had considered dating yet. 'Dating?' I questioned her. 'Oh God, no. I'm not ready for that yet.' She agreed, but then suggested that I at least masturbate no less than once a week. I was starting to get uncomfortable with her, which she must have sensed because she said almost right after she made the suggestion that she only meant it because she believed a healthy sex life—whether with yourself or another person—is a surefire way to relieve stress. And she added: 'Try it with the breathing exercises you've learned. Believe me, you won't be disappointed.'

Later that night, I decided to see if she was right. I ran myself a long hot bath and lit candles all around. I poured myself a nice tall glass of white wine and soaked in the bath for a while. I began masturbating, and as I did, I also practiced some of the breathing I had learned.

'Holy cow!' is all I can say. That night, I had the most wonderful and satisfying orgasms—yes, more than one—which completely blew away the short spasms I had sometimes had with my husband. I found myself thinking that it would really be nice to share this kind of thing with someone again. I was definitely on the mend, and all thanks to some good advice and some great breathing!"

In and Out

As we learned in Chapter 19, one of the benefits of using breathing in sex is that it helps prolong and sustain orgasms. But there's more to it than that.

When we exercise, proper breathing plays a crucial role in our stamina, endurance, and overall workout. Why should it be any different for sex? Think about it: Sex is exercise after all—and it's some of the best exercising there is. If you asked a group of people if they'd rather be pumping away at an exercise bicycle or pumping away at their lovers, most people would probably opt for the latter. So why not give up that hour at the gym tonight and spend it in bed with your lover, getting the workout of your life!

Getting back to the exercise element of sex, how we breathe during sex is very comparable to the way we breathe during a strenuous workout. The best way to breathe during sex is to inhale through your nose, and deeply. As any athlete will tell you, when you inhale through your mouth while exercising, you set into motion the same physiological process that happens when you are gasping for breath. Mouth breathing during any athletic activity cues the body to believe that it is not getting the smooth, steady flow of oxygen that it needs in order to compete at its highest level. Failure to breathe with your mouth closed is actually one of the surprising causes of fatigue.

For that reason, whether you're in bed, on the exercise bike, or sitting at your desk at work, get in the habit of breathing in through your nose. This will give you a much smoother, steadier supply of oxygen, which, after all, is the purest fuel for the human body. Think about it: We can live without water (which is one-third oxygen) a heck of a lot longer than we can live without breathing.

And once you've gotten your breathing pattern down, start taking languorous, relaxed deep breaths while you are making love. This will slow down your physiological response, and decrease the sense of tension and anxiety that so often leads to premature ejaculation for men, as well as the stress for women when they do not feel that they are achieving orgasm quickly enough.

So if you inhale through your nose, where do you exhale? Your choice; however, it is mostly recommended if you are in an intense exercise session—a mile on the treadmill or moving into your fourth sexual position of that session come to mind—that you do exhale through your mouth.

Whether you exhale through your nose or mouth, make a little "mmm" sound with your lips as you exhale. Athletes use this device as a means of increasing the quality of their breathing and performance. We can't tell you how or why it works, only that it works enormously.

If you are finishing up your erotic exercise session, or working towards being very close to orgasm, you'll want to do all your breathing through your nose. Why? Breathing exclusively through the nose will make your orgasms more intense, and you don't have to read any books or manuals (other than this one) in order to perfect the technique.

And remember, in sex, it's not just a matter of breathing through your nose; you must also breathe deeply. Air is free. Take it all the way into the diaphragm, hold it there, and then release it. A series of deep breaths followed by holding the breath in, followed by even longer exhalations, has the effect of cleansing the entire system. It's a great way for the lungs to carry off any of the toxins we take into our bodies on any given day. The cleansing treatment will also put you in a relaxed frame of mind as you approach a session of lovemaking.

> "Sex and death. Two things that come once in a lifetime. But at least after death you are not nauseous."
>
> —Miles Monroe (Woody Allen), Sleeper

Breathing Exercises

Now let's talk about a few other breathing exercises that you alone, or with your partner, may care to try. Keep in mind that deep breathing helps us move from the level of thought (how we operate the rest of the day) to the level of sensation, a thought-free zone into which sex ushers us. We'd like to share with you three techniques for deepening your breathing, and thus your pleasure, as well.

Advanced Breathing Technique #1

Here's a theatrical exercise you might actually remember from your high school drama class.

Lie down, close your eyes, and take deep breaths. Start at the top of your head, and relax every part of your body with each successive thought:

1. Breathe in, and relax your scalp.
2. Breathe in, and relax your forehead.
3. Breathe in, and relax your eyes.
4. Breathe in, and relax your nose.
5. Breathe in, and relax your jaw.
6. And so on down your arms, your trunk, your legs, and your toes.

It's amazing just how much tension we drag into our sex lives. The more tension we can diffuse prior to making love, the better the sex.

Advanced Breathing Technique #2

This is the yoga method of breathing known as "breath of fire."

Sit up straight or lie on your back, close your eyes, breathe in deeply, and then snort repeatedly through your nose. As you snort, forcibly contract your diaphragm. Repeat a dozen times running—a dozen inhalations, a dozen diaphragm contractions and snorts—and you'll picture yourself on the banks of the Ganges, wearing nothing but a loin cloth, ready to make love in the noonday sun.

> "I'm an experienced woman. I've been around. ... Well, alright, I might not've been around, but I've been ... nearby."
>
> —Mary Richards (Mary Tyler Moore), The Mary Tyler Moore Show

Advanced Breathing Technique #3

This comes to us all the way from www.breathing.com, where Gary Hagman, described as a "San Francisco master body worker," offers tips on sex and breathing. According to Mr. Hagman, lovers should warm up for sex by sitting together and scanning their bodies—checking in, as it were, with each of the parts of their bodies. This may come as a new idea, but don't let that scare you. Sit quietly and listen to the signals that your body might give you, if only we would listen to them. Where are we tense? Where do we feel a significant amount of resistance or frustration?

Take some time to notice these places of tension. Then ask your partner to place his or her hands on those tense spots. Nothing more than touching is required. Hagman writes that the idea is not to manipulate, massage, or zap, but to invite compassion, respect, and feeling. Most of us are out of touch with our own bodies. Imagine how much more so we are unaware of what goes on in our lover's body.

Of these three breathing exercises, the first two can be performed alone or with your partner. The extra level of relaxation experienced by virtue of breathing deeply, going within, and getting quiet will put the wind at your back as you seek to increase your combined pleasure. Of course, that's if your partner is willing. If your partner feels self-conscious about doing these exercises, but you feel strongly about continuing, tell him or her that if he or she does this with you, you will do something for him that will more than make it worth his while.

Breathe deeply during sex, and practice breathing with your mouth closed. And you'll find, as the yogis have known for millennia, that more deeply enjoyable sex is in the very air we breathe.

Sexploration Exercise #26

1. Do you ever talk dirty to your partner?
   a. I try to, but he usually gets squirrelly about it.
   b. I'd love to, but I don't know how to get started.
   c. I never would. She's much too conservative for that.
   d. All the time—it helps her climax.

2. Does your partner ever talk dirty to you?
   a. Usually. It's very hot.
   b. He's tried to before, but I just find it gross.
   c. I don't imagine that's something she would ever do in a million years.
   d. Sometimes—and I wish it would be more!

3. If you don't talk dirty to one another and you'd like to try it, which partner do you think will be most into it?
   a. Definitely him.
   b. Definitely her.
   c. Neither of us.
   d. Who knows—after reading this chapter, it could be either of us or both.

4. Have you ever said filthy things to yourself in your head during sex?
   a. Yes, if my partner won't, then saying these things in my head really gets me going.
   b. I never thought about trying that, but I think tonight I might.
   c. Not ever. I have enough to worry about without listening to a lot of voices in my head.
   d. Sometimes—it just gives that little added enhancement needed to push me over the edge.

5. Do you have a favorite dirty word or phrase?
   a. Oh yes, but I'll never tell what it is.
   b. My partner definitely knows it—and uses it often.
   c. I like them all.
   d. I just don't stand for that kind of filthy talk.

chapter 26

Talking Dirty

"Hell, I'd be happy to just find a girl that would talk dirty to me."
—*Goose (Anthony Edwards),* Top Gun

We've all been there: enjoying the feeling of the extreme closeness of our lover's body while getting swept up in the passion, slowly building to climax. And then, out of nowhere, our lover says something to us and somehow we find ourselves driven over the edge. Of course, it all depends on what he or she says.

In bed, talking dirty gets you hot. It's really as basic as that. All of your senses are involved in the act of making love, so when your lover talks dirty to you, it's like a perfectly timed caress or kiss; what you hear is simply another way to be stimulated. Of course, dirty talk can also be a source of humor and a way to alleviate the mounting tension of an intense moment. Certainly, at times there's nothing like a good giggle to bring you closer to your partner and to remind you that what you're doing in that bed should first and foremost be fun!

Of course, just like any of the other suggestions we've made in this book, talking dirty is not for everyone. If you feel self-conscious about saying bad words in front of your lover, then don't do it. You can have perfectly great sex without it. If that is the case, you'll likely want to skip ahead to the next chapter now. If hearing naughty words from your partner is a source of embarrassment for you, you certainly don't want to put yourself in a situation to hear it from strangers.

And that leads us to this crucial word of warning: This chapter may contain language that some may feel is offensive and objectionable. If you have issues with vulgar language, chances are, you'll have skipped this chapter already. If, however, somehow you've made it this far, we must tell you now that there will be words here you don't want to see. If you're on the fence, head to the next chapter. We'll meet you there.

Okay, this is your last chance to turn to the next chapter. Don't say you weren't warned. Just be sure you have your sense of humor—and adventure—firmly intact before you read on!

Charlotte, 52

"My husband, Bob, is so straight-laced, you wouldn't believe it. He's the type that wears a jacket and tie to work every day, even though the rest of his office went casual years ago. He always wears white dress shirts and never colors because he thinks colored dress shirts are 'flashy.' You can imagine how boring his ties are! And if you think that's buttoned-up enough for you, get this: Bob is so conservative, doesn't even like cable TV because he thinks it's immoral, which neither myself or my kids have ever been able to figure out, but we've respected his wishes and gone without it.

So no one could ever blame me that the first time he used a dirty word in bed, I nearly fell on the floor laughing.

My poor husband. I didn't mean to hurt his feelings like that—or make him feel embarrassed that he's finally taken a chance. But the more he reacted, the more I laughed. It was getting really bad. He turned beet red. I had to convince him I liked him talking to me the way he had, I was just taken off guard as I never in a million years would have suspected he ever would. Of course I was surprised. Who wouldn't be?

After lots of comforting and convincing, he finally became relaxed again and we got back into the action. I asked him to say the word again, but he wouldn't. I begged, but he told me no. But I didn't give up. Finally my insistence won him over and he whispered the word into my ear. I didn't laugh. Then he did it again, and added a few more he had thought of, and all I could do was go more and more crazy at the sound of every word. And he knew it. 'You like that?' he asked me. 'You like when a man talks dirty to you when he's doing you?' And of course all I could do was nod. 'You dirty little slut,' he said to me, and it was all I could do not to climax right then and there. 'You filthy little whore,' he said to me while he pounded in and out of me. And I *loved* it.

I still can't say I loved it as much as he loves it when I talk dirty to him—which, I know, is how he must have gotten inspired to do it in the first place.

You see, I have always loved talking dirty—even just talking in general. I'm what you'd call a very verbal person I guess. I talk through everything all the time. I talk to myself—or anyone who will listen to me. My husband tells me I even talk in my sleep, but he'll never tell me what I say! Which is why I guess I love talking in bed. It's just natural to me. It feels really good. When Bob is on top of me, and I scream out 'harder' 'deeper,' 'faster'—I just lose all control. And the dirtier I get, the more insistent his thrusts get—and the more worked up I get, which means the dirtier my talk gets and …. You get it!

I'm always happy when I learn a new word or phrase because I see with Bob that the more surprised he gets, the more turned-on he gets. I think of talking dirty like a jockey hitting a horse with a whip during a race. Maybe I ought to get a whip!

Well, we'll probably have to work a few more years to get up to that point! But I'm just so glad he's decided to join me in my dirty talk. I feel like it really brings us closer together. I can't wait to see what kinds of adventures lie ahead of us. And who knows? This week, smut speak, next week, casual Fridays? I guess we'll just have to find out!"

"There may be some things that are better than sex, and there may be some things that are worse. But there is nothing exactly like it."

— *W. C. Fields*

Free Speech

There are so many reasons to bring dirty talk into your sex life. As happens with all of us, the mundane routine of daily life has a tendency to get in the way sometimes, and we are all prone to sometimes taking ourselves just a little bit too seriously. Dirty talk can help. So while shouting out "Deeper!" or "Harder!" or "Suck it, you filthy wench!" during sex can fuel your fantasies, it can also help you and your partner take yourselves just a little less seriously. Especially if you've known your partner for a long time and generally have a lot of laughs together to begin with, the filthier you speak to one another, the harder it may be to take yourselves seriously, and the more fun you're going to have.

The bedroom is a place where titles, resumes, and other impertinences of modern life simply don't matter. And when two people can comfortably laugh while they're in bed together, then their relationship has what it takes to last.

Another great reason to talk dirty is that it can help you gear up for fantasy and role play—and, you can also be a little mischievous as well. Try whispering sexy sweet-nothings in your lover's ear when you're out in public together. You can make a boring school meeting or social gathering that much more interesting. Pretend to whisper something else into your lover's ear when you're really saying something like "I can't stop thinking about your big throbbing cock" or "When we get home, I'm going to bend you over the dining room table and pummel you into next Tuesday." Who knows? You might find yourselves all revved up and ready for a quickie! Perhaps you'll be inspired to sneak away and enjoy some salacious stand-up sex.

If you have a long ride home, talking dirty to one another will not only make the car trip seem faster, it will also build you up to an immediate release of sexual energy when you finally get home. In this forum—if you are alone in the car, naturally—you can speak out loud and proud, and even get insistent and demanding if the mood strikes. She can role-play as his dominatrix, and tell him that he's not been a very good slave. That when they get home, he will have to find all kinds of ways to make it up to her and get back into her good graces. He can pretend she's a streetwalker he's just picked up, and recite a laundry list of the things he expects from her.

As always with the most fun sex, your imagination will always be your guide. Let loose and be free with the dirty things you say; your lover's unquenchable desire will be your reward.

Smut Speak 101

If you've never tried talking dirty before, why not make tonight the night? Maybe you've been hesitant because you're not quite sure how to go about it—or you don't know what to say. You're in luck. In this section, we'll give you pointers on how to drive your partner absolutely wild with words.

So how do you start talking dirty? Our advice: Start small. Just use one dirty word—insert your choice here—and gauge your partner's reaction. Did he laugh? Did she get really freaked out, slap you across the face, and threaten to leave you? Did she respond with some dirty talk of her own? If you got a positive response, advance to more words, phrases, commands—whatever you can cook up in that brain of yours.

What can you say? There are lots of things—but there are at least two things you must never utter, no matter what kind of situation you are in. These two bedroom buzz killers? Don't call out someone else's name and never, under any circumstances make sexual comparisons with a previous lover. You can think it; just don't let it slip past your lips!

Also, remember to keep the sex talk credible. Ladies, telling a man that he's "huge" when you both know he isn't can be a deflating experience. Simply telling him that "his cock is magnificent" or that you "love the way he feels inside you," whether he's huge or average, should suffice—and quite nicely. Similarly, guys, you'll never go wrong telling a woman "Your body makes me crazy." Naming

"Loretta, I love you. Not like they told you love is, and I didn't know this either, but love don't make things nice—it ruins everything. It breaks your heart. It makes things a mess. We aren't here to make things perfect. The snowflakes are perfect. The stars are perfect. Not us. Not us! We are here to ruin ourselves and to break our hearts and love the wrong people and die. The storybooks are bullshit. Now I want you to come upstairs with me and get in my bed!"

—*Ronny Cammareri (Nicholas Cage),* Moonstruck

specific body parts could actually make her feel more self-conscious than appreciated, worrying about the parts you haven't specifically named.

Casey, 54

"There's nothing in the world I love more than a woman who gets all hot and crazy when I talk dirty to her in bed. When I'm there, in the moment, I just get nuts and I can't control myself. The words just pop out. But when she loves it, too—oh man, is that sex ever hot!

My first wife, Nellie, hated when I talked dirty to her. I always tried to respect her wishes and preferences, but every now and then, I'd let something slip, and holy cow was I ever in for it! Okay, sometimes I let it slip on purpose, but those times, it really seemed she'd be in to it, you gotta believe me. It was especially at those times she'd either slap me across the face, jump right out of bed, or even just start crying. That was the worst thing that could happen. I always felt like such a jerk when she cried.

The marriage had lots of other problems, though. It wasn't just about the sex. We wanted different things. She was kind of stuck in this 1950s place, like where her parents were—at least where they pretended to be. She wanted a domestic wonderland, where people behaved appropriately and followed the rules. I guess I wanted to be an animal—in her terms at least.

After Nellie, I went through a period of meaningless sex with meaningless women. Years and years and years of nameless faces and bodies. And yeah, sure I could talk to them till I was blue in the face. But it just didn't have the same effect as talking filth to someone you love. And then I met Virginia.

From the moment I met her, I knew she was my perfect match. We were both at some work function. I can't lie—even though I know how cliché this sounds—but our eyes really did meet across a crowded room. We were both involved in other conversations, but we couldn't help noticing each other. When we finally met up, we eventually found a few minutes to be alone. She smiled at me and said, 'I know you like me.' I didn't like being put on the spot like that, so I asked her: 'And how do you know that?' She took a sip of her drink and coyly smiled. 'Because I couldn't keep my eyes off your dick.' She nodded down to my undeniably erect penis. 'The cock never lies.'

She had me dead to rights. If she had a mouth like that in a public place with all her clothes on, I couldn't imagine what She was like in bed. I had to have her. My guess was right: She was a sailor—and nearly worse than me! More than ten years later, Virginia and I share a house, two kids, and a sexual dialogue that has never gone flat!"

> "*I'm going to the backseat of my car with the woman I love, and I won't be back for TEN MINUTES.*"
>
> —*Homer Simpson*, The Simpsons

Sexploration Exercise #27

1. Do you have sexual fantasies?
   a. Every minute of every day.
   b. Sometimes a sexual thought will wash over me over the course of the day, but then it goes away as quickly as it cropped up.
   c. Not usually. I don't think about sex very much at all.
   d. I sometimes fantasize about having sex with other people when I'm having sex with my partner.

2. Do you share your sexual fantasies with your partner?
   a. I try to, but I definitely screen some of the details out.
   b. I usually do, because if we share one, we can feed into each other's fantasy, which makes for a red-hot night.
   c. I never do. I tried once and she spent the night crying in the bathroom. It's just not worth it to me if it's going to hurt her.
   d. I'm not really that good talking about stuff like sexual fantasies.

3. Does your partner share fantasies with you?
   a. Never. He says he doesn't have any, but how am I supposed to believe that!
   b. Sometimes. Her fantasies seem toned down. You can tell where's she's editing them to make me feel better.
   c. I think he thinks I'll be angry with him if he does. Every now and then I share with him, but he never seems to budge.
   d. It seems like my partner shares every sexual thought that's ever crossed her head with me. Sometimes it's cool, but other times, I wish she'd keep some of that stuff to herself.

4. Have you and your partner ever acted out any of your fantasies?
   a. That's what keeps our sex life interesting after all these years!
   b. Every now and then, I'll start a game; sometimes my partner will play along, and sometimes not.
   c. I'm too shy to ask my partner. How would you even go about bringing that up?
   d. My partner thinks that role playing is a terribly silly thing to do.

5. Do you have sexual fantasies that you think are too weird to share with your partner?
   a. I sometimes have rape fantasies that I think might be too over the top to share.
   b. I'm a straight male, but every now and then, I fantasize about having another man in my bed with my wife.
   c. I've fantasized before about having a different man in every one of my orifices—and all at the same time.
   d. Let's just say that leather and rope is part of a fantasy I wouldn't risk sharing with my lover.

chapter 27

Fantasy and Role Play

"The moment I meet an attractive woman, I have to start pretending I have no desire to make love to her."
—*Roger Thornhill (Cary Grant),* North by Northwest

The idea of sexual fantasy can be a controversial one. Some say fantasizing about people who are not your partner is actually very healthy and normal. Others think it's a sign of a relationship on the decline, and that fantasizing about others means you are not happy with the situation you are in and wish to be somewhere—anywhere—else.

We say that sexual fantasy is completely normal. Fantasizing about sex with multiple partners, with coworkers, with one's friends' spouses or partners, about any member of the opposite sex, or even members of the same sex is a perfectly harmless practice and actually allows individuals to burn off, as it were, excess sexual energy. The only time it is hurtful or damaging to a relationship is if it actually leaves the realm of fantasy and becomes an ugly reality.

In this chapter, we look at the pros and cons of sexual fantasy and how it can be used to strengthen and improve an already secure relationship. We talk about whether or not it's healthy to share sexual fantasies with each other, and how to enrich your sex life with your partner by acting out fantasy in role play exercises.

Now don't say we didn't warn you: At the end of this chapter, we feature several fantasy and role play scenarios you can use to launch into your own erotic escapades. Just be sure to read these at your own risk, as some are raunchier than others and essentially run the gamut of fantasy play.

George, 50

"I won't lie. I fantasize about sex with every attractive woman I see. Not some. Not most. All of them. And two at a time, if possible. Have I ever told my wife? What am I, stupid? It would only hurt her feelings. The thing is, it has nothing to do with how I feel about her. It's not like I would act on those feelings—I haven't in 25 years of marriage, and I'm not about to start now. But do I enjoy fantasizing about hot women? That would be a yes. A very big yes. And do I tell her? A big fat no!"

Keep It to Yourself, or Not?

Like many men, George has a very active sexual imagination. That's okay. It's normal to fantasize; it's not normal, however, to act out your fantasies with all the random people about whom you fantasize. What's unfortunate about George's situation is that he can't share his fantasy life with his spouse. And he's probably right not to—although sometimes, it can be fun to share. But we'll get into that a little later on. Many people, upon hearing the sexual fantasies of their spouse, might view such thoughts as mental infidelities. They might also question the motives of why their spouse is telling them all these things. Whether or not you share your fantasies with your lover is all up to your particular situation. It can be bad and good to share, just as it can be both bad and good to hold back. Essentially, sexual fantasy is part of human nature. It's harmless, it's fun,

> "As we all know, sex is an empty experience. But as empty experiences go, sex is one of the best."
>
> —Woody Allen

as long as we don't share our fantasies with those who cannot (or will not) accept or fulfill them. The best question one can ask with regard to sexual fantasy is this: How can you translate your fantasy into a situation that will please and delight your lover and yourself, without jeopardizing your relationship?

Role Play

Role play is a great way to introduce your fantasies into your bedroom. If you have a recurring fantasy about being an executive who has his way with all his subordinates or an Amazonian princess whose male servant's only duty is to see to it that her sexual whims are satisfied (or whatever it is the dirty part of your mind thinks about) and your relationship can withstand sharing it, why not bring it to life with some entertaining role play?

Where can you begin? Try thinking about all the many encounters in the course of a normal day in which a man and a woman, hitherto strangers, may become amorous: a visit from the cable guy; an appointment with a new doctor; a policewoman with attitude just itching to issue a ticket. The options are limitless!

"Take home" situations that may have been turn-ons for you during the day. At what point did you have contact with an individual you found sexually desirable? Was it a waiter or waitress? A sales clerk? The parking attendant at the mall? You don't have to tell your lover that you have the hots for your gas meter reader. But there's no reason not to bring home elements of fantasy from real-life situations we encounter during the day.

In the next section, we present a few scenarios that might spark something you want to try out. The most important aspect of all of this—and we can't stress this more—is just have fun! And, as always, if one partner is not comfortable in the scenario, stop it immediately. Sex is never fun if only one party is enjoying it.

> *Tess McGill: "I have a head for business and a bod for sin. Is there anything wrong with that?"*
>
> *Jack Trainer: "Uh, no. No."*
>
> —*Melanie Griffith and Harrison Ford,* Working Girl

Sexy Scenarios

In this section, we're going to get you started in your fantasy life with some favorite scenarios, from mild to wild. However, you're going to have to let your imagination be your guide here. All we can do is get you started; where the fantasy will end up is all up to you and the inner workings of your own devious—and deviant—mind!

Mild

The following scenarios feature couples involved in loving relationships, finding new ways to celebrate and express their love for one another. This in and of itself can produce amazing passion. However, if you're looking for something slightly more salacious, you'll have to move to the next sections!

Caribbean Dream: The very special person you've been seeing has decided to take you on a weeklong Caribbean vacation to celebrate your relationship. You're staying together in a secluded suite that overlooks the water. You don't have to leave the room for anything—not even food, as a gourmet, 24-hour room service promises to bring you anything you want, anytime you want. But your lover insists you leave the room anyway, and takes you on a hike through a densely thicketed rain forest. You feel like you are the only people in the world. When you come to a waterfall, your lover suggests you strip down and take an outdoor shower—and you do.

Honeymoon Redux: You and your brand new spouse have not been spending very much time together lately. Ever since you got back from your honeymoon, it's been work this, social engagements that—heck, you barely have time to even get a good night's sleep. Suffice to say, as much as you crave it, you have not been having very much sex. And the sex that you have been having has been average—at best. You wish you could be on your honeymoon again—skiing in the Alps, sharing hot cocoas in front of a warm fire, and not to mention the other things you did in front of that fireplace in your private chalet.

Apparently, your spouse has also had the same idea and surprises you with the news of a winter weekend getaway. You can't repeat the Alps—you're still paying for that trip!—but you can mimic it, and your spouse knows the perfect place. There's a bed and breakfast located a few hours north of where you live. Still trying to wind down from your all-too-recent hectic state of affairs, you decide to go skiing on your first day. But when you come back to your room, the fire in the fireplace has already been started, and a bottle of champagne has been left by the innkeepers, with wishes for a happy honeymoon. The raging fire immediately brings memories of your honeymoon back, and you strip down and cuddle up together. And then ....

Sunny Day Rain Delay: The women especially will appreciate this one! It's a sunny Sunday afternoon, and your husband or boyfriend is in his usual Sunday spot, perched on the couch with the remote in one hand and a beer in the other. You're starting to get annoyed with this weekend routine. While you hustle around the house, trying to get things ready for the week ahead, he screams at the screen and belches. You complain as you want to do something else—anything else—this Sunday. He tells you that this is the most important game of the season and that maybe you can do something afterward, which you realize is going to be about 8 o'clock—and it's only about 5 o'clock now.

So you get an idea. You decide to strip down to nothing but a pair of pretty pantries and go about your tasks dressed just like that, being sure to walk in front of the TV screen as often as possible. And then you disappear—and into the bedroom. Curiosity fully roused, he stares at you from the bedroom door, shielding his eyes from the sun that pours through the picture window, while he begins to disrobe with his other hand.

'I thought that was a big game?' you ask as he approaches you, hunger in his eyes. He lifts you in his arms, tosses you on the bed, and mumbles 'rain delay' as he pushes himself on top of you. 'But, the sun's—' you try, but it's useless. He looks in your eyes, and more firmly now, he says the words again: 'Rain delay.' Looks like you'll have to believe him.

> "The Bings have horrible marriages! They yell. They fight. And they use the pool boy as a pawn in their sexual games!"
>
> —Chandler Bing (Matthew Perry), Friends

Medium

These fantasies are a little more racy than the ones we just provided. For one, they don't involve your lover—well, not necessarily! These involve random acquaintances—even total strangers! Of course, you can always pretend.

Love in an Elevator: You are so late for your meeting, you're sure you're going to lose your client over it. But what could you do? It was impossible to tear yourself away from the office where you were trying to put out another fire. It seems like lately, that all you ever seem to be doing is putting out fires. But what you really need is to ignite a different kind of fire. Of course, with all the work you've been doing, it's been impossible to go out and actually meet someone to start said fire with.

You nearly miss the elevator—but a sexy stranger on the inside sees you coming and holds it for you. Your client is on the 54th floor, and you wonder if it shows to the stranger how incredibly attracted you feel to him or her, and how badly you wish you could just have your way with him or her. And then it happens. The elevator stops. The lights go out. And all of a sudden you feel someone breathing in your ear, as two hands clench the sides of your hips. 'Do you want me as much as I want you?' And of course, you do.

Are These Melons Ripe? Men will probably like the premise of this fantasy a whole lot! It's Saturday night again—another lonely Saturday night with no plans. All your friends are busy with their wives, and you have a date with a DVD. You look at the clock and realize it's time you went out and found something to have for dinner. You get it into your head that it might be fun to actually cook something for yourself, so off to the supermarket you go.

But what are you going to have? You realize this is a question you should have asked yourself before you left the house as you wander aimlessly through the aisles of what appears to be an empty store. And then it seems that your wandering may not have been such a bad thing when you run into a sexy redhead in the produce aisle. Looks like your possible new friend is also alone, so you walk by and smile. Your smile is returned as you wander over to the cantaloupe bin, trying to effect some skill in picking out the perfect one. Apparently, you've impressed your friend, who has wandered over to you with a cucumber in her hand. As she gets closer to you, you notice she has wonderful breasts—made ever more so by the fact that she is wearing a see-through blouse, through which you can see she isn't wearing a bra.

She puts down the cucumber and picks up a couple of cantaloupes. 'I never know how to choose these,' she coos into your ear, as she brushes behind you and presses her breasts into your back. She lifts the cantaloupes up in front of you. 'Do you think my melons are ripe?' she gasps, as she presses into you. You turn around and kiss her full on the mouth. 'I'm not that good with produce,' she says, as she drops the melons and grabs up the cucumber again. 'For instance,' she says with her knee between your thighs, 'what am I supposed to do with this?' At that, you find an empty corner of the store and ....

Someone Call for a Repairman? Every woman loves a guy who's good with his hands—and every man likes to help a woman in need! In this fantasy scenario, there's something for everyone!

When your refrigerator breaks down for the third time this year, you are fit to be tied! What you'd really like to do is buy a new one, but money's been tight lately. So you get out the phone book and call the repair service—the number that you should really know by heart by now. You're not getting dressed for these guys, you decide. They always send over the smelliest, fattest ones to your place. In fact, you have already decided that this is a prerequisite for the job as you've never seen one out of that mold yet—and you've seen a lot of them!

When you answer the door with your terrycloth robe on and nothing else, you pray that the hunk on the other side of the door is just a hallucination—that there isn't really a six-foot, two-inch Adonis standing in front of you. 'I'm from All-Repair,' he tells you. 'Can I come in?' Right now you're so mad that you didn't get dressed, especially because you're sure he can feel the heat coming off you and smell you getting aroused. When he gives you the once over and licks his lips, you realize you may not be the only one interested.

He starts working and then he does something weird: He starts clicking his tongue and shaking his head. 'What's the matter? What is it?' you ask, the bill running up in your head. 'Well,' he tells you, 'looks like the problem here is gross neglect.' You're confused. 'Pardon?' you ask. 'Yes, well it seems,' he says as he walks over to you, 'that someone is not taking very good care of this machine.' This he says as he starts to unbutton his shirt. 'According to the manual, I'm supposed to teach a lesson to the person who owns it,' he says, now pressed up to you, his arms slipping into your robe. His hands begin running up and down the curves of your naked body. He presses you up against the wall and ....

> Harry Burns: "That's it? Some faceless guy rips off all your clothes, and *that's* the sex fantasy you've been having since you were ten?"
>
> Sally Albright: "Well sometimes I vary it a little."
>
> Harry Burns: "Which part?"
>
> Sally Albright: "What I'm wearing."
>
> —Billy Crystal and Meg Ryan, *When Harry Met Sally*

Wild

The fantasies in this section are as hot as we can print them—and be advised, they are certainly not for everyone. They may involve S&M themes, bisexuality, threesomes, moresomes, and others. Continue reading at your own risk!

The Naughty Secretary:

You knew she wasn't a very good secretary when you hired her. You didn't really need a secretary for your job anyway, so anyone would have fit the bill. So you decided to at least get one you'd like to look at a lot. Someone you'd really like to boss around and give orders to. Someone who looked really nice in a short skirt and a pair of high heels. But this latest offense, this was just too much.

***

You're in a lot of trouble and you know it. The boss was not very happy with the way you did that filing, and now you know, for sure, that he's going to punish you. And it will probably be very stern. He will probably bend you over his knee again and spank you harshly, mercilessly. And then he'll bend you over the desk, no doubt, and …. Oh, dear! How you wish you hadn't forgotten to wear your panties today.

***

That insolent little tart needs to be punished, and this time, it's got to be good. Messing up the files, defying the rules of alphabetical order—her actions were intolerable. And yet, part of you knows that she did it on purpose. That she wants to be punished. That she craves it.

***

When the intercom rings, you jump. He's pressing down so hard, you know he's got it in for you now. You put the meekest look you can on your face you can muster and you walk into his office to face your punishment.

The Tupperware Party: You can't believe you have to go to another one of these inane parties. You never have any fun at them, and yet the neighborhood women always feel like they have to invite you. And, not wanting to insult anyone, you always go. Your hostess greets you at the door. As she takes your coat, her hands linger a little longer than you expect on your shoulders. 'I am so glad you came,' she says, brushing your cheek with the back of her hand.

The party, as expected, is about as boring as it can be. So you excuse yourself, lying about having to go to the bathroom. On the way, you walk by your hostess's bedroom, and for some reason, you feel compelled to enter. As you look around, you begin to hear some women giggling in the bathroom. It's your hostess and one of the other guests. You walk over to the door that's been left ajar, and you peer in. You can't believe your eyes. The other guest is naked on the sink; your hostess is kneeling down in front of her. You gasp, and your hostess hears you. She's not embarrassed. 'I told you I was so glad you came. Why don't you join us?' she asks. You find yourself strangely intrigued by the proposition.

Has Anyone Seen My Wife? You and your wife are new to the neighborhood, so when your next-door neighbors invite you over for a party on Saturday night, you figure, okay. You have no idea what you're getting into, though. Not until you walk through the front door that night. What you see shocks you at first. Couples are sitting around, sipping cocktails, in various states of undress. You look over to your wife to see if she also knows what kind of party this is. You nod to her to see if she wants to leave; she shakes her head, smiles, and pulls you inside. This is something you've talked about trying before, but you never imagined it would ever really come to pass.

Over the course of the night, you and your wife get split up. Every now and then you catch a glance of her talking with different men, and then it looks like she gets propositioned. She looks to you for approval and you nod. Eventually, you get bored of the other women and you search out your wife to go home. And then you walk in on her with another man and his wife. They invite you to join them.

Sexploration Exercise #28

1. How often do you and your partner have sex in your own bed?
   a. Every single time.
   b. We have a large bedroom with many pieces of sturdy furniture, so we shake it up quite a bit.
   c. Mostly we have sex in our bed, but we really love doing it in the master bathroom—especially in the tub.
   d. Our kids are finally grown and on their own, so the least visited place in our home for sex is our bed!

2. Do you and your partner make it a point to try and have sex in other places aside from your own bedroom?
   a. We basically just stick with the bedroom.
   b. Once a month, we send the kids off to their grandparents' house for the weekend and try out as many new places in the home as we can think of.
   c. We have a weekly game. Whoever thinks of the most creative place in the home to have sex gets treated to the first favor!
   d. We used to, but I feel like we're just too old to be going at it all over the house at this point in our lives. It somehow seems undignified.

3. Which of you is more adventurous when it comes to having sex in different locations?
   a. Definitely him.
   b. Definitely her.
   c. We're both pretty even with the suggestions we make.
   d. Neither of us believes it's proper or correct to have sex anywhere else but the bedroom.

4. Have you ever had sex in any of the following places?
   a. Dining room
   b. Garage
   c. Restaurant lavatory
   d. Ski lift

5. Where's the most unusual place you ever had sex?
   a. On a park bench in the middle of the day—while I was wearing a very long skirt.
   b. On the roof of a building in the dead of winter.
   c. On a fire escape during a cocktail party.
   d. In the Tunnel of Love at the amusement park.

28

Location! Location! Location!

Harry Burns: "No man can be friends with a woman he finds attractive. He always wants to have sex with her."

Sally Albright: "So you are saying that a man can be friends with a woman he finds unattractive?"

Harry Burns: "No, you pretty much want to nail them, too."

—Billy Crystal and Meg Ryan, When Harry Met Sally

Earlier on, we suggested that finding a new venue for sex can break up the boredom that affects many marriages. Now, in this chapter, we'd like to give you some more sex-crazed ideas about where to go for a really good time.

Elsie, 43

"Nothing turns me on like having sex where we're not supposed to. The possibility of getting caught is the biggest erotic thrill in the universe. Luckily, I finally divorced my stick-in-the-mud husband of ten years, Larry, who never wanted to do anything exciting sexually. It was all bedroom, all the time. And that meant not even any of the other furniture in the room, but just the bed! Probably the only reason I stayed with him so long is that he would at least do other positions than missionary. But not that often.

A few months ago, I met Rob, who's about fifteen years younger than me, but with the libido of a seventeen-year-old. Honestly, he can't get enough sex—which is great, because neither can I!

Rob and I have had sex everywhere. We've done it at the movies, the ballet, and even the opera. We've gotten it on in my car, his car, the subway, and airplane, and even on a hayride once!

We've been naughty in parks and porticos—and even in a canoe once, but I don't think we'll try that again! We got so incredibly turned on that we capsized and ended up sharing a cold for a week. And certainly that was no cause for complaint, as it allowed us to justify spending a wanton long weekend in the sack! But waterwise, we have had great success on a cruise boat—but I guess who hasn't!—in a sailboat, and my favorite, in a gondola on a hot summer's evening in Venice. Ah, having to insist on having that blanket cover us even though we were wearing sandals and sleeveless shirts because it was so warm out.

We've gotten hot and bothered in baseball stadiums, at poetry readings, elevators—even in the bathrooms of our favorite restaurants.

I hope this crazy train of lust never stops!"

Changing Venue = Sex Beyond Your Wildest Dreams

Elise speaks for many, many people—and not just people in their twenties, either. Although Rob is considerably younger than her, it doesn't seem like he's pressuring her to do anything she doesn't want to do—and her boring husband aside, there are plenty of people in our age group who are ready, willing, and anxious to dance with danger in the name of desire.

To add a little danger definitely spices up a sex life. We think there's nothing like a little grip-and-grin, doggie-style sex over a bathroom sink to reduce or eliminate the cares of the day. We'd like to suggest a variety of other places that can serve as perfect backdrops for your most excellent erotic encounters.

It's *Not* the Bedroom!

Forget the room you have most and probably all your sex in. In this chapter, we are closing the door to that space, locking it, and throwing away the key—okay, well maybe we'll just hide the key from ourselves for a while!

This chapter is about adventures in amour. About frisky frolics in places you may never even have dreamed of, well, frolicking in before. For now, we're going to leave the safety of your bed and see what else is cooking in the rest of the world—starting with your own home.

Dining Room

Have dinner in tonight. The menu? Each other, served with passion right on top of your dining room table.

Missionary style sex is ideal for this situation. Not only will a dining room table typically line up with the hip height of the average man, It provides a stable, sturdy surface on which she can lay flat—and may also afford her a lovely view of a decorative chandelier that hangs overhead. Also, the table will only be supporting her weight, so there's a far less likely chance that it will collapse. Put him on his back on the table and her on top, with a whole lotta shakin' goin' on, and you may find yourselves close to a splintery catastrophe! Rear entry—whether over a chair, the table, or even the sideboard—is also a favorite in this room. Just be sure the fine china isn't in a place where it might get broken!

Kitchen

In the kitchen, it all depends on what you have going on in terms of working surfaces. An island can mean an island paradise, where you're free to flail around at will and are not likely to hit any wall-mounted storage— or walls for that matter. Think of the sink as a waterfall in paradise for you and your lover—just be sure to do the dishes first. Look around your kitchen and use your imagination. You may surprise yourselves with what you come up with! (Word to the wise, stay out of the way of sharp things, like an electric can opener and—especially—a block of knives!

Family Room

This one's essentially a no-brainer. In this room, you've likely got a comfy couch, maybe some chunky chairs, a coffee table at the perfect height to facilitate rear-entry sex.

What you might have in this room that will make it that much more exciting is a pool table, air hockey table, or even foosball table—although special care needs to be taken for where she lays on the last one of those!

Other Options

Your living room may be a pristine haven decked out in white, expensive furniture with antique pieces set about, and therefore, might not be the best place to indulge in a frenzy of wild romping. However, if your living room features a fireplace, an evening of gentle ecstasy in front of its warm glow may be just what you need to keep the embers of your passion aglow.

Other considerations in the home include the laundry room (kill two birds with one stone when you set the washer on "spin" and get busy on top of it— like a vibrating bed in a motel room); the attic or basement; the garage; the stairs; and more. Look around your house. Chances are, there's a nooky nook you have yet to explore.

Auto-Eroticism (Part 1)

The biggest down side of marital sex is that it is completely moral and legal. Who wants moral, legal sex?

The answer seems to be just about nobody. Since a marriage license is a license to commit all the sex you want (with your partner, and with his or her permission), you'd think that married couples would have more sex than anyone. And yet, we all know that's just not so. One of the main reasons is the exciting sense of danger, law-breaking, and fear of getting caught that pervades premarital (and even pre-college) sex. How do we renew that sense of dirtiness and inappropriateness that made sex great when we were young? The answer might be sitting in your driveway: your car.

Why should NASCAR fans be the only people over 25 to have sex in motor vehicles? Get out there and park! If it's cold, you'll be amazed at how quickly the two of you can steam up the windows. Once the glass is sufficiently fogged, there's no limit to what you can do since no one will be able to see in. And unless the two of you combined weigh over 600 pounds, it's not likely the car will be rocking to any noticeable degree. Just be sure to keep a high level of steam on those windows.

You might expect us to say that you should find a place as far away from other people as possible. Quite the opposite. The greater the danger of detection, the better the sex will be. Call it the fear factor, call it a slight case of exhibitionism. We call it good clean fun.

Auto-Eroticism (Part 2)

For an even wilder adventure, don't use your own car—rent a car you don't have and can't possibly ever imagine being able to afford. We're talking Mercedes 500s, Lamborghinis, Ferraris, top-of-the-line Porsches—the kinds of cars that drop jaws when you drive past high schools. Or why not a classic car? Go cruising in a Buick or Ford from the 1950s. If you want to get truly dapper, opt for a true classic from the 1930s. Why? Bigger back seats!

Don't want to do the driving? We understand. Ever rented a limo? Why not go out for a night on the town with your spouse or partner? Let us be clear: You don't want a town car. You want a limo, with a back seat for whatever you can think of. The better ones come equipped with a nice bar, cable TV, and a stereo. Roll down the windows so that the peasants can admire you in all your splendor. Then roll up the windows, open the moon roof, crank up the CD player, and let the good times roll.

Don't worry about the limo driver—he's seen it all before. In any event, there will be a partition that you can roll up, just like in the movies, when you're ready to play.

Theme Parks

An amusement park is a good place for sex for people with good imaginations and flexible definitions of the word "sex." Plenty of these parks feature rides with side-by-side seating with no opportunity for others, close or far, to see what you are doing. This is true for Ferris wheels, roller coasters, and slower, more conventional rides like Tunnels of Love.

Similarly, parks, beaches, planetariums, and libraries all offer the combination of privacy and the hint of danger in being caught that makes life so exciting. Remember that your purpose is not really to get caught but to recapture the sense of excitement and danger that made sex even more thrilling when you were younger.

Department Store Changing Rooms

Not every department store is going to allow couples to enter a changing room together. However, if shopping really turns you on, you may have to go all cloak-and-dagger getting both of you into one changing room.

Work with a sales clerk to find six or eight outfits, then take them all into the booth with you. This is your justification for having all that time in there. If a security person asks how you're doing, let them know you're doing fine.

Just bear in mind that many department stores electronically monitor their fitting rooms. If that doesn't change your mind—if you love the naughty thrill of being watched, and perhaps taped—we're not going to stop you, and chances are, neither is the bored security guard who's watching you. Of course, he could be jealous that his own sex life isn't as exciting and want to take it out on you. Our advice: Just be careful.

Perhaps the worst thing that will happen is you'll be asked to leave the store. When was the last time you saw two fine, upstanding citizens like yourselves on the evening news busted for making love in a department store? Here's one thing you've never heard on the news: "Sex at Sak's. Film at 11."

Airport Lounges

Unless you are a truly frequent flyer, you may be unaware that the major airlines maintain VIP clubs, complete with private showers, at most major airports. If you're flying first or business class, you're in automatically; your ticket is all you need to get in! The rest of you will have to join, which will run you about $300 a year.

If you fly frequently, it makes sense to join so that you can use them for the normal purposes and pleasures of business travelers: a quiet place to think, rest, relax, make phone calls, have a drink, put your feet up and watch TV, or reconfirm your flights with the airline personnel. Generally, it seems that the most experienced, knowledgeable, and adept airline people work in those clubs, and they can find you seats on planes that often no one else can.

That's all well and good, but what does that have to do with sex?

Oh, everything. These places also have private showers, as we've mentioned, where you and your paramour might slip off to for a while, while you await your plane's departure. There's something especially spine-tingling about having sex in an airport lounge, knowing that you are surrounded by thousands of strangers who could not possibly imagine just how much fun you two are having only yards away.

What if you're not flying first class or business class, and you don't want to pony up the annual fee, but you still want to sample the thrill of getting off before you take off? These places will usually allow you to pay a one-time use fee of approximately $25. Worth it? You decide.

> *"Now, just because some-one sees, you know, two naked people asleep in bed together, it doesn't necessarily prove sex was involved. It does, however, make for a very strong case."*
>
> —*Mandy Slade (Toni Collette),* Velvet Goldmine

Parking Structures and Elevators

Every city has them; most people, regrettably, only use them as places in which to park their cars. We think they hold so much more poten-tial! (And you know what we mean, don't you!)

Find a spot deep in the bowels of a parking structure, be it at the airport, downtown, or in a shopping plaza. Your best bet is to go on a weekday when most people are working. This gives you a maximum amount of privacy.

Then, get to work. Stay in your car. Hide out behind one of the cement supports—whatever and wherever you can squeeze in your most-illicit quickie!

Other Options

Once you and your partner start having sex in public and, therefore, illicit places, you'll slowly transform yourselves into location scouts for love. You'll begin to consider the possibilities of every office, building, and public space with an eye toward what you can do, how much time you'll have to do it, and your chances of getting caught.

The mere fact that you're thinking in these terms will put you in a frame of mind to make love either in a newly scouted-out location or when you are home again, safe from the prying eyes of the law. And wasn't that the whole idea, anyway?

Wet and Wild

Virtually every sex book suggests that couples shower or bathe together, either before sex, during it, or afterwards.

Sadly, bathing together vanishes from most marriages right around the two-year mark. It looses its novelty, which is a pity. Of course, the lack of time that all of us seem to suffer from these days certainly contributes to the fact that couples don't bathe together much.

Also, there sometimes creeps into a relationship the need to keep at least *something* private. Performing one's toilette, which we broadly interpret to include bathing or showering, seems to be one of the key things where a spouse or partner wants at least a few minutes of total privacy.

And yet we heartily suggest that you and your beloved explore the old-fashioned pleasure of sitting in a tub as an alternative to renting a movie, going out to dinner, or even (on rare occasions) sex itself. We encourage you to discover the long-lost art of doing absolutely nothing, and doing it together. It's romantic, it's soothing, and more often than not, it will lead you directly to sex.

There are two ways to sit in a bathtub: facing each other and facing away. In either case, the average American bathtub is too narrow to support all but the most insistent couples when it comes to making love. Tubs were simply not built for four knees. We encourage you, therefore, to use your bathtub as a locus of pleasure other than the coital variety. Hang out, relax, soap each other up.

But while it's tough to have sex in a bathtub, it can be very exciting—and easy—to have sex in a shower, although stand-up sex may present something of a physics challenge to many couples, depending on their relative height, strength, and safety concerns. Doggie style while standing—if your shower is big enough, and if you are not leaning on a glass wall that may not be able to bear both of your weight, then go for it. You don't have to have intercourse in the shower to be sexually intimate, however. There are plenty of other things to do in the shower, including soaping each other up and caressing each other. Oral sex in the shower—ever the crowd-pleaser.

A lot of sex manuals talk about the joy of making love in larger bodies of water. Pools are an option; so are lakes, ponds, and oceans. This we leave up to your own discretion. Some couples enjoy having sex this way, while others do not, as they are not able to establish a workable rhythm and a satisfying friction due to the buoyancy one has in the water.

Sexploration Exercise #29

1. Have you ever had phone sex?
   a. My partner travels a lot—what do you think?
   b. I'd be too shy to say those kinds of things over the phone.
   c. I never used to like it before but now I do.
   d. I just don't see the point.

2. Do you use the Internet to download adult material?
   a. We are not interested in pornography.
   b. Yes, but I hope my husband never finds out.
   c. I've thought about it, but I'm sure my wife would kill me if I ever did.
   d. My husband and I have an account together and sometimes download stuff to get us in the mood.

3. Have you ever sent your partner an X-rated e-mail?
   a. Yes—and I hope her boss never reads her e-mail!
   b. No—I'm not really a man of many words. I like action.
   c. I have occasionally. Especially if I know he's having a rough day, I know it will remind him that he has something to go home to.
   d. I would never do that. What if it fell into the wrong hands and started circulating all over cyberspace!

4. Have you ever entered an erotic Internet chat room?
   a. I'm much too scared by all the deviants that might be lurking in there.
   b. I'm curious to try as I'm strangely intrigued by the thought of all the deviants in there.
   c. I'm one of the deviants that lurk in there!
   d. We don't believe in the Internet—too many deviants lurking out there.

5. If you haven't already done so, have you ever thought about ordering adult toys, lingerie, games, or other sexy material off the Internet?
   a. We're members of an erotic book club we found on the Internet.
   b. I've ordered vibrators and that kind of thing. I can keep my privacy by ordering over the Internet.
   c. I would be afraid that everyone in the world would see what I was up to. I don't think the Internet is as secure as people believe it is.
   d. I've done it before, but I prefer the in-person shopping where I can actually see what I'm planning to buy before I buy it.

chapter 29

Technosex

"The Internet is a communication tool used the world over where people can come together to bitch about movies and share pornography with one another."
—*Holden (Ben Affleck),* Jay and Silent Bob Strike Back

As our society becomes increasingly technologically driven, technosex has become an increasingly common phenomenon. Although being in the same bed, or even the same room, with your lover is generally the preferred way to perform coitus, in these days of overbooked schedules and countless business trips, technology has made it easier for all of us to get some, no matter where we are.

For our purposes in this chapter, we are using the term *technosex* as an umbrella term for any kind of sex that relies on technology—such as telephones, e-mail, or the Internet (but not sex toys)—rather than face-to-face, body-to-body contact.

Steven, 52

"I travel for work a lot. My wife, Georgia, really doesn't like that very much. There's nothing I can do about it, really. I've had this job longer than I've known her, and she always knew what she was getting into when she married me. But Georgia, and I mean this with all due respect—and she'd be the first to agree with me—is a total nymphomaniac. She needs it all the time. I mean *all* the time. So maybe now you can see that's all the more reason why it's so hard for her for me to be away as often as I am.

When we were first married, she used to call my hotel room all the time—sometimes even in the middle of the night—and try and have phone sex with me. She's never had to try too hard to get me to go along with her, though! Sometimes we'd stay up all night together, talking about our days, then having hot and heavy phone sex, and then talking about our days again. It could go on all night sometimes. Let's just say there were more than a few morning meetings I went to half asleep because of that.

When technology began to progress, as it is prone to do, and I got my first cell phone, I was in for a rude awakening. That my wife was insatiable was not a secret to me, but I kind of liked to keep it secret from the rest of the world—especially my business associates!

But one day, she called me on my cell phone in a meeting. I knew it was her—she was the only person who had my number, after all—and she knew I would be in a meeting when she called, which is why I picked it up—you know, I figured it was an emergency or something.

'I want that cock and I want it now,' was the first thing I heard after I uttered my pleasant, unassuming greeting. 'I said, get home right now and fill me up with—.' I had to hang up. I was deeply embarrassed. I was able to remain cool with my client—even though my wife had given me a raging hard-on.

I called her when I got back to my hotel room, but before I could discuss it with her, she, well, finished the job. Afterwards, we had a long talk about her behavior putting my job in jeopardy, and she admitted that maybe, on some subconscious level, that's what she was trying to do.

We talked it through for several hours, and I realized my marriage was more important to me than some job. And for a guy my age I was traveling way too much. It was time to let the newbies do the legwork and let the old man do more of the brainwork from home base.

Since I've been traveling less, my marriage has only gotten better. However, I do have to make the odd trip every couple of months or so, just to keep the clients happy.

And now that technology has moved into the realm of text messaging, if my wife needs to be bad, at least there's no way anyone will overhear her. Still, I can't believe I leave it on at all. If you think she talks dirty, you wouldn't believe some of the stuff she writes!"

Porn and the Technological Revolution

Today, you can get porn almost anywhere. We'll get into more detail about this in Chapter 31, but for our purposes here, we'll at least point out some of the technological options that exist today that weren't available thirty years ago, when, if you wanted to see porn, you'd have to visit a seedy theater where sleazy men masturbated into their popcorn boxes.

Porn drove the initial success of the videotape industry. Now, instead of having to "get it on the street," as those who sought it were once inclined to do, porn seekers could drift to the back of the video store, behind the mysterious curtain, and pull out all manner of film. These films they could watch in private, or sometimes even share with their girlfriends or wives, who, chances are, had never seen anything like it before. The backlash against the hardcore stuff that men generally prefer created a whole new softcore industry, tailored to the needs and desires of women. But we'll look into this more in Chapter 31.

When DVDs came along, it made at-home porn that much more enjoyable—and for women and men both. Now, instead of having to rewind and fast-forward over stuff that one or both parties might find objectionable, with the click of a button, you could go to a favorite scene anytime you wanted.

The availability of porn made more men sign up for cable than did the fact that they could get better transmissions of Braves games. Now, with all kinds of channel options available—and more on-the-spot satisfaction with the new "on-demand" most cable providers offer, cable has become a top source for sparking technosex interludes. But more about this in Chapter 31.

Phone Sex

The term "phone sex" can be used to define two separate things. The first has to do with a phone number you dial to have simulated sex with an anonymous party. The second is the same idea, but in this case, you have it with your lover.

Really catching on in the 1980s, the infamous 900 number first became a money-maker for shrewd sex marketers who offered "live chat" or a tape-recorded message of a "just barely legal cheerleader," a "sexy bored feather-duster-toting housewife, perhaps wearing nothing but an apron," "a naughty nurse, just aching to give someone a sponge bath," or some other such fantasy woman.

Despite the proliferation of stuff one can access on the Internet, these numbers remain a popular source for those who have the nine bucks or so a minute to spend, and who are looking to get off on a quickie fantasy.

Masturbation notwithstanding, now that we're well immersed in the age of speaker phones, these numbers can provide a sexy outlet for couples to enjoy together—especially in the case of couples who may have contemplated threesomes. By using these numbers, and chatting with a "live" third party, you can talk and imagine your way through a three-way, without all the emotional damage and physical complications these real-life situations can sometimes cause.

The most fun to have as a couple with the phone, however, is to share phone sex with one another. If one partner travels a lot, or if a couple is enduring a long-distance relationship, this is a fantastic way to stay connected.

How do you have phone sex? Take some tips from the chapters in this book about talking dirty and fantasy and role playing. Set up a scenario for your partner that you know he or she will be dying to enact. If you're the instigator, remember that you're coming into the game already aroused; it's your partner who needs the warm-up, so be extra sensitive to making the experience as arousing for him or her as possible.

The key to mind-blowing phone sex is to develop the fantasy as vividly as you can for your partner—at least at first. As you move along, you're both likely going to get too hot and bothered to even be able to focus on the details anymore!

Your friend, the speakerphone, may be a great solution for you, as it will allow you to keep two hands free for fondling and masturbatory purposes (and yes, of course there's masturbation involved!). However, some lovers—men and women both—prefer to keep the headset up to their ear as it makes them feel like their lover is closer to them, whispering naughty nothings into his or her own ear. Solution: Lie on your back and keep the headset cradled between your shoulder and ear to free up your hands!

Once you've both completed your mission, don't hang up on each other—unless that's part of your game. Spend time talking to one another about what's been going on with you, and what you wish the other person could be sharing with you if he or she wasn't away. It's likely the same thing you'd probably be doing if you were basking in the afterglow in each other's arms.

E-Mail Erotica

Writing and receiving erotic epistles is some of the most fun you can have with your partner—and your home computer—especially if you are both avid readers or aspiring writers.

There are two methods you can use for this: short and sweet, and long and lascivious. What you choose depends on your mood—just like how you actually have sex also depends on your mood.

For short and sweet, you can try instant messaging—or you can send brief sentences or phrases back and forth to each other through regular e-mail, which has been known to prolong the ecstasy as you wonder what your lover will say to you next—or how aroused or shocked your lover was by the last line you sent along! Try sending a command to your lover, such as: "When I get home, I expect you to be naked." Or, start your attack in a less direct fashion, inquiring, the favorite old standby of "What are you wearing?" or "I've been thinking about you." For the latter, when your partner writes back—or even before he or she does, simply type in the single word "naked" and see how he or she responds!

If you have some time on your hands, and you want to test out or hone your short story or essay writing skills, by all means, type out a long and graphic note. You can either start out telling your partner how you feel about him or her, and then move into all the ways you'd like to express that, or you can invent a story about lovers and all the crazy things they've done to each other. Check out collections of erotic fiction stories to get started.

Whatever you choose, no doubt you'll enjoy playing with your lover this way—and you'll also have a written record of dirty talk you can refer to again and again!

Cybersex

The great dotcom shake-out of the last few years has lifted the skirts on that industry's dirty little secret: Practically the only people to make money with stand-alone Internet businesses are providers of pornography.

In cybersex, you can have imaginary sexual relationships with total strangers on the Internet. Instead of touching each other, you and your cyberpartner send each other Instant Messages explaining what you're doing, how the actions of the other person make you feel ("Oh, I love it when you touch me like that"), and ultimately, How It Was For You. In other words, it's a blow-by-blow (pun intended) account, written in real time, by two or more people who are imagining having sex with each other, even though they have never met and are likely never to meet.

When we use the term "cybersex," we also mean downloading and viewing—whether with your partner or not—material high in sexual content off the Internet. For couples and singles alike, this particular experience is no better—nor worse—than watching a pornographic film or leafing through a dirty magazine. If it does it for you, great; if not, like anything else we've talked about in this book, don't. It's just that simple.

Now we're not going to pass judgment here. One man or woman's curiosity is another's essential pleasure. That's one of the things that makes sex interesting. However, there are two things to consider if you are presently—or frequently—engaging in cybersex purely with strangers. While it's true that you are protected from all the messy complications of sex within the confines of a relationship, you may also be missing out on experiencing and enjoying all those things that are fun and fulfilling about a relationship.

If you are single and spending your time downloading porn and typing sex acts to strange members of the opposite sex—or same sex, as you will never know exactly who you are talking with—don't forget that the time you are investing in your cyber sexfest could be spent seeking a relationship with a real person.

If you are currently involved in a relationship, and your partner is not involved in your cyber sexcapades, it may be argued that what you are really doing is cheating. Perhaps the sexual edge has been smoothed down in your relationship, and the time you spend having anonymous screen sex with a stranger could be better spent fixing your own relationship—or taking action to discontinue the relationship so the other person does not get hurt by your actions.

> *"You make love without fading out?"*
>
> —*Tom Baxter (Jeff Daniels)*,
> The Purple Rose of Cairo

Linda, 45

"I can't believe I'm about to admit this to you, but I'm getting to the point that I'll explode if I don't tell someone. Recently, I've gotten myself addicted to cybersex, and it's bad. Well, it's good, but I know the excess I do it in, it can't be great for me!

It all started when I broke up with my long-time boyfriend. We were together for seventeen years—if you can believe it. Greg had never believed in marriage, so I made myself believe that neither did I, so we spent all these years together living a lie. Ugly. One day, I woke up and I realized that there were things in life I wanted that he was never going to provide for me—kids being a biggie. I had to get out.

The breakup was painful and messy, and lasted a long time. There was no legal bind between us; we weren't even living together so there wasn't even common law to contend with. And yet, the process was so taxing, I knew, kids or not, it was going to be a long time before I allowed myself to be in a relationship again. But I still had needs.

A friend of mine was very into the online scene, and recommended I join a chat room if I was feeling lonely. She never recommended the place I landed up in.

The thing about the Internet is, you can mis-strike one little key, get sidetracked on one misinterpreted search word, and you can end up in a world so far from where you were trying to go, it will make your head spin. I was looking for a site on 'female bonding,' a place to go to talk with other women about breakups and moving on. Somehow, I ended up at a site for 'female bondage,' and I was intrigued.

I had heard of S&M before, even had some fantasies of being dominated by men and women both. But I never would act on them. Who with? Greg the 'missionary man?' But here, I was able to investigate this world without leaving the house. Without being afraid of getting mixed up with crazy people who might actually try and physically hurt me the way they write about doing.

I've thought about stopping, but some of the sex I've had, screen to screen, has been better than the skin to skin variety. And, come on, who would ever actually act out those crazy fantasies with me anyway?"

Don't Try This at Work

As much fun as the information age affords us in getting frisky with our partner—or others—when we aren't even in the same room with them, there's still an element of danger involved—and not the kind that makes it sexier to be involved in the naughtiness, but the kind that may end you up on the unemployment line.

Remember, there's nothing wrong with a sexy e-mail to your partner—just so long as you are not sending it to your partner's office. Keep in mind that all office e-mail belongs to the employer. Your employer has a right to monitor e-mail, read it, and, for all we know, post it on the bulletin board behind the water cooler or coffee machine. It's one thing for your lover to know that you really want to "get it on" tonight. It's quite another for the whole department to have that same piece of information.

And if e-mail is risky, don't think phone sex isn't. In this day and age, a lot of employers can, and do, keep phone records of their employees' calls—and may even be listening. So while you think that even if on your lunch hour, you call your significant other with a throaty "What are you wearing" may be innocent enough, be careful how far you take it. Most employers would be annoyed with a casual flirting around the issue; none will be happy if you work yourselves into an all-out masturbation frenzy!

The worst thing you can do is surf the net for smut. If you think it's easy for employers to find out who you've called or sent naughty e-mails to, it's that much easier to tell where you've been fulfilling your daytime urges for cyberporn.

In this hyper-techno world, use and enjoy the outlets provided to you to give your sex life that extra charge, but be sure to be smart and discreet about it. No technosex is worth losing a job over—no matter how much you may hate the job or how hot the technosex is!

Sexploration Exercise #30

1. Have you ever wanted to be tied up during sex?
   a. I love being tied up during sex. There's nothing like it!
   b. I've fantasized about it a lot, but I can't think of how I'd approach my wife about it.
   c. I think it's fine in the fantasy realm, but weird if you ever actually put it into practice.
   d. No way. What if something happened to my partner and I couldn't get out!

2. Have you ever tied up your partner during sex?
   a. He would never allow that.
   b. She can't get enough of it!
   c. I tried tying him up once, but we giggled too much about what we were doing to really get into the action.
   d. Yes, but not that much. I can tell she doesn't really like it even though she'd never tell me differently.

3. In bed, do you find you're more a dominant sexual partner or a submissive?
   a. Definitely dominant.
   b. Definitely submissive.
   c. I can be both—it depends on my mood.
   d. I don't define myself with such terms.

4. Do you and your partner know what a safety word is—and if you do, do you have one?
   a. We love dabbling in light bondage, so we definitely know what it is and have a couple of words—depending on how much we really want the action to stop.
   b. We like to think that we don't need one. We have been together for so long now, we should just know when one of us has had too much.
   c. We don't do that kind of thing.
   d. What's a safety word?

5. In your opinion, spanking is:
   a. Sexy.
   b. Perverted.
   c. Weird.
   d. All of the above—and in the best possible way!

chapter 30

Bondage

"It's the oldest story in the book. Boy meets girl. Boy wants girl to do dominatrix film. Girl says, 'Naked?' Boy says, 'Yeah.' Girl says, 'No way!' Boy says, 'Okay, how about you just wear this rubber dress and beat this old guy with a scrub brush?' Girl says, 'How hard?'
—*Karen Walker (Megan Mullalley)* Will & Grace

There are all kinds of kinky games that lovers can play with one another in a committed, loving relationship. We touch upon many of these in the chapters in this section. In this chapter, we're going to briefly delve into the world of BDSM, or bondage.

Don't be alarmed. While it's true that the term "bondage" can sound a lot worse than it actually is, there are mild forms as well, and this is the type we're looking at in this book.

While in the most extreme situations, so-called lovers are known to do all kinds of things to each other in the name of pain and domination, what we're looking at in this chapter is essentially harmless. If you think this is not something you and your lover would ever be interested in, we invite you to go ahead to the next chapter. However, if a little kinky play is something you might be interested in trying, stick around. You might just learn something that will put an added oomph into your sex lives.

In this chapter, we look at how to bring this highly erotic activity into your bedroom, and how to tailor it to your specific needs and desires.

Victor, 41

"I'm the kind of really conservative guy type who's always dated very conservative girls. No one who knows me would be surprised about that. I'm a walking advertisement for Brooks Brothers, who is usually seen with women who wear pearls and sensible shoes. Mabel, my recent girlfriend, is that kind of woman. Except, I have to admit, in bed.

Everything seemed pretty typical at first. I met Mabel at a club function for singles. Not a cocktail party, mind you, but a high tea, where respectable people gathered to talk about business, books, and the stock market—all in the hopes of meeting that perfect fit to start a normal life with, complete with proper children, specially bred dogs, and private school. We talked the entire afternoon, and when the function ended, we took a nice, polite walk through the park. I invited her out on a date, got her phone number, demurely kissed her on the cheek, and hailed her a cab.

The night of the date, a proper Saturday night date, I made reservations at a top restaurant and picked her up at her apartment—her apartment lobby, I should add, as there was no way I was going to disrespect her by entering her apartment.

Dinner was elegant and chic. We drank a lovely bottle of Sancerre and talked about our future plans. And drank another one. And then drank another. You can imagine that by the middle of the third bottle of wine, we had unraveled from civilized to near savage. And then the conversation took a very interesting turn.

'Do you know what a dominatrix is, Vic?' she asked me, not even annoying me at this point by abbreviating my first name, which is a huge peeve for me. I slugged back another glass of wine. 'You mean those women in the East Village who dress in black leather and whip men into submission?' I laughed, totally shocked that she would even know that word. She regarded me with a quiet stare. 'Yes. Something like that,' she said, as she sipped the last of her Sancerre. And then there was silence between us for a minute or two.

I couldn't help but be intrigued. 'Why do you ask?' I offered as a way to break the uncomfortable silence. 'Well,' she hesitated, 'I asked because I am one.' I laughed so hard, Sancerre sprayed out of my nose. She wasn't laughing. 'It's just a sex thing, Vic. Does it make you uncomfortable?' I had to admit that actually, it did not. 'You ever try out any of that—that S&M stuff?' she asked, so seriously I was instantly sober. 'Uh. No.' She scratched a fingernail on my innocently resting hand. 'You want to?'

Okay, what can I say? I was drunk as a sailor and I went to her apartment that night. And this pristine princess taught me things I never knew about sex. My job is very demanding and I have a lot of responsibility. I have to admit, I liked the feeling of being under her control—of being her slave and catering to all her wishes—weird or not.

We've been dating now for about six months. I think it might be time to propose the kind of life we now dream about: normal house in suburban neighborhood, two or so kids, and plenty of whips and leather stashed carefully away under our antique, Laura Ashley-covered bed!"

Understanding BDSM

As we touched upon in the introduction to this chapter, BDSM, which stands for Bondage Domination Sado-Masochism, is a life style choice some people make. It is a mutual arrangement essentially based on communication, trust, and an exchange of sexual power.

However, for our purposes, and in the terms of what goes on in most bedrooms in this arena, what is meant by bondage is not the type of incredible antics and activities that go on in underground

"Rollin', rollin', rollin', keep them doggies rollin', man my ass is swollen, Rawhide! Round 'em up, ride 'em in, get 'em up, get 'em dressed, comb their hair, brush their teeth, Rawhide! Tie me down, tell me lies, pull my hair, slap my thighs—with a big wet strap of, Rawhide!"

—Mitch Robbins (Billy Crystal), City Slickers

sado-masochism clubs. Rather, it means playful domination and submission—perhaps a little spanking here and there. What's usually meant is a situation where one lover ties up the other, as the inability to move—or to restrain your lover—can be a strong sexual turn-on. In other words, light bondage, the kind we'll look at in this book, involves tying someone up in a playful way, where you're restricting their freedom but not their blood flow.

This is not an activity that everyone enjoys, to be sure. But for those who do, it can add an extra erotic charge to an already electric sexual experience.

Approaching It with Your Partner

How any given person can introduce this concept into their own bedroom really depends on the individual couple. Experts appreciate the delicate challenge and make various recommendations on how to go about it.

The best way to approach it with your partner: Talk about it. Naturally. If you have an open relationship for communication, you and your partner already have an existing forum for sharing fantasies. If this is the case, you're in really good shape. You can simply bring it up as a fantasy you have, and see if your partner would like to try it out. If not, okay. Nothing ventured, nothing gained. Leave it in your fantasy life and keep it at that. If your partner is interested in trying it with you, all the better.

Another way you can approach it is by bringing home a video or magazine with pictures of people involved in this kind of sex play. This can give you an easier way to express what you have in mind than just blurting out over breakfast: "When I get home tonight, I'd like to bind your wrists and feet to the bedposts and do very kinky things to you." The imagination runs wild; what you are envisioning as your partner loosely tied up in his own neckties might be perceived to him as being hog-tied like a colt in the rodeo.

Of course, you can just try and spring it on your partner while you are making love—maybe reach under the bed and pull out a stash of silk scarves you have stowed there, and make corny, eyebrow-raised faces at your partner. But we don't recommend this. Surprise in sex is great—but not when it means that someone's ability to move is going to be compromised. This is the kind of thing you definitely broach before you cross the bedroom threshold.

What's important to stress always is that what goes on in the bedroom stays in the bedroom. Just because one partner typically plays the submissive role doesn't mean that the equality of the relationship outside the bedroom door need—or ever should—be compromised.

Trust Is Everything

Once you've thoroughly discussed the possibility of bringing this new kind of play into the bedroom, and you and your partner are both comfortable with at least trying it out to a small degree, you must set some boundaries. We can't stress enough that if trust is not involved in this type of situation, it can easily become dangerous.

Even the most serious BDSM couple has something called a "safety word." This is a word or phrase that typically the submissive person can utter to stop the action. It is never "no," "stop," or "cut it out, you big jerk." The saying of these types of words and phrases is part of the game, and part of the erotic charge of taking sexual power away from the submissive.

Instead, couples can choose an innocuous word or phrase, and better yet, one that has no place in the bedroom. That way, the saying of this word or phrase will seem so ridiculous at the moment it comes out, that the erotic trance will immediately be broken. Imagine having your tied-up lover, who you are relishing ravishing blurt out "marshmallow," "elephant," or "Julie Andrews." Try to decide upon a word or phrase that will be totally silly for you and your partner both. The confusion alone will be enough to stop the action.

When this word is uttered, it means that playtime is over, no questions asked. If you feel your partner will either forget or worse, disregard this word once it is uttered, than there is no place for this kind of sex play in your relationship.

"And after the spanking, the oral sex!"

—Dingo (Carol Cleveland),
Monty Python and
the Holy Grail

Props for Pleasure and Pain

There are many kinds of props available for BDSM play—on the Internet, in sex boutiques, in the back ads of raunchy magazines. We recommend you not even think about using most of these. They are designed for hardcore play; if you're just starting this kind of play in your sexual relationship, you're much better off using what you have on hand in your bedroom. For example, you can use neckties or silk scarves to tie your lover to the bedposts, or whatever else is at hand. You don't need to invest in a full-scale S&M harnessing system.

Handcuffs are kinky, in theory. There is always the possibility that the key could be misplaced or simply won't work. There's also the problem that handcuffs were not designed for sexual pleasure—they were designed to restrain bad people. With regulation-issue cuffs, there's a certain amount of cutting into the flesh that all but your most diehard bondage lover would likely find objectionable.

Most couples are better off with methods of tying up that do not involve anything metallic. However, your policeman role-playing game might not be complete without a set of cuffs. In that case, some sex shops carry furry cuffs that are much more comfortable for the wrists or ankles. If you or your partner is especially forgetful, some sex-shop handcuffs even come with quick-release features.

For a subtle extra touch, you may also try a light gag in the mouth of your submissive partner. We're not suggesting that you cause someone to gag; we're simply suggesting that you further increase their sense of submissiveness and your own sense of dominance (or the reverse—fair's fair, after all) while they are tied up. Remember, it's all about boundaries. Both partners must feel comfortable every step of the way.

Always remember, that the key to this kind of play is to not cause real pain or discomfort for your lover, or at least more pain than a pain-loving partner might stand. The true pleasure in light bondage comes from the control that the tying partner gets to feel with regard to

> "Intellectual and stimulating? Hmmm …. I could read Shakespeare while you spank me."
>
> —Dennis Finch (David Spade), Just Shoot Me!

the immobile one. Conversely, some immobile partners enjoy the thrill of being powerless.

Also, you should never keep someone tied up for more than half an hour. Experts also recommend that you don't tie anyone up if you, or they, are drunk.

Patricia, 51

"I love to get tied up. That's just fun. But it just sounds creepy when my husband calls it bondage. I just ignore the word and go along with it, though. I'll usually go along with anything, actually. I trust Ralph and his fantasies, and he always respects and fulfills mine—so really, what's in a word anyway?

The other day, though, he nearly creeped me out again. He's been having some trouble at work lately. There have been some layoffs at his job, and his favorite boss was let go. His company brought in this thirty-something witch to clean things up, to get his department working more efficiently. What a taskmistress this one is! I can't even get into it. All I'll say is that everyday, he comes home beaten and demoralized.

And then, in our bed that night, he brought his job home. It all started pretty innocently—like any one of his other games. But how it ended up, well, that was pretty wild.

Ralph leaned over to kiss me goodnight, and then he whispered something in my ear that I couldn't quite make out. So I asked him to repeat himself. What he said was, 'Ms. Smith, I'm afraid you haven't been typing quite fast enough for my standards.' I was taken aback. What could I say? First of all, our last name is 'Franklin.' And I haven't typed a word since writing papers in high school. I'm a painter, after all. But I played along, curious to see where this was going.

'I'm sorry, Mister, um,' I didn't know what to call him. 'Mr. Jenkins. You stupid wench! You've been working here for six months and you still don't know my name yet?' He was almost scarily stern with me. 'And sorry's not quite nearly enough. No. You will have to be punished—and punished severely, I might add.'

Giggling, I leaned over the side of the bed and pulled out the box of silk scarves we keep there for just such an occasion. 'Oh no. You're not getting off that easy,' he scowled, grabbing a fistful of scarves from me. 'Now get on all fours. And pull up that nightie! Haven't I already punished you for wearing such provocative clothing to the office!' At this he nearly laughed, but we continued to play.

Ralph tied me to the bed, hands and feet both. I thought he was going to have sex with me, so you can imagine my amazement when his palm hit my exposed derriere! 'Do you know how much money you cost the company today with your sloppiness and laziness?' he chided, as the hand came down again. 'I should fire you right now. If I didn't love this magnificent ass so much, in fact, that's just what I'd do!'

He must have spanked me twenty times before he reached over and hugged me. 'I love you, baby,' he cooed into my ear. I turned my head around and kissed him. I was totally aroused, I was on fire. 'If you really loved me, you would take me right here and now!' I demanded. And he did.

We haven't done the spanking thing since that night, but I have warned him that one day I might just have a bad day at work and have to, um, take it out on his delicious butt!"

Spanking—and No, We Don't Mean Spanking the Monkey

As Patricia learned from her husband, Ralph, there's more to kink and bondage than just being tied up. Spanking is an activity that for whatever reason can be a gleeful experience for both the spanker and the spankee. Perhaps it's because there's an element of the absurd involved in it—that a grown man or woman can be deemed so naughty or insolent that they need to be taught a lesson over the knee of their for-all-other-purposes-in-life equal? Whatever the reason, it's all sex play, and it's all meant for fun. If this is something you and your lover like to partake in, by all means do; and if you don't, that's the end of the story.

Folks who are very into spanking will either use the front of their hand to spank their lover, or any number of other implements. A paddle is a popular substitute, but a hairbrush, rolling pin, even a rolled-up magazine will also do the trick.

As with the type of bondage we talked about earlier, the idea here is not to cause excessive pain or any kind of bleeding at all whatsoever. You don't need to have actual pain to enjoy this activity; for many, just the act itself is erotic enough. Some may even like to be spanked to the point of having a stinging sensation, or a red bottom. It's all about personal preference—and that means the preference of the couple, not just the individual.

Spanking is another instance where a safety word or phrase is an absolute necessity. If the one being spanked cries out "please stop," or "I'm sorry—it won't happen again," these only fuel the fantasies of the spanker—and perhaps the spankee. Remember—it's more a power exchange, not a total giving up of one's power. Role playing will probably play a big, well, role, in the reason why one person is bent over another's knee. So probably screaming out "dishwasher" or "dictionary" is a better way to stop the action—unless, of course, the one being punished is being spanked because they were naughty and didn't load the dishwasher after dinner, or, within the context of the game, the naughty boy didn't finish his homework before seducing his tutor.

Other implements that people may use in this activity include whips and other like tools. Sex boutiques sell the novelty type variety of these, if you want to take it that far. Again, it's all between you and your partner, your trust level, your personal boundaries, and what really turns you on.

Sexploration Exercise #31

1. Have you and your partner ever watched an adult film together?
   a. Sometimes. They're good for a giggle.
   b. A lot. We've gotten some good ideas from these kinds of films.
   c. Only softcore. I couldn't imagine my wife sitting through some of the stuff I've watched with my buddies!
   d. I've thought about it, but my husband's much too big a prude for that.

2. Have you and your partner ever read "the good parts" of an erotic novel to one another?
   a. Yes. It's a very sexy way to get in the mood.
   b. We have a couple of times and I wish we would do it more. I love the sound of my partner's voice when she gets excited about something especially dirty.
   c. Who wants to read when you can just put in a tape?
   d. What's an erotic novel?

3. Have you and your partner ever used an erotic film to express a sexual need or desire?
   a. Yes. It's the number-one method we use to communicate what we want to each other.
   b. Occasionally. There have been times that we've watched and I've seen something that looked interesting—but it's not like we use them all the time.
   c. Never. We don't watch those kinds of things.
   d. I've heard that couples do that. It might be something to try.

4. Would you ever film you and your partner having sex?
   a. Are you kidding? What if it got out there?
   b. Makes me nervous. What if one of the kids put the tape in?
   c. We've tried it, but it just seems so silly.
   d. Not our style.

5. What's the craziest sexual thing you and your partner ever did on videotape?
   a. We once made a full-scale porno production. We were younger then and had a lot of times on our hands I guess.
   b. I filmed her going down on me.
   c. I filmed him going down on me.
   d. We discreetly made love on a public beach—and even more discreetly filmed ourselves doing it!

chapter 31

A Star Is Porn

*John Van Dyke: "When our children can go to any
street corner in America and buy pornography for
five dollars, don't you think that is too high a price
to pay for free speech?"*
*President Bartlett: "No. On the other hand,
I think that five dollars is too high a price
to pay for pornography."*
—David Sage and Martin Sheen, The West Wing

Pornography is ubiquitous. Whether it's soft-core stuff that
you can rent over your cable system, the hardcore variety
that you can download from the Internet, or even the wiggle-
and-jiggle that you get on the networks during prime time or
soap operas, the video depiction of sex is practically impossible to avoid. A lot of the more hardcore stuff that's out there
is pretty raunchy stuff, with cheap production values, actors
that are not especially easy on the eyes, with action that has
all the mechanical repetitiveness of pistons hammering on a
factory floor.

Of course, that doesn't mean it can't be fun. Single people have watched dirty movies to let off a little sexual steam. Couples have watched together as a way to get warmed up before sex—and even used it as a medium to communicate information about wants, needs, and desires to each other. Adult films exist for entertainment, yes, but there is also an extremely viable market of videos that have been designed for instructional purposes. But just because these were meant to educate does not mean they can't also serve to entertain. Ever watch an instructional sex video with your partner all the way through, sitting demurely on opposite sides of the couch or room? We didn't think so!

In this chapter, we go through the ins and outs (please pardon the pun) of adult-oriented films—whether they're watched alone, with a partner, or even if you and your paramour decide to make your own!

Alice, 44

"I once had a boyfriend, Todd, who was totally into hardcore pornos. It was gross, and it's pretty much why I dropped him. I could never understand what was so hot with all that low-budget stuff. The acting was terrible. The stories were totally stupid. Even the actors were so ugly, you couldn't even look at them—much less watch them actually having sex with each other.

I still shudder at one he made me watch with him—one that involved three paunchy, hairy, downright awful men all having sex with one woman—and all at one time. I couldn't sleep for a week without having nightmares about that one!

So you must understand that when my husband, Marty, suggested that we buy one of these erotic, couples-oriented videos, I was a little queasy. I was like, I'm not going through that again. But he told me to just give it a chance.

I'm glad I did. The first one he brought home was totally different than any video I remember watching with Todd. There was a story—an actual plot—and none of the grotesquely graphic, sweaty, sleazy in-and-out I remembered. And in this film, the women actually looked like they were enjoying themselves—that they were in it for the fun and they were in control, not because they owed some crack dealer some money and they needed a quick way to make cash.

Over time, we started to incorporate these videos into our lovemaking routine—only occasionally, but it was usually a treat—a nice change of pace. A couple of times, there would be something I didn't like, and Marty, fantastic guy that he is, just took the tape out and that was the end of it.

We also stumbled upon some of these instructional videos—you know the kind, where people act out whatever the voiceover says to do and you learn new things and how different techniques can stimulate your lover in different ways? I've developed a special affinity for these.

In fact, I now find myself watching these 'instructional' videos when Marty's away on business trips. Sometimes we'll even have phone sex while I've got the video on. He doesn't always know I'm watching it, though!"

The Hard Stuff

Only for the most graphic tastes, this is what offends most when they think of what's involved in adult films. That said, we won't spend a lot of time in this world.

Essentially, the more hardcore the porn, the more graphic the sex. Hardcore films leave nothing to the imagination. If you don't want to see countless shots of penetration, acts that may be considered degrading to women—like the infamous "money shot," in which the male (or males) ejaculates in the woman's face and the like—and acts that many may perceive as too provocative for their tastes, such as anal penetration, hardcore S&M, and sexual acts involving one woman, several men, and penetration of ever orifice imaginable—and likely, all at the same time, it is wise to avoid this variety of adult films.

The hardcore variety generally appeals to men, as it is based mostly in the visual, nuts-and-bolts brand of sexual acts. If you're looking for a little more "story" and a little less, well "sex," it's recommended that you avoid these types of films. Cable TV stations like Spice, and, at times, The Playboy Channel, will feature films of this nature, but typically, you'll be able to find the most hardcore stuff only on video, DVD, or the Internet.

Softcore—for Couples?

Premiere cable TV channels like Cinemax, Showtime, and HBO sometimes feature adult-oriented films after-hours—mostly after 11 P.M., when these networks believe most kiddie-poos are safely tucked away in their beds, and their parents are alone and looking for a little extra heat in theirs.

The type of adult films these channels typically feature after hours is typically more of the softcore variety of porn. In these films or series, you can watch people having sex, but whether it's simulated or actually being done is a lot more difficult to discern than in the hardcore variety. The mood is far more romantic, and the sexual fantasies depicted in the videos take into account the desires of both men *and* women.

You won't see any actual penetration, and you'll be hard-pressed to find anything close to "gang-bang" action in these films; however, there will be an occasional threesome as well as lesbian sequences. The likelihood of seeing full frontal of men or women is very small. Mostly, it's lots of breasts and buttocks—and not much else.

Geared toward women and couples, softcore adult films typically have better production values than their hardcore components, and you may even come across decent acting and story lines.

Women typically have a more atmospheric sensibility when it comes to sex, versus the strictly visual cravings of the men, and so these films have been known to have great appeal for women who aren't particularly against a little video voyeurism, and may be seeking out a little extra stimulation or titillation.

> "*My Homer is not a Communist ... he may be a liar, a pig, an idiot, a Communist ... but he is not a porn star!*"
> —Grampa Simpson,
> The Simpsons

Couples can enjoy this kind of film together because it presents a forum for sexual experimentation without exploitation or embarrassment.

Be advised, whether you are a woman or man, if you are a partner planning an evening of adult film viewing, you should preview it for yourself prior to bringing the subject up at all. That way, you won't have any nasty surprises. Chances are, if you have been with your partner long enough, you know what he or she likes and doesn't like, and you can avoid any unpleasant surprises by seeing the whole thing in advance.

Intimate Instruction

Another kind of video, specifically aimed at couples, can be found in higher-end sex boutiques, on cable, and online. In these videos, the production values are typically high and the couples more attractive. They also generally feature gentle narration by a reputed "sexpert." Designed to show couples different ways to share and experience sex, these videos are typically geared towards couples, although some have been produced to teach men and women separately. Topics include sexual positions, performing oral sex, mastering the *Kama Sutra* or tantric sex, erotic massage, and the like. While not always particularly graphic in nature, watching this type of video with your sex partner will likely get you revved up and ready for some action—and you might even find that you'll watch these only in segments before you've had enough primer and are ready to join the action.

Adult Magazines

Generally in the purview of men, adult-oriented magazines typically feature full-color, glossy photographs of young, beautiful, and highly air-brushed females. Sometimes these women are alone, sometimes they are depicted doing very naughty things with close girlfriends.

Sometimes these can be shared between couples—it's all up to the individual couple. The pictorial exposes that involve hetero couples—and even those naughty girlfriends—can be exciting to share. Some magazines feature graphic stories, articles, and letters, a la the famous *Penthouse* "Forum," that appeal to both men and women. Again, it's all a matter of particular taste in titillation: As long as no one's offended by the material, there's nothing wrong with sharing it.

Erotica

Another forum for adult entertainment involves no type of film whatsoever. This is erotica, which is an umbrella term that encompasses adult-oriented material in the written word.

Unlike actual pornography, erotica was not invented in this or the past century. You can find erotic writing that dates back centuries—*Kama Sutra,* anyone? Not to mention the classical works of Sappho, Ovid, and many more. Different times have relied heavily on euphemisms, but if you've ever been wondering what John Donne was talking about in his poetry when he said that he and his lover "die" together, wonder no more. It's not that they are so in love that they're ready for a little Romeo-and-Juliet double suicide action: In Elizabe-than times, to die, in this form, actually meant to achieve orgasm. The buttoned-up Victorians were the most prolific purveyors of erotica. Don't believe it? Pick up a volume of Victorian erotica and you'll see what an era of sexual repression can do!

Today's erotic writings can be found in bookstores everywhere—and even through online outlets like Amazon.com. And we're not even talking about those bodice-ripping, randy romance novels here. A whole market has risen up around novels that involve acts more explicit than even the most hardcore films. If for nothing else, try one of these novels out at least for the fantasy fodder they can provide for you—and for your lover.

Erotic nonfiction encompasses sexual self-help, and if you thought dirty magazines featured explicit photographs, you haven't seen anything until you've thumbed through a pictorial erotic manual!

> *"One woman's pornographer is another woman's spiritual leader."*
>
> —Carrie Bradshaw
> (Sarah Jessica Parker),
> Sex and the City

Burton, 48

"I can't explain what came over my wife, Andrea, the other night. We had spent the day visiting our kids at Parents' Day at their camp. She just bought a video camera, and so we took lots of family films and had a really good, wholesome family day.

And then we got home.

Andrea has always been on the tame side in our sex life. I've always been the one to suggest we do new things—to introduce into our bedroom new ways to enjoy each other sexually. It's important you understand this when I tell you what I'm about to tell you.

That day, when we got home, I went into the living room to watch the game. She went into the bedroom to change. When she came out, she was wearing a red-hot red negligee and was holding the video camera in her hand. She took the tape we had made during the day out and put a fresh one in. 'We're going to try something new tonight,' she told me, in the most sultry voice she could muster. She opened a bottle of wine and poured two healthy-sized glasses. I was intrigued. 'Tonight, we're going to make a little movie of our own.'

I didn't need much convincing. In fact, I didn't need to even do that much at all—with the exception of being the best porn leading man I knew how to be. I didn't have to think or plan anything out. She had apparently been thinking about this for a while and had the whole film planned out in her head. She was the dominatrix director; I was her subject, and that was that.

We did things that night I don't ever remember doing in our marriage— and if we had done them, it was so many years ago, that at least I'd long forgotten them. She had purchased a tripod and other peripheral equipment, so neither of us had to be distracted during the fun—or worry about breaking that new expensive piece of equipment that probably could have paid for a week of camp—except when we wanted to be. We found we each had a wonderful experience from time to time holding the camera and filming the other.

Afterward, Andrea admitted that the only reason she had even bought the camera was for this very purpose. That we could have nice family tapes was just a happy accident. She explained that we could do this as often as we liked, but we just had to keep the tapes carefully labeled— and keep our 'special' tapes under lock and key. She had no complaints from me.

I don't think I'll underestimate my wife and the crazy inner workings of her dirty mind ever again!"

Lights, Camera, and Get Ready for the Action!

These days, most people own a video camera. Which, for our purposes, naturally leads to the inevitable question: Should you make your own porn?

Absolutely! Sex is definitely enhanced when *both* partners know that a camera is rolling. Yes, there's a certain amount of self-consciousness to overcome, but it can be enormous fun for both parties to know that every move they make is being captured by the camera.

First and foremost, you'll want to think about how to spring this idea on your partner. Here, a little bit of social lubrication may or may not be in order. Why not pour yourself and your beloved a drink or two (or three) before you bring up the question of making a tape. Be sure to emphasize that no one else will ever see it, that you won't leave it out so that the housekeeper could accidentally put it into *The Sound of Music* box.

Keep the lights turned down low or, if you prefer, you can make the video outdoors. This is strictly a matter of personal taste and there is no one way to go. The discussion of production values can be a delightful aphrodisiac and almost as much fun as the lovemaking itself. Together, you can choose the setting, the lighting, the background music, how much or how little you and your partner will wear, how much or how little you and your partner will show, and so on. You can even give Spielberg a run for his money with special directing ideas. Will the camera be stationary, or will each of you take turns doing the taping while making love? (That's what we recommend!)

Keep in mind that the entire video does not need to be shot in one single take. You could begin in the bathroom, where you video yourselves or each other showering, perhaps through a steamed-up glass door. Or you could begin in the living room, before a blazing fire, and then slowly make your way to the bedroom. Chapter 27 should give you a great start. Where you take it is your own business!

The degree of self-consciousness that you and your partner have about your own bodies should dictate the level of explicitness of the video. You may want to keep covered up. On the other hand, if you feel good about your appearance, then show some skin. Keep in mind that the two of you will be the only observers of this magnum opus, and you've already seen each other naked hundreds of times.

After you've finished your Oscar-worthy production, let it sit for a night before you watch it. Create another special lovemaking event around the experience. Make some popcorn, and for God's sake, make sure that the kids won't be coming home early. Then take a look at what you've got. You're more than likely in for a highly entertaining and erotic evening.

> *Marie Barone: "What is a DVD player? Is it for pornography?"*
>
> *Debra Barone: "Yes, Marie, I bought Ray a porn machine!"*
>
> —Doris Roberts and Patricia Heaton, Everybody Loves Raymond

Proceed with Caution

It may not have occurred to you (that's why we're here, of course) that by making such a video, you have now qualified to enter a hitherto forbidden world of amateur couples who swap their lovemaking videos with others. Thanks to the Internet, there exists a brisk trade in these swapped videos, a (physically) safe way to experience sex with strangers, now that we live in a world of sexually transmitted diseases.

There are, however, risks to entering into swapping relationships. Someone might just decide that your video is really terrific and ought to be downloadable, either for free or for a fee. Don't forget what happened to Pamela Anderson and Tommy Lee! A lot of people would then have access to your artistic masterpiece, perhaps even your teenage kids. Tread carefully if you're getting involved in that whole video-sharing world. You may end up with a little more than you bargained for.

Sexploration Exercise #32

1. When's the last time you performed a striptease for your partner?
   a. Not since I had the body of a twenty-year-old!
   b. I never have! Guys don't strip for their women.
   c. Not for a few years now. Who has the time.
   d. Last night!

2. Have you and your partner ever been to a cabaret club together?
   a. I've wanted to go, but she'd never come along with me.
   b. I've thought about it, but would he think I was a lesbian if I asked him to take me?
   c. No—that's why they call them "gentlemen's clubs." No ladies allowed!
   d. I've been with my friends but never with my husband!

3. Have you ever had a lap dance?
   a. I live for lap dances.
   b. I think lap dances are too much like cheating if you ask me.
   c. I've thought about it, but I'm a woman. Does that make me gay?
   d. I've had one and I'm a straight woman. Let's just say it's really hot, but mostly you just giggle with the dancer.

4. Have you ever performed a lap dance?
   a. My husband loves it when I give him a lap dance.
   b. I'd be too shy to do all that gyrating and stuff on him.
   c. I'd crush my wife if I tried to give her one.
   d. I just bought an instructional tape on how to give a lap dance—we'll see how it goes!

5. What do you find is the sexiest thing about stripping?
   a. The anticipation of what's to come.
   b. The idea that she's doing this all for you.
   c. The part where she's finally naked!
   d. There's nothing sexy about stripping.

chapter 32

Stripteases and Lap Dances— for Her and *Him!*

"Playing strip poker with an exhibitionist somehow takes the challenge away."
—*Nick Smith (Chris Eigeman),* Metropolitan

So you think that you and your partner have done it all by now. The ancient mysteries of the *Kama Sutra* hold no mystery for you any longer. You've twisted yourselves like a pretzel trying out new sex positions six ways to Sunday. You've done it with gravity boots, with trapezes, with mirrors, on the land, in the sea, and in the air. You've made the mile-high club. And now here you are, in the prime of your sex life, wondering if there's anything left you haven't tried.

Well, we've got good news for you. There's always something new to try. As we've told you before, a little imagination goes a long way.

For our purposes right now, try taking your imaginations into the realm of the strip club, where women find inventive, erotic uses for fireman's poles and tassels, and men dressed—and then undressed—like sexy cops, construction workers, or what have you accept fistfuls of dollar bills into the elastic of their barely there G-strings.

This is the world of the exotic erotic. In this chapter, we bring the secrets of exotic dancers, both male and female, right into your bedroom (or living room or kitchen of wherever you'll be when the mood strikes!).

Beth, 42

"I got the idea of going to a strip club with a friend from a magazine. At first the idea really turned me off—I mean, that's where sweaty, slobby men go to drool over girls young enough to be their daughters—right? And wouldn't only lesbians be interested in watching other women strip?

I found out I was wrong when I mentioned the idea to my friend, Sally, from work. She said she had been before and that it's lots of fun—you just have to know the right place to go. So I figured okay, why not? If Sally's gone to this kind of place and she's had fun—and she isn't gay—well, then maybe it'd be good for a laugh.

I felt pretty weird at first when we walked into the place. I was so embarrassed—especially because it seemed like every guy in the audience was looking at us. I wanted to run right out of there—to jump back into my car and get out of there as quickly as possible.

After the initial novelty of two women being in their space wore off, the guys essentially started to ignore us. Maybe they were more embarrassed to see us there than we were to see them. Who knows? Either way, we snuck off to a little table in the back, behind the male customers, and ordered a couple of drinks.

It was quite an education, watching those women undress. Even if they weren't beautiful, they knew how to strip down, and it made me think about how I generally take my clothes off at night before going to bed. Before my husband, Ted, and I make love. Taking it all in, imagining how much more exciting sex could be with this kind of prelude, I decided it was probably time to change all that.

And then Sally really surprised me. She called one of the girls over and whispered something in her ear. The girl took some cash from Sally. She then straddled my friend on the chair and then began to gyrate in Sally's lap and do all kinds of erotic things. I nearly thought I was going to faint. I didn't want to go that far. After the dance was over, Sally asked if I wanted one, too, but I politely declined. We ended up talking to the dancer for a while, and she even showed us pictures of her son. The whole thing was very different than I thought it was going to be, I can tell you that.

When I got home, I was slightly tipsy from the three Cosmopolitans I drank—and, I have to admit, from the whole experience of the evening. I was glad that Ted was still awake. 'Hey sweetie,' he said to me as I innocently kissed him. 'How was your dinner?' (Okay, so I hadn't told him where I went. I wasn't sure he'd understand.)

Then I got my inspiration. I asked him where our daughter was and he said she was spending the night with a friend. Our son was away at college, and as I stumbled through the math—three Cosmos, remember—I finally realized we were alone. 'Living room. Now. Pronto!' Like a good boy, he obeyed. 'Sit down on the couch.' He complied. I went to the CD player, threw in something sexy, and began to act out what I saw tonight, concluding with a fairly hot lap dance.

If you think my husband was pleased, you're right. And not to mention really surprised. 'What did I do to deserve this?' he asked when we had topped off my lap dance with some of the hottest sex we'd ever had in our lives.

I actually admitted to him what I had been up to that night, which he regarded with a pensive stare. 'Are you mad at me?' I asked, as sheepishly as I could get away with after delivering that performance. 'Mad at you? No,' he replied. 'But I will be mad if you don't take me with you the next time!"

> *Maria Portokalos: "Touvla, on my wedding night, my mother, she said to me, 'Greek women, we may be lambs in the kitchen, but we are tigers in the bedroom.'"*
>
> *Toula Portokalos: "Eew! Please let that be the end of your story."*
>
> —Lainie Kazan and Nia Vardalos, My Big Fat Greek Wedding

Stripping for Him

Why do men like watching strippers and receiving lap dances? It's very basic. There's just something very exciting about a woman undressing just for them. But that doesn't necessarily mean that strip clubs are entirely for men and their buddies, and that there's nothing there that could interest a woman, as we saw in the case of Beth and her friend Sally.

A lot of women go to strip clubs from time to time for various reasons. When Beth finally opened her mind and let her inhibitions go, she not only had a fantastic time, but she came home with a few new boudoir tricks with which to dazzle her husband.

If this is something that interests you, grab your partner (it's very likely he will not say no) and or an as-curious close friend and head to a strip club.

Watch the dancers on the stage as they move around and disrobe. Watch a lap dance. Take note of all the moves that the dancer makes. Imagine yourself doing this for your husband. What the heck? It's just for fun. You might even note some of the music playing. If you are feeling especially bold and daring, get a lap dance yourself.

One thing visiting a strip club may do for you is put your mind at rest about what your husband or boyfriend actually does there—and if it can be construed as cheating. In a strip club, limits on contact vary by state and individual clubs, and most are very stringent in an effort to protect the dancers from the wandering hands and advances of the customers.

All of this begs a question: Why should he go out when he can get it at home? In your own home, there are no limits! Ladies, why not give your man his own personal sex show and become an exotic dancer in the privacy of your own home? Scared you won't know what to do? Afraid of a little stage fright? Think you might start to feel a little silly? These are all valid reasons not to give your partner a fantasy dance, but think about what you might be missing if you don't even try.

Your costume can be as simple or as complicated as you want it to be. We're talking new lingerie. We're talking sitting a man down in a chair, dimming the lights, putting some slow, sexy music on the stereo, then slowly, very slowly, performing a striptease.

Getting Ready

To get yourself geared up for your performance, visit a very sexy lingerie shop. You may even want to buy some new perfume for this experience. For fun, you might even try a disguise. While you're out shopping for your bad self, consider adding a wig to your purchases. A wig allows you to step out of your own persona and inhabit an entirely new character.

Don't forget the candles or anything that might give the room an unusual scent. The bedroom or living room in which you perform your lap dance does not have to smell like the beer and cigarette aroma that permeates most strip clubs. Aim higher.

Don't tell him what's going to happen. Just tell him that something special *is* going to happen. Do whatever you need to do to make sure that the house will be empty. And make sure that he understands that he really needs to be home by the appointed hour.

Before he gets home, prepare the room for whatever mood you seek to achieve. You might even pour yourself a nice glass of white wine in order to loosen any remaining inhibitions. When you hear the key in the door, it's show time.

Leave him a note to explain in exactly what room he should meet you. Position a chair appropriately, and make it a chair that can comfortably bear your weight and the G-forces likely to ensue. You might even put a note on the chair that says, "Sit here." Then let the games begin!

> Peter: *"Why didn't you take off all your clothes? You could have stopped 40 cars."*
>
> Ellie: *"I'll remember that when we need 40 cars."*
>
> —Clark Gable and Claudette Colbert, It Happened One Night *(1934)*

Debut Performance

In exotic dancing, the key word for your performance is S-L-O-W. There's no rush. Remember that you don't have to squeeze all of your moves into one three-minute number. Many women report that by the time the first song has ended, they had barely begun to undress. The only rush should be the head rush he gets from watching you.

Don't leave anything out. He'll love you for it. Separate his legs with a knee. Lick your breasts, if you are so constructed. Don't be afraid to be anything that you saw in the strip club, or anything that suddenly crosses your mind. Deep inside every good girl, there's a bad girl just dying to escape. This is your chance to trade matron for Mata Hari—and have a blast!

Rub up against him, unhook your bra, and look your man straight in the eye with neither fear nor favor. Make sure the kids are out of the house for the evening because this is going to be one hell of a night.

The beautiful thing about being in a committed relationship is that it provides a safe, secure outlet for exploring your unconventional side. We would hardly recommend you perform a lap dance on the second date. The results might not be everything you would hope for. You might have the excitement and danger, but you would not have the safety factor that a long-term relationship provides for exploring this naughty part of your nature. So take advantage of the fact that you're married, and do what a single woman might not dare with a man she does not know well. If that one lap dance should turn into a lap ballet, we will be off in the wings, admiring your performance, bearing witness to the fact that a sexy, naughty new star is born.

> *Mr. Burns: "You're fired."*
>
> *Marge Simpson: "You can't fire me just because I'm married. I'm gonna sue the pants off of you."*
>
> *Mr. Burns: "You don't have to sue me to get my pants off."*
>
> —*Harry Shearer and Julie Kavner,* The Simpsons

Jeffrey, 45

"For my wife Sara's recent fortieth birthday, I did something I never in a million years ever imagined I would do. I actually gave her a striptease! Sara and I have been married nearly fifteen years, and in all that time, it's never even occurred to me that she might enjoy a striptease—I mean, one that I gave her. Women are sexy. And a woman taking off her clothes—we'll just say it doesn't get much better than that! But guys, I mean, let's face it. We're bulky if not bulging—and not in all the right places, if you catch my drift. We're hairy, course, tough-skinned—who wants to see that?

Apparently my wife did. When her best friend Gilda turned forty last month, all the women headed right to something called a 'male revue.' Essentially, they spent the night watching guys take off their clothes and shoved dollar bills at them. Sara came home so riled up, I nearly had to fight her advances back for fear of my life. But I gave in, and man did she give it to me good.

I, of course, asked her what had come over her, and she told me that there was just something about the way these men had carried on in the club, and all the excitement they had generated with the women that she was about ready to explode when she walked through the door and was beyond glad that I was home.

Well, I don't have to tell you that it bothered me somewhat that my wife was getting turned on by strange men, so I decided to get to her myself. Before she left for work one morning the following week, I asked her which guy had given her the biggest charge. 'Definitely the motorcycle cop,' she told me.

The day of her birthday, I ended up taking the day off from work—but I didn't tell her that. Once she left, I cleaned the apartment, made reservations at her favorite restaurant, and headed right for the costume shop.

When she got home, she was thrilled about the state of the apartment, and when I told her we were going to Diane's for dinner, she was over the moon. We had a wonderful dinner, but the best part of the night—was about to begin.

I sat Sara down in the living room and I headed into the bedroom to get into character. When I came back out again, she actually erupted in a fit of giggles. But then, when I got tough with her and threatened to write her a ticket if she didn't settle down, she could see I was serious—and she sat back and enjoyed the ride. After my performance, she jumped on top of me and literally knocked me right off my feet—and right out of my boots, so to speak.

I'm going to have to figure out who some of her other favorite characters are and head to the costume shop again soon!"

Stripping for Her

Hey, guys, listen up: Stripping was not just made for a woman to do for your enjoyment as you sit back with your head against your arms with a giant smile on your face. There are a few things you can do for her in this department—and by that we mean rising to the occasion (no, not that!) and giving her a performance she'll never forget. Of course, chances are you outweigh your female partner by more than a few pounds, so a lap dance may be more dangerous than exciting for her; however, a striptease may delight her in ways you've never even considered before.

On a random Friday night in the not-so-distant future, give her a special treat:

1. At least a week beforehand, make arrangements for the kids to stay with their friends overnight—or, if they are young children, see if their grandparents won't want to take them for an overnight visit. If all else fails, a close neighbor may also be glad to help you out.

2. Plan your attack. Tell your partner that you want to make a special night for just the two of you, and that you've already made arrangements for the kids. (This, she will especially love.) Tell her you want to have a candlelight dinner at home—and maybe with a surprise or two for desert.

3. Decide what character you'd like to play—if any. If you're a white collar guy, maybe just for tonight, you could become her blue-collar fantasy man; if you're strictly blue collar, change it up by putting on your best suit, and maybe wear glasses and walk around with a newspaper folded under your arm. (See Chapter 27 for inspiration.) And yes, of course, you can always just be yourself.

4. Pamper your woman. Make sure you get home from work before she does. When she arrives, meet her at the front door with a stiff drink or a refreshing glass of white wine. Take her into the bedroom and help her change into comfy clothes. Remember, you're the sex object for this one, not her, and that means no high heels or constricting

clothing for her. Encourage her to wear a comfy T-shirt and sweats—which maybe, if you're really good, you've already laid out for her on the bed.

5. Lead her to the dining room table where you'll already have dinner set and ready to enjoy. (Whether you cook or order in, it will be nice for her if she doesn't have to worry about it at all.)

6. Let her carry the conversation—unless she's too tired to talk. In that case, you do the talking but make the conversation about her.

7. If she tries to clear the table, stop her immediately. Instead, send her immediately to the living room or bedroom, wherever you've decided to give her your show, and let her relax while you clean up. Go change into your costume, if desired.

8. When you finish cleaning up, head to the room where she waits, and head right to the CD player. Turn on your music, turn down the lights, and let the games begin!

Your woman might be a little surprised at first by everything, but when she sees you're serious about it, she'll be into it! When you're done—and if you don't have back or other physical ailments that might make this difficult—scoop her up in your arms, Rhett Butler style, and take her to the bedroom where you should now both be primed and ready to ravage each other to your hearts' delight!

Sexploration Exercise #33

1. Which best describes your position on sex toys?
   a. They're a great enhancement to a couple's sexual enjoyment.
   b. They're fantastic to use with yourself, but not in the presence of your significant other.
   c. They should be used sparingly as they could get really addictive and turn users off having sex with other humans.
   d. They are distracting to couples and they have no place in the bedroom.

2. Have you ever used a sex toy on yourself?
   a. I never would have had an orgasm if I didn't discover the vibrator.
   b. Sometimes when I masturbate, I'll use a dildo in my anus.
   c. I always wanted to try, but I don't know which one is right for me.
   d. I don't believe in sex toys.

3. Have you ever used a sex toy on your partner?
   a. We always use sex toys with each other. It gives our sex life that added umph it sometimes needs.
   b. There's nothing more erotic than masturbating my wife with her favorite vibrator.
   c. I'd love to use a sex toy to stimulate my husband's prostate as I hear this gives men excellent orgasms, but I'm not sure he'd be in to that idea.
   d. I would never use anything on my wife that wasn't a part of my own body.

4. Do you know what each of the following sex toys is typically used for? (Hint: you'll find the answers in this chapter.)
   a. Butt plug
   b. Dildo
   c. Cock ring
   d. Butterfly

5. What is your favorite sex toy?
   a. Ben-Wa balls
   b. Anal beads
   c. Vibrator
   d. French tickler

chapter 33

Sex Toys

Alvy Singer: "With your wife in bed, does she need
some kind of artificial stimulation,
like, like marijuana?"
Old Man on the Street:
"We use a large vibrating egg."
—Woody Allen and Albert Ottenheimer, Annie Hall

Whether you choose to use sex toys or not is up to you and your partner. Just keep in mind, there's nothing abnormal or unhealthy about loving or hating sex toys. It's completely a personal preference.

A lot of people are squeamish about sex toys. There's a sense that if you can't do it on your own, it's cheating to use a battery-operated or plastic device. Many women who love vibrators are not comfortable sharing the experience with their lovers. Other couples will use a vibrator as a means of increasing stimulation of the clitoris during vaginal love-making. If you like it, great; and if you don't, then that should be the end of the discussion.

Many couples have never tried toys, for the simple reason that one or both parties are simply too squeamish to make the purchase, or to share it with a lover. That's okay. We're in the electronic age now. You can find sex toys online and through mail order as well as in adult sex boutiques—so you can't let that be what gets in your way of trying out some of these truly delightful devices anymore!

In this chapter, we look at what the options are in the sex toy arena—and perhaps open you up to a new experience by getting you to try some of them out for yourselves!

Doug, 41

"Recently, my wife, Loretta, got involved with a new group of women. Let me tell you this. When she first started hanging around them, I didn't like it one bit. Now, with all the stuff we've gotten to do together because of what she's learned from them ... Well, let's just say I'd like to kiss each and every one of them!

What happened was Loretta lost her job after slaving away at the same company for like twenty years. I kept encouraging her to get a new job, that employers just don't reciprocate the loyalty you feel for them any-more, but she was comfortable and settled and thought for sure this was the place she would retire. Let me jump in here right now and tell you that my Loretta really doesn't like change, never has, which was why I was so shocked when she first started making all these weird suggestions—but, I digress. I'll get to that in a minute.

Anyway, what happened was Loretta went to work on an ordinary Wednesday, got her coffee, as usual, started to eat her lemon poppy seed muffin as she did every day, and then got called into her boss's office. And then poof! Within twenty minutes, she was packing up her desk, saying good-bye to her stunned colleagues, and out the door. The boss said it was something about her making too much money for the company to afford—some bad economy bull.

Anyway, Loretta was devastated. She spent days just moping around the house. Our sex life essentially stopped.

One Sunday, I saw an ad in a our church bulletin for a women's sup-port group—a forum for recently unemployed women to gripe and network and all that stuff. Believe it or not, that ended up being the group that gave her all the racy ideas.

Even after her first meeting, Loretta started to get her sex drive back. And then she started, little by little, to make some pretty zany suggestions. One thing I knew, we weren't having any sex at all. Next, we were doing it all the time and in positions I can't even explain. And then one day, she brought *it* home.

It was a purple wand-like thing that came with batteries and three different speeds. A vibrator! I had to draw the line then and there. Certainly I wasn't going to complain about all the sex we were having, but I'd be damned if we were going to have a third party of any kind join in the fun. She said she understood and put it back in the box.

A few days later, I came home early from work, and walked in on her, sprawled out on the bed, using the thing on herself. She was so wrapped up in *it*, she didn't even hear me come in. And then the weirdest thing happened. I started to get really turned on watching her get so turned on. I couldn't take my eyes off of her. Sure, she'd masturbated in front of me before—but it was never anything like this.

When she finally came out of her trance, she looked up and saw me there. She was much too flushed already to show any embarrassment at all. 'Want to try it out with me?' she gasped. And I did. And it was great!

Now I'm not going to say we're going to start getting into all kinds of other kinky sex, but I have to say, I am intrigued to see what she's going to come home with and want to try out next!"

Gallery of the Most Common Sex Toys

In this section, we'll look at some of the most basic sex toys. True, some are more adventurous than others, but isn't that what keeps sex interesting? That is, taking it to the next level again and again. Don't know the difference between a vibrator and a dildo? Curious about all the various anal toys available? Thought some of these devices only existed in fiction? Think again. This section will give you a primer on sex toys; where you take it? Now that's up to you!

Anal Beads

Anal beads are typically used to enhance orgasms—not to provoke them. Before sexplay, they are inserted into her or his anus. When she or he is about to climax, an attentive partner can delicately and carefully pull them from the anus, one by one, during the contractions of orgasm.

Essentially, anal beads look just as you imagine they would—like a necklace that hasn't been closed. They are, essentially, a string of beads linked together with a nylon cord. Some are made with cotton cords, but these should only be used once as they are impossible to clean properly.

Made of all kinds of materials, from plastic to silicone to jelly to rubber, anal beads also come in several different sizes, from "shy" (imagine the size of a blueberry) to "oh-my-goodness-you're-going-to-stick-that-where" (okay, now imagine a bead about the size of a typical orange).

Anal Probes

These work along the same lines as dildos (see below), except that they come in different shapes and sizes than most dildos, and can be flexible or quite stiff. Used, of course, in anal play, they sometimes even vibrate. Some may even contain bumps that simulate the feeling of anal beads, and can thus be used in the same way.

Ben-Wa Balls

Japanese in origin, Ben-Wa balls consist of a pair of marble-sized spheres that a woman inserts in her vagina. One of the balls is solid, and is placed far up in the vagina, near the cervix. The second one, which is hollow but typically filled partially with mercury or ball bearings, is placed in the vagina next to the solid one. They come in lots of different nonporous materials, including acrylic, silver, steel, and, for the Rockefellers among us, gold.

How do they work? When the women wearing them moves even slightly, the mercury-filled ball will clang into the solid one, and create a vibrating sensation in the vagina. These can be worn during typical sex play, but many women like to wear them at other times, such as when they're running errands like grocery shopping or picking up dry cleaning. Others like to wear them to the office or while exercising. Possibly doing laundry is a good time to wear them—especially if you're passing the time by sitting on top of the washer with a good book.

Like everything else in sex, it's all about personal preference. Some women swear by Ben-Wa balls; others don't derive the same pleasurable sensations from using them and essentially don't get the point of using them.

Butt Plugs

This toy is just like a dildo, except it is especially designed to be used in the anus. A butt plug is narrow at the top and base and larger in the middle. It is inserted and left in the anus during sex play. It can be smooth and straight, or ridged, almost like a corkscrew. Made in all kinds of interesting shapes and sizes, the butt plug has a specially designed base whereby it will not be able to get lost, um, up there. The vaginal canal ends at the cervix; there's not a whole lot of space to lose something there, although it has been known to happen. The anus, which is connected to the rectum, which is connected to miles of intestines, is quite another thing. Always be careful with things being inserted into the anus. It's not a conversation most of us really want to have with the emergency room doctor!

Butterflies

This interesting device has all the benefits of a vibrator—and an added bonus. It's essentially "hands-free," except that it is controlled by a remote device you hold. The butterfly, sometimes also known as a bumble bee, is essentially worn like pair of panties. It's strapped around the pelvis, with the vibrating mechanism placed in front over the clitoris.

Cock Rings

Cock rings are devices designed to limit the blood flow to the penis, therefore increasing a man's staying power. They can be made from leather, metal, or rubber, and are generally about one and a half to two inches in diameter. The cock ring is worn around the base of the penis—and sometimes around the testicles, and also serves to create a more intense and powerful erection. Some cock rings are fitted with a stimulation device known as a French tickler (see below).

Be careful when using this device, however. It should never be worn for longer than a half an hour at most—and it should not be worn too tightly. Why? We'll give you one word that will, in this context, very likely stay with you forever: *tourniquet*.

Duotone Balls

These are very much like Ben-Wa balls and are designed for her pleasure. They are inserted into the vagina. They bounce against each other inside the vagina to create pleasurable vibrations. However, they are much bigger than Ben-Wa balls. These are more like golf balls. Usually made from lighter—nonporous—materials than Ben-Wa balls, they are also weighted and come with a nylon pull string. Also, a women can wear either two or four of these at a time—it all depends on her mood!

Dildos

Dildos are among the most common—and favorite—sex toys for women and men. Dildos have been used as sex toys since the dawn of time. Don't believe us? Check out some of the racy illustrations in the *Kama Sutra!*

What is a dildo? Essentially, it's a fake penis. And like penises, dildos come in all shapes and sizes—and girths, from an inch to two inches in diameter. Unlike human penises, however, dildos are made in every material imaginable—from silicon and rubber to jelly and hard plastic to glass. Also unlike penises, dildos can be two-headed: straight, for sharing with a partner, or curved, like a horseshoe, to stimulate the vagina and anus simultaneously.

As we mentioned before, dildos can be highly arousing for men and women, for vaginal and anal play. A dildo can be used on a man to stimulate the infamous prostate gland. Inserting a dildo into a woman's vagina while she is being stimulated clitorially will bring her to new heights of ecstasy. Inserting a dildo into her anus during vaginal intercourse can make the sex experience that much more satisfying and complete.

Food

Long vegetables like carrots, cucumbers, and zucchini are sometimes used as substitute dildos. Just be careful: Vegetables are a lot more malleable than traditional dildos and can snap and break. Also, be especially cautious when using these in anal play. Unlike butt plugs, these devices were not designed by nature with any kind of stoppage device!

French Ticklers

Almost like condoms, but not designed to prevent STD transmission or pregnancy—so don't use them solely for these purposes—French ticklers fit over the penis. They are designed with ridges and small bumps to stimulate the vagina and clitoris. Unlike condoms, they are reusable, but, like all sex toys, should be cleaned thoroughly between uses.

> "Give a man a free hand and he'll run it all over you."
>
> —Mae West

Penis Thickeners and Extenders

These are used just like you think they are. A penis thickener fits around the shaft of the penis, and leaves the all-sensitive tip exposed, so it promises pleasure for women and men both. A penis extender is also a hollow device, but one that is added to the tip of the penis to give it length. It is secured by straps or a harness that fits around his hips.

Remote Control Panties

The ultimate in naughty date wear! These are essentially panties, worn by a woman, with a built-in clitoral stimulation device in front. They are operated by a remote control that is operated by the lover of the wearer and therefore can be enjoyed anywhere.

Shower Heads

No, the folks at Kohler are not in the sex toy business, but any woman who has a particularly strong showerhead—and preferably detachable for greater mobility and concentration—knows the remarkable benefits of this handy household device!

Sleeves

Used by men as masturbatory implements, these are essentially just as they sound. Some are made of latex and are special tubes that may or may not be fitted with small pearl-like bumps for added stimulation. They are designed to fit over the head and shaft of the penis and are operated with a remote control device.

Tongues

The next best thing to a vibrator, this device, made of a soft rubber, latex, or jelly, is used to simulate oral sex for a woman.

Vibrators

The first vibrators were created to cure "hysteria"; a condition, it was believed, in which a woman's uterus began to float freely through the woman's body, causing her all kinds of stress and mental anguish.

There really is a vibrator for everyone. They come in all shapes and sizes and are made from countless materials, from hard plastic to soft rubber designed to feel as natural as a man's penis or fingers. Most women use vibrators for clitoral stimulation, and not penetration as many men are apt to believe. Another thing that men erroneously believe is that their lovers' vibrators will replace them. Not true. A vibrator is a sexual aid and nothing more. The best orgasms a woman has are the ones she shares with her partner—so stop worrying!

They can be battery-operated, which is the most common type on the market, or can be plugged into electrical outlets. Most come with speed and intensity control, which is important as overusing a vibrator for an extended session can actually have the opposite effect it was designed for—it can actually over-stimulate and numb the clitoris.

> *Narrator: "Amélie still seeks solitude. She amuses herself with silly questions about the world below, such as 'How many people are having an orgasm right now?'*
>
> *Amélie: "Fifteen!"*
>
> —Andre Dussollier and Audrey Tautou, Amélie

Here's a tip for the gentlemen out there: The key to buying a vibrator for your wife is very simple. Spend the most money you can, buy only the top of the line, and don't hesitate to ask the sales clerk with the pierced nose for guidance—she's the one most likely to possess the knowledge you seek.

Keep It Clean

One of the most important things you can do for yourself and your toys: Be sure to keep them clean! And this goes especially for toys that have been used in anal play.

Most sex toys can be cleaned using a gentle, antibacterial soap and warm water. There are also special cleansers on the market you can order when you order your sex toys or lubes. Check manufacturer's directions for suggestions.

Whatever you do, don't bring out the Clorox for cleaning your sex toys! Especially for toys made of more porous materials, there's no guarantee of rinsing them totally clean. Remember: Clorox burns—and not in a pleasant way!

Also, check your toys regularly for tears, cracks, and other imperfections, which can trap bacteria and lead to a pretty nasty infection for the user. And be sure to dry toys thoroughly before putting them away. Mold and mildew are about as sexy as bacteria.

Denise, 45

"If you ever told me even two years ago that my husband, Joel, would ever be into any kind of anal play, I would have laughed in your face. But once we discovered Waldo, well, everything changed.

I have to explain to you who Waldo is. He's not human—and in fact, we're not even sure if he is a he. More like an *it*. Waldo is a dildo, and a throwback from my bachelorette party about five years ago. It was something I brought home and we laughed about. We never thought we'd actually use the thing!

Then, a couple of years ago, our sex life was starting to get a little stale. I had read in a women's magazine that introducing new elements into lovemaking could give old lovers a new lease on sex, so I decided to take it out of the closet where it's been stored since the day I took it home. I read that lube was necessary, so I went to the local pharmacy to purchase the recommended brand, Astroglide, and I waited for Joel to come home.

While I was waiting, I lit some candles around the bedroom to let him know I was in the mood. When he arrived, he got the hint, and we started going through the motions of our very vanilla sex life. And then I whipped out Waldo.

He was quite shocked at first, but somehow, I was able to get him to agree to use it on me. He went down on me, while penetrating me vaginally with the dildo, and let me tell you, we were both very impressed with our new friend! Since that time, we've brought out Waldo quite a few times, and started getting closer and closer to each other.

And then one day, Joel came home with a men's magazine rolled up in his hand. I wasn't sure what he was planning to use that for—maybe some kind of S&M play? Who knew? But then he unrolled the magazine and opened it up to an article about how to stimulate the prostate. 'What do you think?' he asked me. I gave him an incredulous look. 'You do know where your prostate is, right?' which was kind of a silly question, because he was certainly at the age to have had it examined. He smirked, shrugged his shoulders, and nodded his head.

We had a great time with Waldo that night! Joel reported having the most intense and amazing orgasm of his life. Now, Waldo is strictly used on him. But I'm not that sad. We recently went out and bought 'Wanda' for me!"

"A woman's body is a work of art. A man's body is utilitarian. It's for gettin' around. Kinda like a Jeep."

— *Elaine Bennis (Julia Louis-Dreyfuss)*, Seinfeld

Sexploration Exercise #34

1. Which of the following is not an aphrodisiac?
   a. Strawberries.
   b. Chocolate.
   c. Pasta.
   d. They all are—any food can be sexy if you know what to do with it!

2. Have you and your partner ever incorporated food into your love play?
   a. Always
   b. Sometimes
   c. Rarely
   d. Never

3. Which best describes your attitude about food and sex?
   a. They are as natural together as air and water.
   b. I don't like to get crumbs in my bed, so I guess you could say I'm pretty much against it.
   c. Sex only gets better when you bring food into the equation.
   d. It's just not hygienic to mix food with sex.

4. Have you ever made a "meal" of your partner, so to speak?
   a. One of the best desserts I ever had was to cover my wife in whipped cream, head to toe, and lick off every luscious bite.
   b. What—you mean like a cannibal?
   c. I like to pour honey on my hubby and swirl my finger all around in it till he gets all hot and bothered.
   d. I once made a banana split with ....well, you know. Ultimately, the ice cream was too cold and it was a huge disaster until I cleaned his, um, banana off with my tongue.

5. What's your favorite aphrodisiac?
   a. Oysters
   b. Champagne
   c. Avocados
   d. Lobster

chapter 34

Food and Sex

"Oh, my god! Don't you realize what happened?
Because you started eating while having sex, you
associate food with orgasms!"
—*Jerry Seinfeld,* Seinfeld

They say you are what you eat—and so if you eat sexy, than you will become sexy, right? We say right! Food and sex have been linked together as a winning combination since the beginning of time. Sexual symbolism through food happens all the time. Take the biblical story of the Garden of Eden for instance. What do you think that apple was really meant to symbolize?

Aphrodisiacs are food, drugs, or scents used to stimulate sexual arousal. Named for Aphrodite, the ancient Greek goddess of love and passion, they come in all shapes and forms—and may be hiding in places where you least expect it!

In this chapter, we look at some of the most popular aphrodisiacs there are and see how they can be used to enhance your sexual satisfaction.

Robert, 49

"My wife, Amy, and I recently enrolled in a cooking class, and I have to tell you, it's the best thing we've ever done. Though I never realized before a certain Saturday night kitchen adventure why the class we were taking is called 'Cooking for Lovers.'

At first I really wasn't interested. I didn't like to cook and didn't know how to do anything more adventurous than scramble an egg. Weekend breakfasts were always my domain—that's what the guy does and that's just the way it goes. Dinner, the only food you ever really need to cook, that's the woman's job. My father didn't cook. His father before him didn't cook. I was not about to break this proud tradition.

But Amy didn't seem so happy with us lately, so I signed up with her to try and change that.

It wasn't really as hard as I thought it was going to be, and it was actually fun to spend this time with my wife. Then it hit me: We really hadn't been spending that much time together at all since the layoffs at my job—and all the new work left for the lucky survivors—had forced me to work really long days. When we were in class, she was happy.

Once I got good at it, I started helping Amy put dinner together in the evenings when I could. I realized this was a good chunk of time I had been wasting stupidly vegging out in front of the TV, thinking I was too tired to do anything else. And Amy was smiling again.

One Saturday, I decided it was time to take a huge leap and prepare a meal for just her and me, right off our assignment list. I sent her shopping with the kids during the day. For nighttime, I had made arrangements with her sister to take the kids so we could be alone.

When Amy came home to find her sister standing in the foyer with a bag packed for the kids, she was elated. She turned them right around again, walked them through the door and to the car, and nearly skipped back into the house, she was so thrilled.

That kind of got ruined when she came into the kitchen and saw what a disaster zone it had become, thanks to my efforts. 'What the …?' she started to ask but stopped dead in her tracks when she saw me emerge from the pantry, wearing nothing but an apron. 'Dinner will be ready in ten minutes,' I lied, naturally, because I had ruined the whole meal, and I was going to be taking her out that night instead. 'Who needs dinner?' she asked, as she ran up to me and threw her arms around my neck. 'I want dessert. Now!'

That night I finally learned why the class was called 'Cooking for Lovers!'"

Frisky Foods

In this section you find descriptions of the aphrodisiac powers of some of your favorite foods. How many of these can already be found in your kitchen or garden—and how many will be added to your grocery list this weekend? There's a common theme that runs through lists of most aphrodisiacs: They are finger foods. It's a lot more fun to lick food off of one another's fingers than it is to fill a dishwasher or wash utensils in the kitchen sink. Savor the experience of feeding and being fed by your lover with your hands—and the stickier and juicier the food is, the better.

Apricots

A highly sensual food when eaten correctly—that is, shared when the fruit is ripe and bursting with juice—the ancient Chinese were firm believers in the sexual power of apricots.

Asparagus

Many have touted the virility-inspiring ability of this vegetable, especially the French. During Victorian times, it was believed that a man should consume as much asparagus as possible the night before his wedding to get the stamina to please his bride—over and over and over again.

Bananas

There is great sexual imagery in the act of a woman peeling back the skin from a banana and biting it as a whole. The size and consistency of this particular fruit leaves very little to the imagination. Just remember: A pre-peeled, pre-sliced banana just won't do!

Carrots

Like bananas, carrots, when left whole, are just the right shape and size to make imaginations run wild. This was a favorite seductive food of lovers during the Middle Ages.

Caviar

Part of the reason this decadent treat is considered an aphrodisiac is that it is best enjoyed with chilled liquid aphrodisiacs: vodka and champagne. However, it is mainly thought of as such because caviar is essentially fish eggs, and eggs are a symbol of fertility.

Chocolate

Most people agree: There is no better aphrodisiac than chocolate. But it isn't just because it tastes so sweet and creamy and luscious. There's actually real science involved. Chocolate contains a chemical called phenylethylamine (PEA), which helps the brain release seratonin, which is at least one of the reasons we feel so wonderful when we eat chocolate! Many cultures have celebrated its aphrodisiac qualities, including the Aztecs!

> "You know why God is a man? Because if God was a woman she would have made sperm taste like chocolate."
>
> —Comedienne Carrie Snow

Cucumber

A favorite sex toy for those too shy to actually purchase a dildo, it's also been scientifically proven that the scent of cucumbers is arousing to women.

Grapes

As Mae West sexily and suggestively cooed: "Peel me a grape." She just never got into the rest of why these can be such a sexy food. There's the obvious reason that grapes are used to make wine, and we all know how romantic wine makes us feel. But also, like cucumbers, grapes are nature's sex toys—or can be used as such by creative imaginations.

Honey

The sticky and sweet qualities of this substance make it a lot of fun to lick off your lover—and because it is so sticky, it might take a long time to do so! Honey has been used as an aphrodisiac since the dawn of time and by various cultures throughout the world. One custom many cultures share is to spread honey on the palms of brides and grooms and have them lick it off each other—hopefully an activity that won't be forgotten in their marriage!

Lobster

Because of the association of Aphrodite being born from the sea, most seafood can safely be considered aphrodisiac in nature—not to mention that it contains high levels of phosphorous and iodine—each noted to increase sexual potency. Of course, we all know that's not what makes lobster sexy—it's actually the act of eating it!

Mango

An episode of HBO's famous adult TV show, *Real Sex*, featured a segment for a class on how to perform oral sex on a woman. The prop used to simulate the female? A ripe, juicy mango!

Peaches

Just like nectarines and the X-rated mango, peaches, when properly ripe, are soft and fleshy, juicy and sticky. A perfect "sharing" food (see also, apricots).

Pomegranate

This ancient fruit has many sexual connotations. This was the fruit that Persephone ate in Hades, the reason she had to return to Hades half the year. You don't need to read too far into that symbolism. Also, the pomegranate is featured in the most famous sex bible of all time, the *Kama Sutra*.

Shellfish

If it looks like a duck and acts like a duck, it has to be a duck, right? It doesn't take that much imagination to make the connection to what an oyster or clam or mussel looks like. Oysters especially are known around the world as food for seduction.

> *"I know you're probably busy having mind-blowing sex, but I feel you need to know that your good friend, Miranda Hobbes, has just taken a piece of cake out of the garbage and eaten it. You'll probably need this information when you check me into the 'Betty Crocker Clinic.'"*
>
> Miranda Hobbes (Cynthia Nixon), Sex and the City

Herbal Ecstasy

Not only can the foods we eat increase our desire, arousal, and stamina, but the herbs that we flavor them with can also be used to great effect. Try slipping some of these herbs in your kitchen concoctions and see how long it takes you to finish your meal and head for your bed!

Basil

Sure, it's very popular in Italian cooking, but did you know that basil is also used in Haitian voodoo love ceremonies?

Cardamom

This is a great one for the guys. Herbalists suggest that cardamom both helps erectile functioning and stops premature ejaculation.

Fennel

Fennel has, since ancient times, been considered to increase sexual desire.

Garlic

So many ancient cultures swore by the aphrodisiac qualities of garlic, including the Chinese and Japanese, and the ancient Egyptians, Greeks, and Romans—and their descendants continue to prize this strong seasoning.

Ginger

Believed by herbalists to combat impotence, ginger is popular throughout Asia for its aphrodisiac qualities.

Pine Nuts

A very popular aphrodisiac of ancient cultures of the Mediterranean and the East, you can find references to pine nuts in everything from Ovid's list of aphrodisiacs in his *Art of Love*, to the Arabic *Perfumed Garden* love manual.

Saffron

This Mediterranean herb is said to intensify the sensitivity of erogenous zones.

> "You know, I am an artist the way I combine my business and my pleasure: Money's my business, eating's my pleasure and Georgie's my pleasure, too, though in a more private kind of way than stuffing the mouth and feeding the sewers, though the pleasures are related because the naughty bits and the dirty bits are so close together that it just goes to show how eating and sex are related ...."
>
> Albert Spica, the Cook (Michael Gambon), The Cook, the Thief, His Wife & Her Lover

Lusty Libations

We all know that booze is an aphrodisiac—but only if you don't have too much of it! Sexual side effects of excessive alcohol consumption include erectile difficulty for the man and clitoral desensitization and vaginal dryness for the woman. You don't need a degree in physics to figure out that under these circumstances, not only is it not going to work, it will likely be a messy, clumsy, disappointing affair if it does. However, a controlled quantity of alcohol—a glass of wine or champagne, a pint of beer, an ice-cold martini or margarita—can curb inhibitions and enhance desire.

Greta, 51

My husband, Lars, would kill me if he knew I was telling you this, but I just can't help myself. Last night we had what appears to be called a 'bedroom picnic.' It was so incredibly hot; I'm still all aglow with afterglow!

It all got started when I read an article in a woman's magazine about ways to spice up your marriage. There were all kinds of things I wouldn't be caught dead doing, but I figured what they called a bedroom picnic might be harmless enough—even if it got messy, the cleaning lady was going to be due in the next day. So I took the chance.

The article recommended getting lots of snack-like foods that are easily eaten with fingers. That made sense. Imagine trying to eat a lasagna dinner in bed! Also, it recommended having on hand a lot of tasty condiments—not things like ketchup, mustard, and mayo, but honey, whipped cream, and chocolate sauce—and a few rolls of paper towels, if needed.

Grocery shopping that day wasn't the boring task it usually is because I had a lot to look forward to. I also kind of liked it that no one else knew what I was up to. I was just some middle-aged broad picking up provisions for an early bird supper—not a crazed sex kitten revved up and ready for a night of sticky sweet lust!

I bought just what they told me to buy: strawberries and grapes; cheeses that could be cut into cubes and crackers; peaches and mangos; caviar and chocolate; and lots of succulent oysters!

When I got home, I chilled a bottle of champagne and went about the task of transforming our sleeping space from boudoir to banquet. I put clean sheets on the bed—why I'll never know because they were an absolute mess when we were through—and lit several small votive candles. The article also said that scents could be very sexy, and it listed a few. So I also lit a jasmine candle I got as a gift and was saving for a special occasion.

Lars finally got home and I was ready for him. He called out my name looking for me and finally arrived in the bedroom. He was not expecting to see all this food around—or me draped across our chaise lounge wearing nothing but Saran wrap. I'd love to tell you more, but I know you wouldn't believe me anyway. You'll just have to try it for yourself!"

Amorous Aromas

As we said in the beginning of this chapter, an aphrodisiac can be something you eat, but it can also be a scent. Some of the most popular scents for lovers include jasmine, ylang ylang, clary sage, sandalwood, patchouli, black pepper, coriander, cinnamon, and champaca.

The most popular form for these scents are essential oils. Use these in a romantic bath or even dab a drop or two on yourself. You can also get these wonderfully wanton aromas by using scented candles—and then you can kill two ambience birds with one stone: sensual scent and romantic lighting!

Afterword

Congratulations! You've finally gotten through your lessons, and now it's time for the fun part—to put everything you've learned to use. And we hope that you will do just that to-night, tomorrow night, every morning before work—heck, as frequently as possible. This old adage is especially true when it comes to mind-blowing sex: Practice makes perfect. So practice as much as you possibly can!

One thing we hope you will always remember is that your mind is your most powerful and effective sex organ. With it, you can transcend physical limitations—through fantasy and improvisation. You can imagine a whole world of ways to excite, arouse, entice, and satisfy your partner. Most impor-tantly, with your mind, you can connect with your partner in realms that far surpass the physical.

Don't even for one small second believe that just because you've reached middle age, you now have to settle for middle-of-the-road, humdrum, vanilla sex. A world of options and experimentation is open to you and your partner to enjoy. Be sure to savor the destination itself—as much as or more so than you do the reward. The orgasm, after all, is only an element of sex—it's not the absolute purpose.

So what are you waiting for? It's time to track down your partner, strip down your sexy selves, and sizzle your way into the night!

appendix

Further Reading

Arnott, Stephen. *Sex: A User's Guide*. Delta, 2003.

Barbach, Lonnie, Ph.D. *For Each Other: Sharing Sexual Intimacy*. Signet, 2001.

Berman, Jennifer; Berman, Laura; and Bumiller, Elisabeth. *For Women Only: A Revolutionary Guide to Reclaiming Your Sex Life*. Owl Books, 2002.

Birch, Robert W. and Ruberg, Cynthia Lief. *Pathways To Pleasure: A Woman's Guide to Orgasm*. PEC Publishing, 2000.

Blue, Violet. *The Ultimate Guide to Fellatio: How to Go Down on a Man and Give Him Mind-Blowing Pleasure*. Cleis Press, 2002.

Bodansky, Steve and Bodansky, Vera. *The Illustrated Guide to Extended Massive Orgasm*. Hunter House, 2002.

Chia, Mantak. *Taoist Secrets of Love: Cultivating Male Sexual Energy*. Aurora Press, 1984.

Chia, Mantak and Abrams, Douglas. *The Multi-Orgasmic Man: Sexual Secrets Every Man Should Know*. Harper, 1997.

Comfort, Alex. *The New Joy of Sex and More Joy of Sex.* Simon & Schuster, 1998.

Finz, Iris and Finz, Steven. *Erotic Confessions: Real People Talk about Putting the Spark Back in Their Sex.* St. Martin's, 1999.

Fulbright, Yvonne K. *The Hot Guide to Safer Sex.* Hunter House; 1st edition, 2003.

Gabriel, Bonnie. *The Fine Art of Erotic Talk: How to Entice, Excite and Enchant Your Lover With Words.* Bantam Doubleday Dell, 1996.

Gray, John. *Mars and Venus in the Bedroom: A Guide to Lasting Romance and Passion.* HarperCollins, 1997.

Heiman, Julia. *Becoming Orgasmic.* Fireside, 1987.

Henderson, Julie. *The Lover Within: Opening to Energy in Sexual Practice.* Barrytown Ltd, 1999.

Hicks, Donald L. *Understanding the G-Spot and Female Sexuality: A Simple 10-Step Guide for Unleashing the Ultimate in Female Ecstasy.* Universal Publishers, 2001.

Hutcherson, Hilda, M.D. *What Your Mother Never Told You About Sex.* Putnam Pub Group, 2002.

Hutchins, D. Claire. *Five Minutes to Orgasm Every Time You Make Love: Female Orgasm Made Simple.* JPS Publishing, 2000.

Joannides, Paul and Gross, Daerick (Illustrator). *The Guide to Getting It On! (The Universe's Coolest and Most Informative Book About Sex).* Goofy Foot Press, 2000.

Keesling, Barbara. *The Good Girl's Guide to Bad Girl Sex.* M Evans & Co., 2001.

Keesling, Barbara. *How to Make Love All Night and Drive Your Woman Wild.* Perennial Press, 1995.

Kline-Graber, Georgia and Graber, Benjamin, M.D. *Woman's Orgasm: A Guide to Sexual Satisfaction.* Warner, 1998.

Lacroix, Nitya. *Tantric Sex: The Tantric Art of Sensual Loving.* Southwater, 2000.

Laken, Keith and Laken, Virginia. *Making Love Again: Hope for Couples Facing Loss of Sexual Intimacy.* North Star, 2002.

Leman, Keith. *Sheet Music: Uncovering the Secrets of Sexual Intimacy in Marriage.* Tyndale House, 2003.

Leonardi, Tom. *Secrets of Sensual Lovemaking: The Ultimate in Female Ecstasy.* Signet, 1998.

Love, Patricia, M.D. and Robinson, Jo. *Hot Monogamy: Essential Steps to More Passionate, Intimate Lovemaking.* E P Dutton, 1994.

McCarthy, Barry W. and McCarthy, Emily J. *Rekindling Desire: A Step by Step Program To Help Low-Sex and No-Sex Marriages.* Brunner-Routledge, 2003.

McMeel, Andrews. *Best Sex You'll Ever Have.* Carlton, 2002.

Page, Susan. *How One of You Can Bring the Two of You Together: Breakthrough Strategies to Resolve Your Conflicts and Reignite Your Love.* Bantam Doubleday Dell, 1998.

Paget, Lou. *How to Give Her Absolute Pleasure: Totally Explicit Techniques Every Woman Wants Her Man to Know.* Bantam Doubleday Dell, 2000.

Penner, Clifford J. and Penner, Joyce. *52 Ways To Have Fun, Fantastic Sex—A Guidebook For Married Couples.* Thomas Nelson, 1993.

Penner, Clifford J. and Penner, Joyce. *Restoring the Pleasure: Complete Step-by-Step Programs to Help Couples Overcome the Most Common Sexual Barriers.* Word Publishing, 1993.

Rako, Susan. *The Hormone of Desire: The Truth About Testosterone, Sexuality, and Menopause.* Three Rivers Press, 1999.

Raskin, Valerie. *Great Sex for Moms: Ten Steps to Nurturing Passion While Raising Kids.* Fireside, 2002.

Reichman, Judith. *I'm Not in the Mood: What Every Woman Should Know About Improving Her Libido.* Quill, 1999.

Rosenau, Douglas E. *A Celebration of Sex: A Guide to Enjoying God's Gift of Sexual Intimacy.* Thomas Nelson, 2002.

Ryan, M. J. *Attitudes of Gratitude in Love: Creating More Joy In Your Relationship.* Conari Pri, 2002.

Schnarch, David. *Constructing the Sexual Crucible: An Integration of Sexual and Marital Therapy.* W. W. Norton & Company, 1991.

Schnarch, David. *Passionate Marriage: Love, Sex, and Intimacy in Emotionally Committed Relationships.* W. W. Norton & Company, 1997.

Schnarch, David and Maddock, James. *Resurrecting Sex: Resolving Sexual Problems and Rejuvenating Your Relationship.* HarperCollins, 2002.

Sonntag, Linda. *The Bedside Kama Sutra: 23 Positions for Pleasure and Passion.* Fair Winds Press, 2001.

Stains, Laurence Roy and Bechtel, Stefan. *What Women Want: What Every Man Needs to Know About Sex, Romance, Passion and Pleasure.* Rodale Press, 2000.

St. Claire, Olivia. *203 Ways to Drive a Man Wild in Bed.* Harmony Books, 1993.

St. Claire, Olivia. *227 Ways to Unleash the Sex Goddess Within.* Harmony Books, 1996.

Weiner-Davis, Michele. *The Sex-Starved Marriage: A Couple's Guide to Boosting Their Marriage Libido.* Simon & Schuster, 2003.

Wheat, Ed. *Intended for Pleasure: Sex Technique and Sexual Fulfillment in Christian Marriage, Third Edition.* Fleming H Revell Co., 1997.

index

self-pleasure. *See* mas-
turbation
shellfish, 319
shower heads, 309
showering, 176, 260
simultaneous orgasms
(69 orgasms), 206
sixty-nine position.
See 69 position
sleeves (toys), 309
softcore pornography,
286
spanking, 280
spirituality
orgasms, 177
tantric sex, 174
spooning position,
137-139
standing positions,
141-148
examples, 145
lubrication, 144
movement, 143
penetration, 147
rear-entry, 144
variations, 143
Kama Sutra, 168
stimulants, 315
stimulating
manual, 70-74
penises, 72
perenium, 75
strip clubs, 293, 296

striptease, 293
pacing, 297
stroking, 84
surrender (tantric sex),
172
suspended position, 168
swallowing (oral sex),
194
swan sport position, 166
sweats, 20-21

T

talking dirty, 235, 238
e-mail, 267
examples, 239
tantric sex, 171-175
breathing, 174
examples, 178
learning, 174
meditation, 176
orgasm, 177
spirituality, 174
technosex, 263
testosterone, 25-26
theme parks, 258
timers, 10
tips
anal sex, 215
communicating, 35
fondling penises, 73
massage, 104
missionary position,
114

oral sex, 185, 195
females, 181
rear-entry sex, 134
tantric sex, 176
woman-on-top
position, 126
toys, 303
anal beads, 306
anal probes, 306
Ben-Wa balls, 306
bondage, 278
butt plugs, 307
butterflies, 307
cleaning, 310
cock rings, 307
dildos, 308
duotone balls, 308
French ticklers, 309
sleeves, 309
spanking, 280
vibrators, 310
two bodies as one
(tantric sex), 175

U–V

undressing, 84
unity (tantric sex), 175
unresolved problems, 6
upright sex. *See* standing
positions
upside-down squat
position, 158

vagina
  arousal, 88
  clitoris, 88
  dryness, 20-21
vertical sex. *See* standing
  positions
vibrators, 310
video recording, 290
videos (pornography), 33

W–X–Y–Z

wall sit position, 157
wheelbarrow position,
  154
widows, 41
  dating, 42
woman-on-top position,
  121-128
  examples, 123
  facing away, 127
  penetration, 125
  tips, 126
  variations, 126
women. *See* females
workaholics, 17

yoga, 142
  breathing exercises,
    232
  tantric sex, 171
yoni, 165

The times, they are a-changin'

The *Boomer's Guide* series offers practical knowledge and advice about the really important things in life, geared specifically to the needs of baby boomers. You know—those of us now 40- or 50-something who have teen- or college-age children, aging parents, maturing marriages (or perhaps a new single status), looming retirement, investment and property responsibilities, new health and fitness concerns, and a realization that we are finally becoming our parents.

Boomer's Guide to
Getting the Weight Off... For Good
Roberta Schwartz Wennik, M.S., R.D.

1-59257-160-3 • $16.95

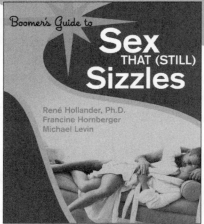

Boomer's Guide to
Sex THAT (STILL) Sizzles
René Hollander, Ph.D.
Francine Hornberger
Michael Levin

1-59257-155-7 • $16.95

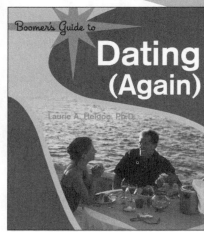

Boomer's Guide to
Dating (Again)
Laurie A. Helgoe, Ph.D.

1-59257-164-6 • $16.95

Coming Summer of 2004:

Boomer's Guide to
Divorce

ALPHA

From the publishers of *The Complete Idiot's Guide®* series